D0225843

Civil Rights and Civil Liberties in America

Books in the **Contemporary World Issues** series address vital issues in today's society such as genetic engineering, pollution, and biodiversity. Written by professional writers, scholars, and nonacademic experts, these books are authoritative, clearly written, up-to-date, and objective. They provide a good starting point for research by high school and college students, scholars, and general readers as well as by legislators, businesspeople, activists, and others.

Each book, carefully organized and easy to use, contains an overview of the subject, a detailed chronology, biographical sketches, facts and data and/or documents and other primary source material, a forum of authoritative perspective essays, annotated lists of print and nonprint resources, and an index.

Readers of books in the Contemporary World Issues series will find the information they need to gain a better understanding of the social, political, environmental, and economic issues facing the world today.

Civil Rights and Civil Liberties in America

A REFERENCE HANDBOOK

Michael C. LeMay

 ABC-CLIO®

An Imprint of ABC-CLIO, LLC
Santa Barbara, California • Denver, Colorado

Library of Congress Cataloging-in-Publication Data

Names: LeMay, Michael C., 1941- author.
Title: Civil rights and civil liberties in America : a reference handbook / Michael C. LeMay.
Description: Santa Barbara, California : ABC-CLIO, an imprint of ABC-CLIO, LLC, [2021] | Series: Contemporary world issues | Includes bibliographical references and index.
Identifiers: LCCN 2020052200 (print) | LCCN 2020052201 (ebook) | ISBN 9781440867293 (hardcover) | ISBN 9781440867309 (ebook)
Subjects: LCSH: Civil rights—United States. | Liberty. | United States—Politics and government. | United States—History—Sources.
Classification: LCC JC599.U5 L417 2021 (print) | LCC JC599. U5 (ebook) | DDC 323.0973—dc23
LC record available at https://lccn.loc.gov/2020052200
LC ebook record available at https://lccn.loc.gov/2020052201

ISBN: 978-1-4408-6729-3 (print)
      978-1-4408-6730-9 (ebook)

25 24 23 22 21   1 2 3 4 5

This book is also available as an eBook.

ABC-CLIO
An Imprint of ABC-CLIO, LLC

ABC-CLIO, LLC
147 Castilian Drive
Santa Barbara, California 93117
www.abc-clio.com

This book is printed on acid-free paper ∞

Manufactured in the United States of America

Contents

Civil Rights and Civil Liberties in America: A Reference Handbook focuses on the more than 200-year history of struggle in the United States to give meaning and reality to the bold experiment in self-governance and the inspirational goals articulated in the Bill of Rights and subsequent amendments to the Constitution. The Bill of Rights sought to limit government power and authority to guarantee certain inalienable rights for all citizens. It was a revolutionary approach to government. It was also very much a work in progress. The civil rights and liberties guaranteed in the Constitution had to be clarified as to their meaning and, over time, had to be incorporated, by the Fourteenth Amendment, to bind state and local governments to the limits on the national level of government. As this historical narrative makes clear, it took the struggle of many individuals and groups to continuously press government to secure those rights. It required further enactments by legislative bodies (the U.S. Congress and state legislatures) to expand upon what is meant by the various clauses of the Constitutional amendments. It took executive actions (proclamations and executive orders) to bring practical meaning to those lofty goals. It took literally hundreds of court decisions to do so as well.

The arc of history bending toward freedom had to be wrought by the sweat, blood, and tears of countless advocates. The march to actuate those fundamental civil rights and liberties was constant, but it proceeded in fits and starts, and sometimes steps backward followed steps forward. The historical narrative documents the perennial struggle of countless minority groups and leading activists to achieve those rights and to protect and maintain them as technology and other developments worked to undermine or threaten them.

As do all the volumes within the Contemporary World Issues series, this volume follows a prescribed format. Like the other books in the series, this book is aimed at high school, college, public, and university libraries. It presents a synthesis of current studies of the issues raised by that perennial struggle to "create a more perfect union."

Chapter 1 discusses the historical background of government attempts to give life and meaning to the goal of guaranteeing the fundamental rights and liberties of citizenship. It shows how the very definition of who was, is, or ought to be a citizen had to be further defined and clarified. It shows precisely what privileges and immunities that status confers on an individual and what limits it imposes on government. The chapter seeks to present that narrative in an even-handed manner so as to better enable readers to form their own judgements of the issues raised.

Chapter 2 describes and discusses the most vexing problems associated with the attempt by a continuous stream of newly ascribed minority groups to struggle to achieve their civil rights and liberties. It addresses efforts by government to seek, at times, to suppress those rights. It explores the controversies aroused by the struggle of minority groups to have their rights recognized and their grievances addressed. It describes efforts by governments, through laws, administrative rules and regulations, and landmark decisions by federal courts, to "resolve" solutions to those often thorny problems that tend to defy easy solutions.

Chapter 3 presents ten original essays by scholars involved in civil rights and liberties matters and jurisprudence to add their voices and perspectives to the complex politics inherent in these issues and matters. These essay contributors are drawn from diverse disciplinary perspectives to enrich the view that this author brings to the discussion.

Chapter 4 describes an extensive array of organizations and activists in the arena of politics in which the struggle for civil rights and liberties are played out. They are best perceived as stakeholders in the struggle to shape the debates, to enact or reject proposed reforms in the laws and governmental practices designed to put into practice the guarantees of the constitutional amendments to ensure those fundamental rights. These participants shape the policy debates and are key to understanding the adoption of or opposition to proposed solutions to the perceived problems.

Chapter 5 presents data and documents that focus on the discourse on civil rights and liberties in law and in practice. A dozen tables of data are presented to enable the reader to assess the struggle depicted in chapters 1 and 2. Ten documents are presented in full or are excerpted to represent events in the struggle over civil rights and liberties across the decades of U.S. history. The documents are selected to illustrate why the problems are so complex and the solutions so difficult to achieve or maintain as U.S. society and its politics changed so dramatically over time, as the United States evolved from thirteen mostly rural and sparsely populated states huddled along the nation's Atlantic shores to span the continent and emerge as a highly industrialized and urbanized world superpower.

Chapter 6 is a resource chapter. It presents and annotates 185 books and more than twenty scholarly journals that provide sources of information for future study of the topics that are raised herein. It also presents a number of feature-length films that touch on the subjects and individuals presented in earlier chapters. They are suggested for readers to consult to give "life" to the topics and a "face" to the individuals.

A chronology of key events in the history of the struggle for civil rights and liberties is then presented. Finally, a glossary provides easy access to definitions of key terms and concepts used, often in legal jargon, in civil rights and liberty debates discussed throughout the volume. It is followed by a comprehensive subject matter index.

Civil Rights and Civil Liberties in America

Etched by Albert Rosenthal 1888.

Introduction

The Bill of Rights, comprising the first ten amendments to the Constitution of the United States, was finally and legally ratified in December 1791. They are collectively the lofty statement of the protection of basic rights of all citizens. They guarantee freedom of speech, press, and assembly; free exercise of religion; and the right to fair legal procedures. They protect the right to bear arms. They assert that powers not delegated to the federal government would be reserved for the states and the people of the United States. The Bill of Rights was influenced by English common law, expressed in the 1689 Bill of Rights, and also drawn from the Virginia colony's Declaration of Rights. They were drafted by George Mason in 1776 and comprised twelve stipulated basic rights. Mason was a lifelong champion of individual liberties, and in 1787 he attended the Constitutional Convention as a delegate from Virginia. Mason criticized the final document for lacking constitutional protections of basic rights. During the struggle to ratify the constitution, Mason and other critics agreed to support the Constitution only in exchange for the assurance that amendments would be passed immediately. On December 15, 1791, Virginia became the tenth of fourteen states to ratify the Bill of

Founding Father George Mason is widely held as the author of the Bill of Rights. (New York Public Library)

Rights, thereby assuring the ratification necessary to make legal the U.S. Constitution (Labunski 2006; Wood 2009).

Civil rights may be defined as the rights of *citizens* to political and social freedoms and equality. These rights are stipulated to ensure people's physical and mental integrity and the right to privacy; protecting life and safety; and protection against discrimination based on protected characteristics such as race, gender, sexual orientation, national origin, color, age, ethnicity, religion, and disability. *Civil liberties* are basic freedoms contained in the Bill of Rights, particularly by the First Amendment's rights of religion, speech, press, assembly, and to petition the government. Taken together, the civil liberties articulated in the Bill of Rights form the cornerstone of democracy as perceived by the Founding Fathers. They articulate the goals of the American experiment in democracy, or the right of citizens to self-government. They are general statements of rights that require further elaboration and understanding in law and through jurisprudence in the courts of law (Labunski 2006; Levy 1995; Wood 2009).

Human rights are rights believed to belong to every person. Human rights have been articulated most specifically in the *Universal Declaration of Human Rights* promulgated by the United Nations in 1948 (see table 5.1). They are exemplified by such declarations as the right to equality; freedom from discrimination; right to life, liberty, and personal security; freedom from torture and degrading treatment; right to marriage and family; right to retain one's own things; freedom of thought and expression; freedom of assembly; and right to democracy, social security, and some basic workers' rights.

The first amendment addresses freedom of religion, speech, and the press, and the rights of assembly and petition. It reads: "Congress shall make no law respecting an establishment of religion, or prohibiting the free exercise thereof; or abridging the freedom of speech, or of the press, or of the right of the people peaceably to assemble, and to petition the Government for a redress of grievances." This chapter examines the civil rights and liberties guaranteed by the first through the tenth amendments as well as the fourteenth, fifteenth, nineteenth, and twenty-sixth amendments. These amendments delineate basic civil rights and civil liberties that have been further defined, refined, and evolved by subsequent laws enacted over time as the conditions faced by U.S. society evolved. They have been defined by court decisions handed down over the past two hundred years as jurisprudence addressed local, state, and federal laws. Those laws impacted the basic civil rights and civil liberties as those concepts were perceived by the people as the nation changed dramatically over the course of its history. Each amendment, and the laws and court decisions associated with them, are discussed in turn to exemplify how basic concepts of civil rights and liberties changed in response to historical developments (Killian and Costello 2000).

Supreme Court decisions have been rendered in a number of landmark cases that concern a number of laws enacted by the United States Congress. They reflect developments in American history during times historians have distinguished as eras for the understanding of civil rights and liberties. During the pre–Civil War period (1789–1865), the focus was on actions of the national government. The Bill of Rights was then viewed as applying only to the federal government. During Reconstruction (1864–1877), Congress and the Supreme Court began applying those rights to state governments. The post-Reconstruction period (1877–1890s) saw the extension of Jim Crow laws and the social and legal enforcement of segregation. The Progressive Era, the 1890s to 1920s, saw a focus on economic rights and the continued application by the Supreme Court of the doctrine of incorporation. The Bill of Rights was viewed as binding on state governments as well as the federal government. The interwar years and the Great Depression, from the 1930s to the mid-1950s, have been characterized as the New Deal era. It was a time noted for the struggle between the civil and economic rights emphasized by the Roosevelt administration and a conservative Supreme Court reluctant to embrace an expansive view of civil rights. The period of the greatest expansion of civil rights was from 1960 to mid-1970, the years when the Supreme Court was at its most liberal ideologically under the leadership of Chief Justice Earl Warren. It was then that the modern civil rights movement formed and agitated for reforms in custom and law. That era was followed by the resurgence in conservative ideology, both in Congress and the presidential administrations, and by the Supreme Court under Chief Justice William Rehnquist, roughly from 1975 to 2000. The Rehnquist Supreme Court was notably a "conservative activist" court that was every bit as activist as the Warren Court had been. The most recent period of significance has been since 2000, when the United States can be characterized as constructing "Fortress America." During this most recent era, civil rights and liberty concerns took a backseat to national security and protection against international terrorism (Killian and Costello 2000). The following sections discuss each of the amendments and how jurisprudence and legislation have interpreted and refined the perception of those fundamental rights. It also shows which citizens they were increasingly aimed at protecting.

The First Amendment—Religion, Speech, Press, Assembly, and Petition

The First Amendment states, regarding freedom of religion, speech, press, assembly, and petition: "Congress shall make no law respecting an establishment of religion, or prohibiting the free exercise thereof; or abridging the freedom of speech, or of the press, or the right of the people peaceably to assemble, and to petition the Government for a redress of grievances."

The U.S. Supreme Court has issued hundreds of decisions on cases concerning the First Amendment. Regarding the Establishment Clause, for example, between 1925 and 2011, the Court rendered more than a dozen cases that challenged federal or state laws on the constitutionality of aid to church-related schools, from *Pierce v. Society of Sisters* (268 U.S. 510, 1925) to *Arizona Christian School Tuition Organization v. Winn* (563 U.S. 125, 2011). Religions involved in these cases challenging laws on the basis of the Establishment Clause included Anglicans, Congregationalists, Roman Catholics, Evangelicals, and the Church of Jesus Christ of Latter-day Saints (more commonly known as the Mormons). The Court ruled on the role of religion in public education in nearly a dozen landmark cases between 1948 and 2000, in such notable decisions as *McCullum v. Board of Education* (330 U.S. 203, 1948) and *Mitchell v. Helms* (530 U.S. 783, 2000). The Establishment Clause prohibitions were at issue in a number of cases dealing with government-sponsored religious displays, such as the Ten Commandments in courthouses or Christmas crèche scenes in public spaces, exemplified by such cases as *Lynch v. Donnelle* (465 U.S. 668, 1984), and *Van Ordern v. Perry* (545 U.S. 677, 2005). The use of prayers in public schools being challenged on Establishment Clause grounds are exemplified by such cases as *Wallace v. Jaffree* (472 U.S. 38, 1985) and *Elk Grove Unified School District v. Newdow* (542 U.S. 1, 2004).

The Establishment Clause was also the constitutional issue in cases regarding state and local laws known as Sabbatarian laws (or more commonly, Blue Laws). Sabbatarian laws were challenged by adherents of Judaism and the Seventh-Day Adventists, for example, in such cases as *McGowan v. Maryland* (366 U.S. 420, 1961) and *Gallagher v. Corwin Kosher Super Market of Massachusetts Inc.* (366 U.S. 617, 1981). Roman Catholics and Hasidic Jews were challenged as religious institutions functioning as a government agency (a zoning board or a school district board) in such cases as *Larkin v. Grendel's Den* (459 U.S. 116, 1982) and *Board of Education of Kiryas Joel Village School v. Grument* (512 U.S. 687, 1994). That clause was also at issue regarding tax exemption to religious institutions, exemplified by *Walz v. Tax Commission of the City of New York* (397 U.S. 664, 1970), which concerned Catholic parochial schools, and Jehovah's Witnesses in *Texas Monthly Inc. v. Bullock* (489

U.S. 1, 1989). A religious institution's standing to sue on Establishment Clause grounds was addressed in two cases: *Flast v. Cohen* (392 U.S. 83, 1968) and *Valley Gorgges and People Christian College v. Americans United for Separation of Church and State* (454 U.S. 464, 1982). And finally, the Establishment Clause was at issue in teaching creationism in public schools in *Edwards v. Aguillard* (482 U.S. 578, 1987) and government's unequal treatment of religious groups in *Larson v. Valente* (456 U.S. 228, 1982).

The Free Exercise Clause of the First Amendment was the basis for constitutional challenges by the adherents of the Old Order Amish and the Old Order Mennonites, by Jehovah's Witnesses, by Latter-day Saints, and by members of the Society for Krishna Consciousness. They challenged state and local laws regulating the solicitation by religious groups in such landmark cases as *Cantwell v. Connecticut* (310 U.S. 296, 1940) and *Heffron v. International Society for Krishna Consciousness* (452 U.S. 640, 1981).

Religious tests being required in order to receive public benefits or services were challenged on Free Exercise Clause grounds in a half-dozen cases ruled on by the U.S. Supreme Court in such landmark cases as *Chaplinsky v. New Hampshire* (315 U.S. 568, 1942) and *Bowen v. Roy* (476 U.S. 693, 1986). The Amish challenged state compulsory education laws on Free Exercise grounds in the landmark case of *Wisconsin v. Yoder* (406 U.S. 205, 1972). And that clause was also the basis for the challenge in *Rosenberger v. Rector and Visitors of the University of Virginia* (515 U.S. 819, 1995), which mandated that student groups with religious motivations had to be given equal access to the university's public forums.

Religion versus Right to Work laws were at issue in a half-dozen cases handed down by the U.S. Supreme Court between 1963 and 1990, exemplified by *Sherbert v. Verner* (374 U.S. 398, 1963) and *Employment Division v. Smith* (494 U.S. 872, 1990). The Free Exercise Clause was used concerning government intrusion into churches' internal controversies as exemplified in such decisions as *Kedroff v. Saint Nicholas Cathedral* (344 U.S. 94, 1952), which involved the Russian Orthodox Church, and in *Hosanna-Tabor Evangelical Lutheran Church and School v. EEOC* (565 U.S. 171, 2012). The power of local government to use eminent domain versus the free exercise of religion was involved in several cases, such as *Lyng v. Northwest Indian Cemetery Protective Association* (485 U.S. 439, 1988) and *City of Boerne v. Flores* (521 U.S. 507, 1997). The Free Exercise Clause versus the right to freedom of speech is well exemplified in *Gonzales v. O Centro Espirita Beneficente Uniao do Vegetal* (546 U.S. 418, 2006). The LDS tenet to practice polygamy versus state bigamy laws was at issue in two U.S. Supreme Court cases, both of which ruled in favor of the state and against the Mormons: *Reynolds v. United States* (98 U.S. 145, 1878) and *Davis v. Beason* (133 U.S. 333, 1890). Finally, the Free Exercise Clause was used as the basis to defend a minority religion group versus a local government ordinance regarding the ritual sacrifice of animals (in this case, chickens) in *Church of Lukumi Bahalu Aye v. Hialeah* (508 U.S. 520, 1993).

Freedom of Assembly and Association was at issue in ten U.S. Supreme Court decisions handed down between 1937 and 2011. These cases are exemplified by *DeJonge v. Oregon* (299 U.S. 353, 1937) and *Christian Legal Society v. Martinez* (561 U.S. 61, 2011). Likewise, the Court ruled on ten landmark cases with regard to Freedom of the Press. These cases stretched from *People of New York v. Crosswell* (3 Johns Cas 337 New York, 1804) to the famous Pentagon Papers case of *New York Times v. U.S.* (403 U.S. 713, 1971) to the case of *Hazelwood School District v. Kuhlmeier* (484 U.S. 260, 1988).

There have been nearly two dozen U.S. Supreme Court rulings on cases challenging government laws and actions with regard to freedom of speech issues. Those cases ranged from *Schenck v. U.S.* (249 U.S. 47, 1919) to as recently as *Janus v. AFSCME* (585 U.S.____ 2018). More details on these many cases based on First Amendment rights can be found in LeMay (2020).

The Second Amendment—The Right to Bear Arms

The Second Amendment to the U.S. Constitution states simply: "A well-regulated militia, being necessary to the security of a free State, the right of the people to keep and bear Arms, shall not be infringed." The meaning of the Second Amendment is not especially self-evident, and some ten Supreme Court decisions handed down since the late 1800s through 2010 have refined its meaning (see table 5.2). Those Supreme Court cases dealt with a number of questions as to its meaning and limitations. Does it primarily refer to the right of *militia* members to have their own arms? Is it applicable solely to the national government, and therefore not binding on state or local governments? Or is it the right of an individual, and therefore binding on all levels of government? How absolute are its restrictions on government? What laws enacted by government to regulate or control the possession of firearms and the nature of those firearms (and ammunition for them) are constitutionally permissible (Bogus 2000; Cress 1982; Holbrook 1989; Malcolm 1994; Spitzer 2008; Tushnet 2007)?

In early nineteenth-century America, when the population of the young nation was predominantly agricultural and rural, and when the vast majority of its people owned and used guns for hunting, the Second Amendment was uncontroversial. It was viewed as applying solely to the national government and was uncontested before the Supreme Court (Bogus 2000; Cornell 2008; Cress 1982; Malcolm 1994; Uviller and Merkel 2002). The first important Supreme Court decision on the matter was during the Reconstruction Era, *United States v. Cruikshank* (92 U.S. 542, 1875). In *Cruikshank*, the Court ruled that the Second Amendment had no other effect than to restrict the power of the national government. And again in *Presser v. Illinois* (116 U.S. 252, 1886), the Court reiterated that the Second Amendment only limited the power of the Congress and the national government and did not apply to the power of the states. The Court reached that same conclusion in *Miller v. Texas* (153 U.S. 535, 1894). The Supreme Court held that various constitutional rights cannot be understood literally and absolutely in *Robertson v. Baldwin* (165 U.S. 275, 1897). It ruled that the Second Amendment was not infringed upon by state laws prohibiting the carrying of *concealed* weapons. Although the Supreme Court regularly employed the incorporation doctrine to use the due process clause of the Fourteenth Amendment to apply the guarantees of the Bill of Rights to the states, it did not do so with respect to the Second Amendment until *Mapp v. Ohio* (367 U.S. 294, 1961). The Court did not specifically rule that gun rights are *individual rights* until its decision in *District of Columbia v. Heller* (554 U.S. 570, 2008).

Some gun control is constitutional, and the Supreme Court has upheld some limitations on the Second Amendment as constitutional. Federal legislation has outlawed the possession of certain types of firearms and ammunition. Congress has passed laws limiting the possession of firearms (1) by convicted felons, (2) by persons convicted of domestic violence and under a restraining order, (3) by persons committed to a psychiatric institution or labeled mentally ill under a court ruling, (4) by undocumented immigrants, (5) by illegal drug users, (6) by former military members who have been dishonorably discharged, and (7) by certain restrictions on the buying and selling of guns (Uviller and Merkel 2002).

Between 1934 and 2005, the United States Congress enacted half a dozen laws regarding gun control that stipulated some limits on the scope of the Second Amendment (see table 5.3). For example, in 1934 Congress put limits on machine guns (aka "Tommy guns") and sawed-off shotguns. The Federal Firearms Act of 1938 required firearms licensees to maintain customer records and made it illegal to transfer firearms to certain classes of persons, such as convicted felons.

Two laws were passed in 1968 when the assassinations of Dr. Martin Luther King Jr. and Senator Robert Kennedy (then a leading candidate for nomination for the presidency) increased awareness of the lack of control over the sale and possession of guns in the United States. They were enacted when the civil rights movement was in full swing. These two laws were major accomplishments of President Lyndon Johnson's war on crime. The Omnibus Crime Control and Safe Streets Act of 1968 (42 U.S. 3789) had among its provisions the prohibition of the interstate trade in handguns and a provision that increased the minimum age for buying handguns to twenty-one. The Gun Control Act of 1968 (82 Stat. 1213) banned mail-order sales of rifles and shotguns and prohibited felons, drug users, and the mentally incompetent from buying guns.

However, those two laws had "loopholes" that rendered their enforcement problematic and limited in impact. The Firearm Owners Protection Act (100 Stat. 449, 1986), moreover, relaxed some of the federal restrictions during the years that the Supreme Court's Chief Justice was William Rehnquist. The 1986 law redefined "gun dealer" by excluding those making only occasional sales or repairs, and it repealed some recordkeeping requirement on the sale of ammunition, although the law retained the requirements regarding the sale of armor-piercing ammunition.

The Brady Handgun Violence Protection Act (107 Stat. 1536, 1993) was passed following the attempted assassination of President Ronald Reagan and the near-fatal wounding of his aide, James Scott Brady. The Brady Act mandated federal background checks on firearms purchases in the United States and imposed a five-day waiting period for the legal purchasing of a firearm. It also established the National Instant Criminal Background Check System. The Violent Crime Control and Law Enforcement Act (108 Stat. 1796, 1994) imposed a ten-year ban on the sale of so-called "assault weapons." Weapons that met the criteria as to what was legally and technically an "assault weapon" however, were still permissibly sold and easily modified by the purchaser to act like assault rifles. The law, moreover, was allowed to expire in 2004, when the Republican-controlled Congress responded to vigorous lobbying by the National Rifle Association (NRA). Likewise, the Protection of Lawful Commerce in Arms Act (119 Stat. 2095, 2005) protects firearms manufacturers and dealers from being held liable when crimes have been committed with their products (Tushnet 2007; Spitzer 2008).

Today, the civil liberty of citizen ownership of guns is a divisive political issue. Proponents of individual rights to own firearms and ammunition of any kind argue that any limits on firearm ownership are a real and symbolic intrusion of government that is a first step toward tyranny. At the other extreme, some Americans believe that public safety requires strict limits on who can own a firearm. In 2018, after a deadly school shooting in Parkland, Florida, surviving students organized a national effort to support legislation designed to reduce gun violence.

The Third Amendment—The Housing of Soldiers

The Third Amendment states succinctly: "No soldier shall, in time of peace, be quartered in any home, without the consent of the Owner, nor in time of war, but in a manner to be prescribed by law." The amendment had its roots in English law. The English Bill of Rights (1689) prohibited maintaining a standing army in time of peace without the consent of Parliament. The Third Amendment was a direct reaction to the English Crown's Quartering Acts (1765 and 1776), which authorized British troops to take shelter in colonial homes by military fiat (order). They were used extensively during the Revolutionary War. The first Quartering Act required American colonies to pay for the British troops fighting to protect their colonies. The Second Quartering Act removed restrictions on where British troops could stay. The colonists referred to these two Parliamentary Acts as "the Intolerable Acts." The Second Quartering Act was essentially home invasion, whereby British soldiers not only took over homes but demanded food as well. It was a basis for the 1776 Declaration of Independence that assailed the king for quartering large numbers of troops among the colonies and for keeping a standing army without consent of the *colonial* legislatures. Similar amendments were contained in the Delaware Declaration of Rights (1776), the Maryland Declaration of Rights (1776), the Massachusetts Declaration of Rights (1780), and the New Hampshire Declaration of Rights (1784). The Third Amendment has been the least often litigated amendment in the Bill of Rights. It has only been applied to a handful of situations since adoption of the Constitution. Indeed, so seldom has the Third Amendment been used in courts that the American Bar Association (ABA) has referred to it as the "runt piglet" of the Constitution (Levy 1999). However, it has been cited in court cases concerning the protection of American citizens' *right to privacy*, for example, in *Griswold v. Connecticut*, 381 U.S. 479, 1965). A more recent case that involved a Third Amendment challenge was in a federal court case, *Engblom v. Carey* (677 F2d, 957, 1982). The plaintiffs were working as corrections officers in New York and sued the governor of New York and several prison officials, alleging that their due process and Third Amendment rights had been violated by the defendants during a statewide strike, when the National Guard had been activated to cover their positions in state prisons. Many of the corrections officers lived in employee housing owned by the state. During the strike, the National Guard members were housed in these residences without giving prior notice to, or seeking the permission of, the corrections officer residents. Ultimately, the District Court granted the defendant's motion for dismissal, holding that the state was the owner of the residences, not the corrections officers, and therefore the latter had no standing to sue on Third Amendment challenge.

The Fourth Amendment—Search and Arrest Warrants

If the Third Amendment is the least litigated of the Bill of Rights Amendments, by contrast, the Fourth Amendment is one of the most often litigated. Some five dozen cases involve challenges to federal, state, and local laws on the basis of the Fourth Amendment. Most of those cases occurred after the Civil War with the enactment of the Fourteenth Amendment. The Supreme Court used the incorporation doctrine to apply the Fourth Amendment guarantees to state and local governments. As the vast majority of criminal law is enacted at the state and local levels of government, it is not surprising that most search-and-seizure cases involve those levels (see table 5.4 for a sample of some two dozen Fourth Amendment–related cases).

The Fourth Amendment states: "The right of the people to be secure in their persons, houses, papers, and effects, against unreasonable search and seizures, shall not be violated, and no Warrants shall be issued, but upon probable cause, supported by Oath or affirmation, and particularly describing the place to be searched, and the persons or things to be seized." It is the only amendment relevant to civilians' control over their homes and property. The amendment raises a number of questions about which problems and issues are concerned and about which the Supreme Court had to render decisions that provided for some resolutions to those issues. For example, what is "unreasonable" seizure? As developments in technology enabled the government to "electronically" enter a citizen's private property, the very method of "seizing" evidence became a question. Does the collection of metadata constitute a seizure? When do citizens have, or not have, a reasonable expectation of privacy? When, if ever, can a person be searched without a warrant? What provides "probable cause" for securing a warrant to search? Can a car seat be searched? Can evidence be seized when it is in "plain view"? Are there exigent circumstances that justify a warrantless search and seizure? Are searches permissible when they are incident to a lawful arrest? Are there exceptions for searches at U.S borders? Are there exceptions for searches conducted in public schools, for example, of students' lockers? Using supercomputers, can the federal government search "metadata" (Issacharoff, Karlan, Pildes, and Persily 2016; Kilman and Costello 2000; LaFave, Israel, King, and Kerr 2017; Lasson 1937; Nowak and Rotunda 2012)?

Exemplary cases dealing with those questions will be discussed further in chapter 2. This section highlights a dozen cases from different time periods to illustrate the development of "search and seizure" jurisprudence.

In the landmark Supreme Court case of *Schenck v. United States* (249 U.S. 47, 1919), the Court upheld the use of evidence seized from the Socialist Party regarding their opposition to the draft. The majority opinion of the Court was written by Justice Oliver Wendell Holmes Jr. The decision upheld the enforcement of the Espionage Act of 1917 during World War I. It notably articulated the "clear and present danger" test. It was subsequently overruled by *Brandenburg v. Ohio* (395 U.S. 444, 1969).

Olmstead v. United States (277 U.S. 438, 1928) concerned whether the use of wiretapped private telephone conversations obtained by federal agents without judicial approval could be used as evidence in court, or whether such use as evidence constituted a violation of the defendants' Fourth Amendment rights. Olmstead and the other defendants were bootleggers convicted of possessing, transporting, and selling alcohol in violation of the National Prohibition Act (41 Stat. 305, 1919; also known as the Volstead Act). Chief Justice William H. Taft delivered the majority opinion of the Court. In its 5–4 decision, the Court ruled that the Fourth Amendment forbade the introduction of evidence obtained in violation of it. However, the decision concluded that wiretapping as occurred in this case did not amount to a search or seizure within the meaning of the Fourth Amendment.

Brinegar v. United States (338 U.S. 160, 1949) was a 6–3 landmark Supreme Court decision that used a "reasonableness test" in warrantless searches, concluding that such a search must always be reasonable. The majority opinion was written by Justice Wiley Rutledge and joined by Justices Vinson, Black, Reed, Douglas, and Burton. The dissenting opinion was written by Justice Robert Jackson, joined by Justices Frankfurter and Murphy. In assessing using probable cause to conduct an arrest, the Court held that the Fourth Amendment still required a reasonable ground for belief of guilt whenever a judge or court evaluates a warrantless search (LaFave 2012; Howard 1999; Tushnet 2008).

During the Chief Justice Earl Warren years, the Supreme Court handed down *Mapp v. Ohio* (367 U.S. 294, 1961), a landmark decision that established the "exclusionary rule." This rule or judicial doctrine prevents prosecutors from using evidence that was obtained in violation of the Fourth Amendment by using the incorporation of the Fourteenth Amendment's due process clause to apply the Fourth Amendment's guarantees to the states. The majority opinion in *Mapp* was written by Justice Tom Clark, joined by Chief Justice Earl Warren and Justices Black, Douglas, and Brennan. The dissent was written by Justice John Harlan, joined by Justices Frankfurter and Whitaker (LaFave 2012; Long 2006; Tushnet 2008; Zotti 2005).

Also during the Warren Court era, in *Katz v. United States* (389 U.S. 347, 1967), the Supreme Court redefined what constitutes "searches and seizures" with regard to the Fourth Amendment. The decision set forth what became known as the *Katz* test that asks whether a person has a "reasonable expectation of privacy." It has been used subsequently in thousands of cases as advancement in technology has constantly posed new questions as to expectations of privacy (LaFave 2012). The majority opinion in *Katz* was written by Justice Potter Stewart, joined by Chief Justice Earl Warren and with Justices Douglas, Harlan, Brennan, White, and Fortas. The sole dissent was written by Justice Hugo Black.

In the 8–1 decision rendered in *Terry v. Ohio* (392 U.S. 1, 1968), the Supreme Court held that the Fourth Amendment's prohibition of unreasonable search and seizure is not violated when a police officer stops a suspect on the street and frisks him without probable cause to arrest if the police officer has reasonable suspicion that the person is committing or is about to commit a crime and believes that the person "may be armed and presently dangerous." The majority opinion in *Terry* was written by Chief Justice Earl Warren, joined by Justices Black, Brennan, Stewart, Fortas, Marshall, Harlan, and White. The sole dissent was by Justice William Douglas (LaFave 2012; LaFave, Israel, King, and Kerr 2017; Tushnet 2008).

The Supreme Court under Chief Justice Warren Burger turned notably more conservative than the Warren Court. *United States v. Matlock* (415 U.S. 164, 1974) is a 6–3 Supreme Court decision that ruled that the Fourth Amendment's prohibition on unreasonable search and seizure was not violated by police obtaining *voluntary consent* from a *third party* who possessed common authority over the premises to be searched. The majority opinion was written by Justice Byron White, with Chief Justice Warren Burger and Justices Stewart, Blackmun, Powell, and Rehnquist. The dissenting opinion was written by Justice William Douglas, joined by Justices Brennan and Marshall.

In *United States v. Ross* (456 U.S. 798, 1982), the Supreme Court ruled 6–3 on whether a legal warrantless search of an automobile allowed for the search of a closed container (and thus not in "plain view") in the trunk of the car. Was it constitutionally permissible to be searched as well? The Court held that such a search was constitutional. The *Ross* decision set the precedent of the "automobile exception," a doctrine based on the car's "practical mobility" that made it impractical to take the time to get a warrant, and that vehicles have a lower expectation of privacy than does a house or office. The majority opinion was written by Justice Stevens, joined by Chief Justice Warren Burger and Justices Blackmun, Power, Rehnquist, and O'Connor. The dissent in *Ross* was written by Justice Byron White, with Justices Marshall and Brennan.

Ohio v. Robinette (519 U.S. 33, 1976) ruled that the Fourth Amendment does not require police officers to inform a motorist at the end of a traffic stop that they are free to go before seeking permission to search the car. The majority opinion, held by Chief Justice Rehnquist and joined by Justices Sandra Day O'Connor, Antonin Scalia, Anthony Kennedy, David Souter, Clarence Thomas, and Stephen Breyer, was that the touchstone of the Fourth Amendment's "reasonableness" must be measured by the totality of the circumstances. The dissenting opinion in *Robinette* was written by liberal Justice Ruth Bader Ginsburg, joined by Justice John Stevens.

The decision in *United States v. Drayton* (536 U.S. 194, 2002) clarified the Fourth Amendment's protection against warrantless search and seizure when that search and seizure occurred on buses (in this case, on a Greyhound bus in Florida) as part of a drug interdiction effort. The search found that two passengers had taped packages of cocaine to their legs. In a 6–3 decision, the majority opinion was written by Justice Anthony Kennedy, with Justices Rehnquist, O'Connor, Scalia, Thomas, and Breyer. The dissenting opinion was written by Justice David Souter, with Justices Stevens and Ginsburg.

The technological development of GPS tracking devices was at issue in *United States v. Jones* (132 U.S. 945, 2012). The question was whether installing (planting) a GPS tracking device on a vehicle to monitor the vehicle's movements constituted a search under the Fourth Amendment. It was used in a drug trafficking case. The Court ruled unanimously that planting a GPS device on Jones' personal effects (his car) was per se a search. The decision held that the *Katz* test of a "reasonable expectation of privacy" did not displace the common-law trespassing test that preceded it. The unanimous decision was written by Justice Antonin Scalia.

Finally, in *Carpenter v. United States* (585 U.S.____ 2018), the Court ruled on the use of historical cell phone location records. In a 5–4 decision, the majority of the Court held that the government violated the Fourth Amendment by accessing, without a legal search warrant, historical records containing the physical location of a cell phone. The majority opinion was written by Chief Justice John Roberts, joined by the liberal justices of the Court, Ruth Bader Ginsburg, Stephen Breyer, Sonia Sotomayor, and Elena Kegan. The dissenting opinion was written by Justice Anthony Kennedy, joined by the conservative justices of the Court, Samuel Alito, Clarence Thomas, and Neil Gorsuch.

The Fifth Amendment—Rights in Criminal Cases and Compelling Self-Incrimination

The Fifth Amendment states:

> No person shall be held to answer for a capital or otherwise infamous crime, unless on a presentment or indictment by a Grand Jury, except in cases arising in the land or naval forces, or in the Militia, when in actual service in time of War or public danger, nor shall any person be subject for the same offense to be twice put in jeopardy of life or limb, nor shall be compelled in any criminal case to be a witness against himself, nor be deprived of life, liberty, or property, without due process of law; nor shall private property be taken for public use, without just compensation.

There have been seventeen Supreme Court cases in which the Fifth Amendment was at issue (see Table 5.5). This section presents ten illustrative cases. They exemplify court decisions across various time periods and concern various aspects of the Fifth Amendment.

Marbury v. Madison (5 U.S. 137, 1803) is a landmark decision that is important because it established the principle of judicial review, giving U.S. courts the power to strike down laws, statutes, and government actions that the court determines violate the Constitution of the United States. The decision, written by Chief Justice John Marshall, is considered to be one of the foundations of U.S. constitutional law. It secured the Supreme Court's primary role in constitutional interpretation. Marbury had been appointed as Justice of the Peace by outgoing president John Adams, but the commission had not been delivered before incoming president Thomas Jefferson took office. The Court decided that Marbury had the right to the commission as Justice of the Peace and that the refusal to deliver the commission to him was a violation of his right (i.e., denying his right to property) without due process of law. The sticking point was whether the Supreme Court had jurisdiction over the case. Chief Justice Marshall ruled that the Constitution only gave the Supreme Court jurisdiction over cases brought by states, not individuals, thus declaring the Judiciary Act of September 24, 1789 (1 Stat. 73) (which expanded the cases the Supreme Court could hear), unconstitutional. This established the Court's power to review laws created by Congress. The principle of judicial review was important to the checks-and-balances system. In Justice Marshall's words, "a law repugnant to the constitution is void, and that the courts, as well as other departments, are bound by that instrument" (Brest et al. 2018; Chemerinsky 2019; Epstein 2014; Miller 2009). During this pre–Civil War period, the Court held the view that its limitation applied only to the federal government.

In the case of *Dred Scott v. Sanford* (60 U.S. 393, 1857), Chief Justice Roger Taney, writing for the majority, held that all people of African descent, free or slave, were not U.S. citizens and therefore had no right to sue in federal court. The 7–2 decision stated that the Fifth Amendment protected slave owners' rights because slaves were their legal property (Fehenbacher 1981; Tushnet 2008; Levy 1986).

Blockburger v. United States (284 U.S. 299, 1932) was a unanimous decision written by Justice George Sutherland. By this decision, the Supreme Court set important standards to prevent double jeopardy. The Court held that the defendant had not been subjected to double jeopardy for selling different drugs to the same person. In Sutherland's words, "Each of the offenses created requires proof of a different element. The applicable rule is that, where the same act or transaction constitutes a violation of two distinct statutory provisions, the test to be applied to determine whether there are two offenses or only one is whether each provision requires proof of an additional fact which the other does not."

What conditions may result in compelling a person to self-incriminate? That was at issue in the landmark decision *Chambers v. Florida* (309 U.S. 227, 1940). The case concerned whether the extent to which police pressure resulted in a criminal's confession violated the due process clause. The majority opinion was written by Justice Hugo Black. The Court ruled in favor of the defendants (four Black men) and overturned their convictions, holding that their confessions were compelled and therefore inadmissible. This decision was the first time in which the Court held that treatment short of actual physical violence should result in the suppression of evidence.

Similar reasoning was used in *Ashcraft v. Tennessee* (322 U.S. 143, 1944). By a 6–3 decision, the Court held that the confessions of E. E. Ashcraft and his codefendant, John Ware, to the crime of murder of Ashcraft's wife were extorted from them. Ware, a Black man, asserted that he confessed to the crime because he feared mob violence. Ashcraft confessed to the crime after being continuously questioned for thirty-six hours with only one five-minute break, claiming he was threatened and abused. The majority opinion was written by Justice Hugo Black, with Justices Stone, Reed, Douglas, Murphy, and Rutledge. The three dissenting justices were Jackson, Roberts, and Frankfurter.

The decision in *Fong Foo v. United States* (369 U.S. 141, 1962) upheld the protection against double jeopardy by the federal government, holding in the opinion delivered *per curiam* that reversed a decision of the Court of Appeals on the grounds of the Fifth Amendment's double-jeopardy provision. The Court held that the Fifth Amendment prevented the federal government from bringing a defendant to trial twice on the same charge.

Miranda v. Arizona (384 U.S. 436, 1966) was a landmark Supreme Court decision that ruled that detained criminal suspects, prior to police questioning, must be informed of their constitutional rights, including the right to an attorney and the right against self-incrimination. The *Miranda* decision established the precedent of the "Miranda warning" as part of police routine procedure to ensure that a suspect are informed of his rights. The 5–4 majority opinion was written by Chief Justice Earl Warren, with Justices Black, Douglas, Brennan, and Fortas. In dissent were Justices Harlan, Clark, Stewart, and White (Levy 1986; Stuart 2004).

Roe v. Wade (410 U.S. 113, 1973) was yet another landmark civil rights decision by the Warren Court. By a 7–2 decision, the Court ruled that the U.S. constitution protects a pregnant woman's liberty to choose to have an abortion without excessive government restrictions. It struck down a Texas law banning abortion. *Roe v. Wade* effectively legalized the abortion procedure across the United States. The majority opinion by Justice Harry Blackmun asserted that a woman's right to an abortion was implicit in the *privacy right* of the Fifth Amendment, and the Court applied it to state laws using the Fourteenth Amendment (Reagan 1996).

The issue of how the Supreme Court should view what constitutes double jeopardy was the concern in *United States v. Felix* (503 U.S. 378, 1992). In its 7–2 decision, the Court held that an offense and a conspiracy to commit that offense are not the same offense for the purpose of double jeopardy. The majority opinion was written by Chief Justice William Rehnquist, with Justices White, O'Connor, Scalia, Kennedy, Souter, and Thomas. The two dissenting justices in *Felix* were the ideologically über-liberal Justices Stevens and Blackmun.

The Fifth Amendment's protection of the right to privacy and the issue of homosexual behavior and its applicability to state laws forbidding that activity were at the heart of the case of *Lawrence v. Texas* (539 U.S. 558, 2003). It was a landmark case in the LGBT rights movement. The *Lawrence v. Texas* decision held that laws prohibiting private homosexual activity between consenting adults are unconstitutional infringements on the Fifth Amendment's right to privacy. The case involved a large number of *amicus curiae* briefs. The 6–3 decision's majority opinion was written by Justice Anthony Kennedy, with Justices Stevens, Souter, Ginsburg, Breyer, and O'Connor. In dissent were Justices Scalia, Rehnquist, and Thomas. The *Lawrence* decision overturned a prior case on the matter, *Bowers v. Hardwick* (478 U.S. 186, 1986) (Carpenter 2012; Chemerinsky 2015; Nowak and Rotunda 2012).

In the post-9/11 world, with its heightened fear of international terrorism, the Supreme Court rendered a landmark decision in *Hamadi v. Rumsfeld* (542 U.S. 507, 2004). This complex case involved both noncitizen detainees as enemy combatants and U.S. citizens also detained as enemy combatants. The decision in *Hamadi* was rendered by a plurality vote, with justices concurring and dissenting on different aspects of the case and the applicability of Fifth Amendment protections regarding procedural matters. In *Hamadi*, the Court held that the federal government had the power to detain enemy combatants, including U.S. citizens, but that U.S. citizen detainees must be given the rights of due process to challenge their enemy combatant status before an impartial (appellate) authority.

The Sixth Amendment—Rights to Fair Trial

The Sixth Amendment states:

> In all criminal prosecutions, the accused shall enjoy the right to a speedy and public trial, by an impartial jury of the State and district wherein the crime shall have

been committed, which district shall have been previously ascertained by law, and to be informed of the nature and cause of the accusation; to be confronted with the witnesses against him; to have compulsory process for obtaining witnesses in his favor, and to have the Assistance of Counsel for his defence.

Quite literary, hundreds of cases have been heard based on Sixth Amendment challenges as to what is meant by a "fair" trial, and exactly what protections afforded by the Sixth Amendment impose limits on state and local government criminal procedures. The Sixth Amendment raises numerous questions and problems, and the Supreme Court has rendered hundreds of "resolutions" to those concerns, many of which are discussed more fully in chapter 2. Given those many questions, the Sixth Amendment has been, arguably, the most litigated of the Bill of Rights amendments.

Sixth Amendment cases concerning what is a *fair trial* have dealt with such issues as the following: What constitutes proof beyond a reasonable doubt? Is the use of false evidence ever permissible? What expenses for indigent defendants must be provided by the state in order for the trial to be fair? How does the mental competence of the defendant affect the fairness of a trial? What burdens does the state have to disclose any exculpatory material? What right does a defendant have to present a defense? How does racial discrimination in the jury pool and venire affect the fairness of a trial? In order to ensure an impartial jury, must the jury represent a fair cross-section of the community? What is the effect of discriminatory peremptory challenges? What limitations as to the availability and impartiality of a jury are necessary to satisfy the fairness of the trial? Do criminal trials always need a unanimous jury verdict?

This section briefly reviews ten cases that are illustrative of the Supreme Court's decisions over time and on the basis of several of those questions raised by the Sixth Amendment protections and prohibitions of federal, state, or local laws, or by lower court decisions. They illustrate how jurisprudence on the Sixth Amendment evolved over time.

In *Beaver v. Haubert* (198 U.S. 1905), the Supreme Court decided that the constitutional right to a speedy trial, and by a jury in the district where the offense was committed, relates to the time, and not to the place, of a trial. The Court held that "speedy" depends on the circumstances; public trial does not mean right away, but that if there are valid reasons for some delays. The Court ruled that Sixth Amendment is not an absolute limit as to place in order to enable a change of venue that is sometimes necessary in cases that are particularly "notorious" criminal cases to ensure an "unbiased" jury pool is available.

Pyle v. Kansas (317 U.S. 213, 1942) held that (1) habeas corpus is a remedy available in the state courts of Kansas to persons imprisoned in violation of rights guaranteed by the Federal Constitution, and (2) a petition for a writ of habeas corpus alleging that the petitioner is imprisoned upon a conviction obtained through the use of testimony known by the prosecuting officers to have been perjured, and through suppression of the evidence favorable to him (exculpatory material), and sufficiently alleges a deprivation of rights guaranteed by the federal constitution, and the denial of the petition without a determination as to the truth of the allegation, was in error. The Court reversed the lower court's decision not to grant a writ of habeas corpus. Granting a writ of habeas corpus is viewed as a remedy for a prosecutor acting in bad faith, which can be ascertained or determined upon review by an appellate court.

In *Avery v. Georgia* (345 U.S. 559, 1953), the Supreme Court reversed the conviction of the petitioner, an African American, by the state of Georgia. He was convicted of rape. The Court held that the petitioner showed discrimination in the selection of his jury panel, in which all the jurors selected to the jury panel where white, even though many African American potential jurors were available in the jury pool. It was one of the early cases of the civil rights era wherein African Americans increasingly used federal courts to address the discriminatory actions of state and local governments and courts.

"Speedy" is not the only factor for a *fair* proceeding. In *United States v. Ewell* (383 U.S. 116, 1966), the defendants had been indicted on certain drug charges and then convicted and sentenced. When they appealed, the original indictments were thrown out because they were not prepared correctly. Nineteen months later, the federal government brought new, corrected indictments on the same charges. The Supreme Court found that the nineteen-month delay was not a violation of the Sixth Amendment because the defendants were not just sitting in prison; they were using the court system to be heard. The Court ruled that rushing that process would be just as damaging as intentionally delaying it.

Klopfer v. North Carolina (386 U.S. 213, 1967) concerned Peter Klopfer, a civil rights activist and Duke University biology professor, who had been protesting segregation in a restaurant. He was indicted for criminal trespass. The jury was unable to reach a verdict at trial. The prosecutor in the case used a North Carolina law for a "nolle prosegui with leave," a procedure to keep the case open indefinitely, and to restore the case for trial without further judicial permission. By a 9–0 decision, the Supreme Court held that the North Carolina law was unconstitutional and that there was nothing to sustain the use of the procedure in either the North Carolina statute or in common law. The Court applied the Sixth Amendment's speedy trial protection to the state.

In *Baker v. Wingo* (407 U.S. 514, 1972) the Court held by a unanimous decision that a determination as to whether or not the right to a speedy trial was violated must be made on a case-by-case basis. The Court set forth four factors to be considered in making that determination. The majority opinion by Justice Lewis Powell asked: How long is too long? Its four factors were as follows: (1) length of the delay, (2) reason for the delay, (3) time and manner in which the defendant has asserted his right, and (4) the degree of prejudice to the defendant caused by the delay. The Court upheld Baker's conviction, noting that his case was not prejudiced by the delay.

What expenses can an indigent person reasonably require the state to bear? In *Ake v. Oklahoma* (470 U.S. 68, 1985), the Court found that the due process clause of the Fourteenth Amendment and certain expenses for an indigent defendant being borne by the state were required by the Sixth Amendment. Specifically, the Court held that the state had to provide a psychiatric evaluation to be used on behalf of an indigent defendant if he needed it. The 8–1 majority opinion was written by Justice Thurgood Marshall, with Justices Brennan, White, Blackmun, Powell, Stevens, O'Connor, and a concurrence by Chief Justice Warren Burger. The sole dissent was by Justice William Rehnquist.

The requirement of "proof beyond a reasonable doubt" in order to have a fair trial was at issue in *Schlup v. Delo* (513 U.S. 298, 1995). In this 5–4 decision, the Supreme Court expanded the ability to reopen a case in light of new evidence of innocence. Justice John Stevens, writing for the majority with Justices O'Connor, Souter, Ginsburg, and Breyer, held that: "A condemned man can bypass the procedural bar on a successive federal habeas corpus petition if he shows that a constitutional violation has probably resulted in the conviction of one who is actually innocent." The dissenting opinion was written by Chief Justice Rehnquist, with Justices Kennedy, Thomas, and Scalia.

Sell v. United States (530 U.S. 166, 2003) dealt with the issue of mental competence necessary to stand trial. In its 6–3 decision, the Supreme Court imposed stringent limits on the right of a lower court to order the forcible administration of antipsychotic medication to a criminal defendant who had to be found competent to stand trial for the sole purpose of making him competent and able to be tried. The Supreme Court determined that the lower court had failed to determine that all the appropriate criteria had been considered before issuing a court order to forcibly medicate the defendant. The lower court's decision was reversed. The majority opinion was written by Justice Stephen Breyer, with Chief Justice Rehnquist, and Justices Stevens, Kennedy, Souter, and Ginsburg. The dissenters were Justices Scalia, O'Connor, and Thomas.

Finally, in *Felkner v. Jackson* (131 U.S. 1305, 2011), the Court dealt with a case in which a California jury convicted Steven Frank Jackson of numerous sexual offenses in an attack on a seventy-two-year-old woman who lived in his apartment complex. Jackson's lawyer filed an appeal arguing that a comparative juror analysis revealed that the prosecutor's explanation for the removal of certain potential jurors was pretextual, and that a non-Black juror who had negative experience with law enforcement was allowed to remain on the jury. After the California Supreme Court denied Jackson's petition for review, Jackson appealed. The U.S. Supreme Court reversed the decision of the Court of Appeals for the Ninth Circuit and remanded the case for further proceedings consistent with the Supreme Court's opinion.

The Seventh Amendment—Rights in Civil Cases

The Seventh Amendment reads as follows:

> In Suits at common law, where the value in controversy shall exceed twenty dollars, the right of trial by jury shall be preserved, and no fact tried by a jury, shall be otherwise re-examined in any Court of the United States, then according to the rules of the common law.

Two U.S. Supreme Court cases dealt with the Seventh Amendment. In *The Justices v. Murray* (76 U.S. 274, 1869), the plaintiff, Patrie, brought a suit for assault and battery and false imprisonment against Murray and Buckley in the Supreme Court of New York. The state Supreme Court refused to return the case to the lower court on the basis of a writ of error. The U.S. Circuit Court then issued a writ of mandamus, a court order issued by a judge or an appellate court at a petitioner's request that compels someone to execute a duty they are legally obligated to complete. The Supreme Court ruled that the clause in the Seventh Amendment prohibiting the reexamination of any fact found by a jury is not restricted in its application to suits in common law tried before juries in courts of the United States; it also applies equally to cases tried before a jury in a state court. Justice Samuel Nelson wrote the majority opinion for the Supreme Court. The case is the first one in which the Supreme Court applied the Seventh Amendment to the states.

In *Feltner v. Columbia Pictures Television Inc.* (523 U.S. 340, 1998), the Supreme Court ruled that if there is to be an award of statutory damages in a copyright infringement case, then the opposing party has the right to demand a jury trial. In *Feltner*, the question before the Court was whether the statutory damages (for copyright infringement by broadcasting television shows after the license to do so was revoked), which equaled $8,800,000 in damages, was tried in the form of a bench trial in a court of law, or a trial in a court of equity? After examining the historical practice of copyright infringement cases, the Supreme Court held that it had been in a court of law, not equity, and thus Feltner was entitled to a jury trial on the issue of the amount of statutory damages. The judgment was reversed and sent back to a jury trial. After a jury trial, the award was increased to $31.68 million. In the 8–1 decision of the Supreme Court, the majority opinion was written by Justice Clarence Thomas. The sole dissent was by Justice Antonin Scalia.

The Eighth Amendment—Bails, Fines, and Punishments

The Eighth Amendment is quite short. It reads: "Excessive bail shall not be required, nor excessive fines imposed, nor cruel and unusual punishments inflicted." It has been subject to many challenges. Four cases concerned the excessive bail clause. More than four dozen cases concerned the cruel and unusual punishment clause. The cruel and unusual punishment cases have most often been on the basis of challenging capital punishment. Among those, some have been on the basis of the *method* used for capital punishment and others on the basis of the characteristics of the individual sentenced to death (such as the mental capacity of the person) and several more on whether extenuating or aggravating circumstances are considered by a judge or by a jury. This section will briefly highlight the four cases concerning excessive bail. Ten of the four dozen cases concerning capital punishment are presented as representative of them across the period of time in which the case was held, or on characteristics of the individual sentenced to capital punishment. States vary as to their having capital punishment: twenty-eight states have it, but four of those also have a governor-ordered moratorium on actual executions; and the remaining twenty-two states have no death penalty law (see table 5.7). Federal criminal law does allow for the death penalty, but it was not used for some time. The federal penal system began to again utilize the death penalty in July 2020, carrying out three executions.

The excessive bail cases are the following. *Stack v. Boyle* (342 U.S. 1, 1951) involved twelve members of the Communist Party charged with conspiracy to violate the Smith Act. Bail for them was set at $50,000 each (roughly equivalent today to more than $500,000). The defendants moved to reduce their bail. The Supreme Court held 8–0 (with one justice not taking part) that the bail set was excessively high, and no evidence was presented by the state (California) that they would flee before the trial date, and therefore the bail was ruled unconstitutional. The majority opinion was written by Chief Justice Fred Vinson. In *Schilb v. Kuebel* (404 U.S. 357, 1971) the Court held that the Illinois bail system did not violate equal protection or excessive bail by its retention of a 1 percent charge as an administrative fee, as the fee was imposed on all, guilty and innocent alike, who seek it. In *Murphy v. Hunt* (455 U.S. 478, 1982) the Court decided for Murphy, *per curiam*, 8–0. The

Court did not rule on the constitutionality claim as it became a moot issue following his conviction and imprisonment in the state of Nebraska. In *United States v. Salerno* (481 U.S. 739, 1987), the Court, in its 6–3 ruling, held that the United States Bail Reform Act of 1984 permitting federal courts to detain an arrestee prior to trial, if the government could prove that the individual was potentially dangerous to others in the community, was constitutional with respect to both the equal protection clause of the Fifth Amendment and the excessive bail clause of the Eighth Amendment. The majority opinion was written by Chief Justice William Rehnquist with Justices White, Blackmun, Powell, O'Connor, and Scalia. The dissenting opinion was by Justice Thurgood Marshall, with Justices Brennan and Stevens.

Ten capital punishment cases, from among the more than four dozen such cases, are briefly cited here to illustrate decisions over time, the characteristics of the convicted person sentenced to death, or based on some procedural matter—such as whether a judge or the jury made decisions on mitigating or extenuating factors. In *Wilkerson v. Utah* (99 U.S. 130, 1879, the Supreme Court, in a unanimous decision, upheld as constitutional death by firing squad. *In re Kemmier* (136 U.S. 436, 1890) was the decision in which the Court unanimously held that execution by electrocution was constitutional. In *Powell v. Alabama* (287 U.S. 45, 1932), the Court, by a 7–2 decision, reversed the sentence of nine Black men, holding that courts are required to ensure that, in capital cases, indigent defendants who do not represent themselves must be appointed counsel. In *Furman v. Georgia* (408 U.S. 238, 1972), the death sentences were held unconstitutional by a 5–4 decision in which each justice wrote a separate opinion. The *Furman* decision resulted in all death sentences pending at the time to be reduced to life imprisonment, and made all previous capital punishment laws void. It was followed by *Gregg v. Georgia* (428 U.S. 153, 1976), which reinstated the death penalty but required all death penalty statutes to provide for a bifurcated trial in capital cases:

one trial to decide guilt and a separate trial to decide on punishment. In *Beck v. Alabama* (447 U.S. 625, 1980), the Court held 7–2 that a jury must be allowed to consider lesser punishments, not just capital offense or acquittal. In *Edmund v. Florida* (458 U.S. 625, 1982), by a 5–4 decision, the Supreme Court ruled the death penalty unconstitutional for a person who is only plays a minor role in a felony crime and does not kill, attempt to kill, or intend to kill. *Ford v. Wainwright* (477 U.S. 399, 1986), by a 5–4 decision, ruled that execution of an insane convict is unconstitutional. The age of the person at the time of committing a crime was at issue in *Thompson v. Oklahoma* (487 U.S. 815, 1988). The Court decided, 5–3, that capital punishment for crimes committed at age fifteen or younger was unconstitutional. In *Ring v. Arizona* (536 U.S. 584, 2002), the Supreme Court ruled, in a 7–2 decision, that a death sentence where the necessary aggravating factors are determined by a judge violates a defendant's constitutional right to a trial by jury. *Ring* mandated that the jury should determine if there are such aggravating factors sufficient to allow for the death penalty to be imposed. Finally, in *Baze v. Rees* (553 U.S. 35, 2008), in a 7–2 decision, the Court held that Kentucky's lethal injection method using sodium thiopental was constitutional. Table 5.6 presents data for more such capital punishment cases to illustrate the basis for the decision, the time of the case, the vote by the Court's members, and such aspects as whether it was for a federal case or a state case.

Table 5.8 presents additional information on capital punishment cases and rulings over the years from 1905 to 2016. The table presents a dozen such additional exemplary cases.

The Ninth Amendment—Rights Retained by the People

The Ninth Amendment states: "The enumeration in the Constitution, of certain rights, shall not be construed to deny or disparage others retained by the people." Nine Supreme Court decisions handed down between 1923 and 1992 have addressed

Ninth Amendment questions. Several upheld a state law, essentially deferring to the Ninth Amendment's rights retained by people/state, and several overturned a state law on other constitutional grounds.

In *Meyer v. Nebraska* (262 U.S. 390, 1923), the Court ruled that a 1919 Nebraska law (the Simon Act) restricting foreign language education violated the due process clause of the Fourteenth Amendment. The 1919 Nebraska law reflected the xenophobia aroused by World War I. In his dissent, Justice Oliver Wendell Holmes Jr. raised the issue of whether the Ninth Amendment would allow the state the right to enact the law (Tushnet 2008). *Pierce v. Society of Sisters* (268 U.S. 590, 1925) struck down an Oregon statute that required all children to attend public schools, thereby extending the due process clause to states, recognizing the principle of *personal civil liberties* (Abrams 2009; Alley 1999). Both *Meyer* and *Pierce* are often cited as cases in which the Supreme Court used *substantive due process* in the area of civil liberties (Ross 1994).

Personal rights to use contraception were at issue in *Griswold v. Connecticut* (481 U.S. 479, 1965). The *Griswold* case concerned Connecticut's "Comstock law" that prohibited any person from using "any drug, medicinal article, or instrument for the purpose of preventing conception." The Supreme Court held, 7–2, that the Connecticut law was a violation of the right to privacy (Johnson 2005). Similarly, in *Doe v. Bolton* (410 U.S. 179, 1973), by a 7–2 vote, the Supreme Court overturned the abortion law of Georgia (and on the same day, of Texas, in *Roe v. Wade)* on the right-to-privacy grounds. The Georgia law allowed abortion only in cases of rape or where there was possible fatal injury to the mother. Justice Blackmun wrote the majority opinion (Cushman 2001).

The question of personal civil liberty rights versus the right of a state to criminalize private homosexual behavior (using a state sodomy law) was at issue in *Bowers v. Hardwick* (498 U.S. 186, 1986). The Supreme Court, by a 5–4 vote, upheld the constitutionality of a Georgia law criminalizing oral and anal sex between consenting adults. That decision was over-turned, however, in 2003, in *Lawrence v. Texas* (Carpenter 2012; Eskridge 2008; Nussbaum 2010; Shilts 1993).

Two state abortion laws refined the standards set in *Roe v. Wade*. In *Webster v. Reproductive Health Services* (492 U.S. 490, 1989), the Supreme Court upheld a Missouri law imposing limits on state funds, facilities, and employees in assisting with or counseling on abortions. In a unanimous vote on some of the law's provisions and dissent on some of its other provisions, the Court held that the law's provisions requiring testing for viability of the fetus after twenty weeks were constitutional, but that those limiting abortion in the second trimester of pregnancy were unconstitutional. Dissenting opinions were by the liberal Justices Blackmun, Brennan, Marshall, and Stevens. Similarly, in *Planned Parenthood v. Casey* (505 U.S. 833, 1992), the Supreme Court upheld Pennsylvania's Abortion Control Act of 1982. The Court upheld the right to abortion as per *Roe v. Wade* but refined standards for analyzing restrictions on that right by crafting the "undue burden" standard for restrictions. It overturned the *Roe v. Wade* first trimester standard by a plurality decision. The majority vote was by Justices O'Connor, Kennedy, Souter, Blackmun, and Stevens; dissenting were Chief Justice Rehnquist and Justices White, Scalia, and Thomas.

The Tenth Amendment—Powers Retained by States and the People

The Tenth Amendment states succinctly: "The powers not delegated to the United States by the Constitution, nor prohibited by it to the States, are reserved to the States respectively, or to the people." Eleven Supreme Court decisions ruled on challenges to federal or state laws that involved conflicts between federal and state laws pitting the Tenth Amendment against other amendments (fourth, sixth, fourteenth; see table 5.9). This section will briefly discuss seven of those cases (four others have been discussed previously regarding other Bill of Rights amendments).

In *The Slaughter House Cases* (83 U.S. 36, 1873) the Supreme Court resolved that the "citizens privileges and immunities," as per the Fourteenth Amendment, were limited to those spelled out in the federal Constitution regarding federal citizenship and did not include many rights given by individual states regarding state citizenship. The cases involved a state of Louisiana law limiting which slaughterhouses were allowed to operate; nonapproved butchers claimed they were deprived of the privilege of doing business. The majority opinion was by Justice Samuel Miller, with Justices Nathan Clifford, William Strong, Ward Hunt, and David Davis concurring. The dissenting opinion was by Justice Stephen Field, with Chief Justice Salmon Chase and Justices Noah Swayne and Joseph Bradley (Foner 1990; Gutzman 2007).

In *Lochner v. New York* (198 U.S. 45, 1905) the Supreme Court, in a 5–4 decision, held that a New York law limiting work time to ten hours per day and sixty hours per week was a violation of the due process clause of the Fourteenth Amendment, which the majority members of the Court viewed as containing a right to "freedom of contract." The majority opinion was written by Justice Rufus Peckham, with Chief Justice Melville Fuller and Justices David Brewer, Henry Brown, and Joseph McKenna. In dissent were Justices John Harlan, Edward White, and William Day, and, in a separate dissent, Justice Oliver Wendell Holmes Jr. The dissenting opinion of Justice Holmes became one of the most famous dissenting opinions in U.S. legal history, as he accused the majority of judicial activism (Bernstein 2012; Kens 1998; Tushnet 2008).

In *Brown v. Board of Education of Topeka, Kansas* (347 U.S. 483, 1954), the Court handed down a landmark decision that ruled that a Topeka, Kansas, segregation law in public schools violated the equal protection clause of the Fourteenth Amendment, pitting the Tenth Amendment's "states' rights" provision versus the Fourteenth. The unanimous Supreme Court decision was written by Chief Justice Earl Warren. *Brown* over-turned the separate-but-equal doctrine established in *Plessy v. Ferguson* that gave a constitutional blessing to segregation. *Brown* gave constitutional protection to desegregation laws and policy. It launched a frontal attack on "de jure" Jim Crow laws and spurred the modern Black civil rights movement (Fireside 2003; Keppel 2016; LeMay 2009; Ogletree 2004; Tushnet 2008).

Gideon v. Wainwright (372 U.S. 335, 1963) extended the right to counsel as required under the Sixth Amendment rights to defendants in criminal cases. The unanimous decision held that indigents who are unable to afford their own counsel must be provided counsel paid for by the state. *Gideon* gave great impetus to the use of a public defender position. It affirmed rights under the Sixth, Tenth, and Fourteenth Amendments. The majority opinion of the Court was written by Justice Hugo Black.

In *Regents of the University of California v. Bakke* (438 U.S. 265, 1978), the Court ruled 5–4 that the University of California's use of racial quotas in its admissions process was unconstitutional, but the use of affirmative action to accept more minority applicants was constitutional as long as it was one of several factors. The decision held that the quota provision violated the Fourteenth Amendment's equal protection clause (Ball 2000; LeMay 2009).

Finally, in *Bond v. United States* (564 U.S. 211, 2011), the Supreme Court ruled that individuals, just like states, may have standing to sue to raise a Tenth Amendment challenge to a federal law—in this case, the federal Chemical Weapons Convention Implementation Act of 1998—for a local assault that used a chemical irritant. The unanimous opinion of the Court was written by Justice Anthony Kennedy. It sets a precedent obviously relevant to their increased use in 2020 by the Trump administration in reaction to protests led by Black Lives Matter movement organizations to protest against abuse of police power and excessive use of force.

The Fourteenth Amendment—Civil Rights

The Fourteenth Amendment addresses many aspects of citizenship and the rights of U.S. citizens. It was ratified by the states on July 9, 1868, after the U.S. Civil War and, along with the Thirteenth and Fifteenth Amendments, is considered a Reconstruction Amendment. Section 1 of the amendment states:

> All persons born or naturalized in the United States, and subject to the jurisdiction thereof, are citizens of the United States and of the State wherein they reside. No State shall make or enforce any law which shall abridge the privileges and immunities of citizens of the United States; nor shall any State deprive any person of life, liberty, or property, without due process of law; nor deny to any person within its jurisdiction the equal protection of the laws.

Section 1 of the Fourteenth Amendment contains the most commonly used and often litigated phrase in the amendment: the "equal protection of the laws." The Fourteenth Amendment has been addressed in such landmark cases as *Brown v. Board of Education* (re: racial discrimination), *Roe v. Wade* (re: reproduction rights), *Bush v. Gore* (re: election recounts), *Reed v. Reed* (re: gender discrimination), *University of California v. Bakke* (re: racial quotas in education), *Elk v. Wilkins* (re: Native American citizenship), *United States v. Wong Kim Ark* (re: Chinese American citizenship), *United States v. Guest* and *United States v. Morrison* (re: state actions), *The Slaughter House Cases* (re: privileges and immunities), *Board of Regents v. Roth* (re: procedural due process), and *Lochner v. New York* (re: economic rights). It contains such important concepts as state action, privileges and immunities, and citizenship (LeMay 2009).

The Fifteenth Amendment—Black Suffrage

Section 1 of the Fifteenth Amendment states: "The right of citizens of the United States to vote shall not be denied or abridged by the United States or by any State on account of race, color, or previous condition of servitude." Section 2 states: "The Congress shall have the power to enforce this article by appropriate legislation." Five important Supreme Court cases handed down between 1876 and 2013 have dealt with challenges to laws of the United States and laws of three states based on the Fifteenth Amendment and the Voting Rights Act of 1965.

In *United States v. Reese* (92 U.S. 214, 1876), the Supreme Court heard its first voting rights case under the Fifteenth Amendment and the Enforcement Act of 1870. The Court, in a 7–2 decision, held that suffrage cannot be restricted based on race, color, or having previously been a slave. The Court held that the Fifteenth Amendment did not confer the right of suffrage, but it prohibited exclusion from voting based on race. The majority opinion in the case was written by Chief Justice Morrison Waite. The two dissenting opinions were by Justices Nathan Clifford and Ward Hunt.

In *Guinn v. United States* (238 U.S. 347, 1915), by an 8–0 decision, the Supreme Court found that the state of Oklahoma's grandfather clause exception to a literacy test for voting rights was unconstitutional based on the Fifteenth Amendment. Justice White's majority opinion found that the Oklahoma grandfather clause, which required Blacks to take the literacy test but excluded those whose grandfathers could vote (effectively, only whites) was "repugnant to the Fifteenth Amendment and therefore null and void." Justice James C. McReynolds, who hailed from Tennessee, did not take part in the decision.

The Supreme Court split on a strictly partisan basis in the highly controversial decision in *Bush v. Gore* (531 U.S. 98, 2000). The Supreme Court settled a dispute regarding the Florida recounting of ballots cast in the 2000 presidential election in four Florida counties: Volusia, Palm Beach, Broward, and Miami-Dade. They are all counties that traditionally vote Democratic and presumably would have tipped the balance of the Florida recount to Democrat Al Gore, thereby assuring him of 271 electoral-college votes and the presidency. In a *per curiam* decision, 5–4, the Court ended the recount process and awarded Florida's electoral college votes to George W. Bush, thus ensuring his victory. The five Republican-appointed justices voted for the majority, and the four Democratic-appointed justices voted against the decision (Ackerman 2002).

In *Shelby Country, Alabama v. Holder* (570 U.S. 529, 2012), the Court ruled 5–4 that the coverage formula in section 4(b) of the Voting Rights Act of 1965 was unconstitutional because the formula was based on forty-year-old data. The majority opinion was written by Chief Justice John Roberts, with Justices Scalia, Kennedy, Thomas, and Alito. The four liberal justices of the Court—Ginsburg, Breyer, Sotomayor, and Kagan—all dissented (Issacharoff, Karlan, Pildes, and Persily 2016).

Finally, in *Arizona v. Inter-Tribal Council of Arizona* (570 U.S. 1, 2013), the Supreme Court, by a 7–2 vote, held that Arizona's controversial voting rights law regarding registration requirements was unlawful because the requirements preempted federal voting law. The majority opinion was written by Justice Antonin Scalia, with Chief Justice Roberts, and Justices Ginsburg, Breyer, Sotomayor, Kagan, and Kennedy. The two dissenting opinions were by Justices Thomas and Alito.

Civil Rights Acts by the U.S. Congress

In the aftermath of the U.S. Civil War and in an effort to legislate Reconstruction and in furtherance of the protections of guaranteed by the Fourteenth and Fifteenth Amendments, the U.S. Congress enacted what eventually became a series of Civil Rights Acts (see table 5.10). The first such act was passed in April 1866. It had been passed in 1865 but vetoed by President Andrew Johnson. In 1866, the Congress passed the Civil Rights law overriding President Johnson's veto. The Civil Rights Act of April 6, 1866 (14 Stat. 27), was the first federal law to define citizenship and to affirm that all citizens are protected by the law. It was enacted to protect the rights of persons of African descent, both freedmen and former slaves emancipated by the Civil War and Lincoln's Emancipation Proclamation (January 1, 1863) (Foner 1990; Rutherglen 2013; White 2012).

The Civil Rights Act of March 3, 1875 (18 Stat. 335), is also known as the Enforcement Act. It was part of the Reconstruction era and was enacted to guarantee African Americans equal treatment in public accommodations, public transportation, and to prevent their being excluded from state and local trials. It was signed into law by President Ulysses S. Grant. It was essentially gutted in its effects by the Supreme Court's ruling in *Plessy v. Ferguson* that public accommodation discrimination could not be prohibited because such discrimination was a private, not a state, act. It had very little impact in the South, where state and local governments and social customs enforced Jim Crow laws for racial segregation (Friedlander and Gerber 2018; Finkelman 2013; Howard 1999).

One of the earliest leaders of a political strategy to fight for the civil rights of African Americans was the brilliant W. E. B. Du Bois, a historian and sociologist at Atlanta University. In 1905, Du Bois and a small group of Black intellectuals met in Niagara Falls, Canada. The Niagara Movement opposed the moderate, compromising position advocated by Booker T. Washington. The Niagara Movement called for radical change ending Black inferior social status. They advocated, for example, (1) against the loss of voting and civil rights due to Jim Crow laws, (2) for the end to segregated schools, (3) against the inhumane conditions in Southern prisons, (4) against the denial of equal job opportunities, and (5) against the segregation of the armed forces of the United States (Brooks 1996; LeMay 2009). The National Association for the Advancement of Colored People (NAACP) emerged out of their advocacy. The NAACP was established on February 12, 1909, the 100th anniversary of President Abraham Lincoln's birthday. Over the years, the NAACP led the campaign for Black civil rights through legal action, sponsoring suits, and supporting others with *amicus curiae* briefs. In 1915, the NAACP achieved its first major victory in one of hundreds of cases pursued at all levels of government when the Supreme Court declared unconstitutional the grandfather clause of the Oklahoma constitution in *Guinn v. United States* (238 U.S. 347, 1915). The NAACP won a greater victory in 1954, in *Brown v. Board of Education of Topeka, Kansas*, which finally overturned the "separate-but-equal" doctrine established in *Plessy v. Ferguson*. Importantly, the *Brown* decision gave a constitutional blessing to desegregate the United States, effectively beginning the end of de jure segregation (segregation by law) (Finkelman 2013; Howard 1999; Keppel 2016; Ogletree 2004).

In using federal courts to achieve civil rights changes, the NAACP was following the example set by the American Civil Liberties Union (ACLU), founded in New York City on January 19, 1920. The ACLU led the way in civil rights litigation, advocacy, and education, and either sponsored suits or supported others by writing amicus briefs in literally hundreds of cases with or on behalf of a wide variety of minority ethnic, racial, religious, and sexual-orientation groups (LeMay 2018).

The NAACP's victory in *Brown v. Board of Education* inspired the modern Black civil rights political activist movement from the late 1950s throughout the 1960s. The movement is best exemplified by establishment of the Southern Christian Leadership Conference (SCLC) in Atlanta, Georgia, on January 10, 1957. SCLC was led by arguably the most prominent Black civil rights activist in the United States, the Reverend Dr. Martin Luther King, Jr. (LeMay 2009). SCLC advocated for various Congressional civil rights laws passed in the late 1950s and 1960s, achieving considerable success before MLK's assassination in 1968. SCLC's success inspired a host of other civil rights groups that followed the direct-action protest strategy, such as Cesar Chavez's Chicano Movement, the American Farm Workers in 1962; the National Women's Political Caucus in 1971; and the American Indian Movement (AIM) in 1968 (LeMay 2009).

The Civil Rights Act of August 9, 1957 (71 Stat. 634), was a voting rights bill, the first passed by the U.S. Congress since the Civil Rights Act of 1875. The administration of President Dwight Eisenhower proposed it to protect the right to vote by African Americans, who had effectively been disenfranchised by Jim Crowism. The law established the Commission on Civil Rights and created a civil rights division within the U.S. Department of Justice. It authorized the U.S. Attorney General to seek federal court injunctions to protect the civil rights of Blacks, for example, in the desegregation efforts with regard to the Little Rock, Arkansas, high school in 1957. More effective laws were passed in 1964 and 1965 (Finley 2008).

The Civil Rights Act of May 6, 1960 (74 Stat. 89), established federal inspection of local voter registration polls and set up penalties for obstructing someone from registering to vote. It essentially closed loopholes in the Civil Rights Act of 1957 (Barsdolph 1971).

The Civil Rights Act of July 2, 1964 (78 Stat. 241), was a landmark law that banned discrimination on the basis of race, color, religion, sex, or national origin. It prohibits unequal application of voter registration requirements and racial segregation of schools, employment, and public accommodation. It was signed into law by President Lyndon Johnson (LBJ), in part to honor the "martyrdom" of President John F. Kennedy, whose administration first drafted the bill before his assassination in November 1963. It was the most sweeping civil rights legislation of the era (Finley 2008; Gregory 2014; LeMay 2009; Woods 2006).

The Civil Rights Act of August 6, 1965 (79 Stat. 437), also known as the Voting Rights Act, is widely considered the most important federal law aimed at prohibiting racial discrimination in voting. It was passed during the height of the civil rights movement and also signed into law by LBJ. It is considered by some scholars as the most effective piece of federal civil rights legislation ever enacted (Berman 2015; Bullock, Gaddle, and Wert 2016; Finley 2008).

The Civil Rights Act of April 11, 1968 (82 Stat. 73), has two common names: the Fair Housing Act and the Indian Civil Rights Act, each after major sections of the law. It was signed into law by LBJ during the riots following the assassination of Dr. Martin Luther King Jr. It is a landmark law that prohibits housing discrimination (in selling or renting) to anyone on the basis of race, color, religion, or national origin. Its Titles II through VII apply many of the guarantees of the Bill of Rights to Native American tribes. Titles VIII through IX are also known as the Anti-Riot Act (Graham 1990; Hannah-Jones 2012; Squires 2017; Wunder 1996).

The Civil Rights Act of November 21, 1991 (105 Stat. 1071), prohibited discrimination of job applicants and workers based on race, gender, religion, color, or other ethnic characteristics. It modified some procedural and substantive rights provided by federal law in employment discrimination cases. It was signed into law by President George H. W. Bush.

The Civil Rights Act of May 20, 1993 (107 Stat. 77), is also known as the National Voter Registration Act. It was signed into law by President William Clinton. The law requires state governments to offer voter registration to any eligible voter who applies to renew a driver's license or who applies for public assistance, and it requires the U.S. Postal Service to mail election materials of a state as if the state was a nonprofit by U.S. Postal Service regulations.

The Nineteenth Amendment—Women's Suffrage

The struggle to ensure the right to vote by women, known as the suffrage movement, and their civil rights as citizens was a nearly century-long effort for equality for women. The suffragettes, women who led the battle, were often associated with the abolition and the temperance movements. Agitation for a woman's right to vote began in the 1830s, but it is marked historically in the United States by the

Seneca Falls, New York, Convention held in 1848, which produced the Declaration of Sentiments calling for women to be given the right to vote. After the Civil War and ratification of the Fourteenth and Fifteenth amendments, leading suffragettes such as Susan B. Anthony, Elizabeth Cady Stanton, Carrie Chapman Catt, Lucy Stone, and Lucretia Mott formed the National Woman Suffrage Association to fight for a universal suffrage amendment to the U.S. Constitution. The suffragettes also fought for the franchise on a state-by-state basis. Several states allowed women to vote in state elections prior to 1919. During the Progressive Era and World War I, the suffragettes advanced their argument and activity. Their movement culminated in the Nineteenth Amendment, passed by the U.S. Congress on June 4, 1919, and ratified on August 18, 1920 (Marlow 2001; Pankhurst 1959; Raeburn 1974).

The Nineteenth Amendment states succinctly: "The right of citizens of the United States to vote shall not be denied or abridged by the United States or by any State on account of sex. Congress shall have the power to enforce this article by appropriate legislation." The amendment was challenged in *Leser v. Garnett* (258 U.S. 130, 1922). In *Leser*, the Supreme Court unanimously held that the Nineteenth Amendment had been constitutionally established. The Court's majority opinion was written by Justice Louis Brandeis.

The Twenty-Fourth Amendment—Poll Taxes

The Twenty-Fourth Amendment reads:

> The right of citizens of the United States to vote in any primary or other election for President or Vice President, for electors for President or Vice President, or for Senators or Representatives in Congress, shall not be denied or abridged by the United States or any State, by reason of failure to pay poll tax or other tax. The Congress shall

have the power to enforce this article with appropriate legislation.

The Twenty-Fourth Amendment was proposed by Congress on August 27, 1962, and ratified on January 23, 1964. During the Jim Crow era in the South, eleven Southern states adopted the poll tax. In some states it was made retroactive—that is, a citizen desiring to vote had to pay the poll tax not only for that year but also for all past years for which he or she had been eligible to vote (LeMay 2009). The poll tax had been upheld as constitutional by the Supreme Court in *Breedlove v. Suttles* (302 U.S. 277, 1937). In 1962, five states still retained a poll tax: Alabama, Arkansas, Mississippi, Texas, and Virginia. Historically, the poll tax was one of several devices the South used to disenfranchise Black voters—the others being the literacy test, the grandfather clause, and the white primary. The literacy test was developed in the North (in Connecticut and Massachusetts) and aimed at immigrants, especially those from Eastern Europe. It was then used in the South as an effective device to disenfranchise Black voters. The literacy test was upheld as constitutional in *Williams v. Mississippi* (170 U.S. 218, 1949) by a unanimous decision written by Justice Joseph McKenna. The Supreme Court ruled that the Fourteenth Amendment allowed the government to declare the use of the literacy test as unconstitutional in *Kazenbach v. Morgan* (384 U.S. 641, 1966). The Supreme Court also reversed itself and declared the poll tax invalid in *Harper v. Virginia* (383 U.S. 663, 1966). In *Harper*, the Supreme Court upheld the Twenty-Fourth Amendment, ruling that Virginia's poll tax was unconstitutional under the equal protection clause of the Fourteenth Amendment. The majority opinion was written by Justice William Douglas, with Chief Justice Earl Warren and Justices Clark, Brennan, White, and Fortas. The dissenting opinions were by Justice Hugo Black, with Justices Harlan and Stewart (Lawson 1976; LeMay 2009). Most recently, in a July 16, 2020, decision, the

U.S. Supreme Court held 6–3 that the state of Florida can enforce a law barring ex-felons from voting if they still owe court fines or fees that they are unable to pay associated with their convictions. The majority based their decision on the basis of a distinction between a poll tax and a required payment of court fees. In the dissenting opinion written by Justice Elana Kagan, the liberal justices (Sonia Sotomayor, Ruth Bader Ginsburg, and Elena Kagan) argued that the Court's order prevents thousands of otherwise eligible voters from voting in Florida's primary election. They decried the Court's trend of condoning disenfranchisement.

The Twenty-Sixth Amendment—Suffrage for Eighteen-Year-Olds

Student activism within the civil rights movement, influenced by the Vietnam War, advocated for change in the age requirement for voting from twenty-one years old eighteen years old. The movement's common slogan was (if you are) "old enough to fight, old enough to vote." The Twenty-Sixth Amendment to so change the law was proposed by the U.S. Congress on March 23, 1971, and ratified on July 1, 1971. That was the quickest ratification of an amendment to the Constitution in U.S. history.

The Twenty-Sixth Amendment states: "The right of citizens of the United States, who are eighteen years of age or older, to vote shall not be denied or abridged by the United States or any State on account of age. The Congress shall have the power to enforce this article by appropriate legislation." The amendment's constitutionality was challenged in *Oregon v. Mitchell* (400 U.S. 112, 1970). By a split 5–4 vote, the Supreme Court ruled that Congress could set the voting age requirement for federal elections but not for state or local elections. In the majority opinion written by Justice Hugo Black, four justices joined him for allowing eighteen-year-olds to vote in federal elections (U.S. House of Representatives,

Senate, Vice President and President), but four voted against it for state elections.

Conclusion

The march toward establishing and effectively ensuring civil rights and civil liberties in the United States to fulfill the lofty goals articulated in the U.S. Constitution, and especially in its Bill of Rights, has been a continuous, long, and complex march. It has often moved in fits and starts, and at times taking a step or two backwards after advancing a step forward. It has involved adopting additional amendments to the U.S. Constitution (the Thirteenth, Fourteenth, Fifteenth, Nineteenth, Twenty-Fourth, and Twenty-Sixth). It has depended upon landmark U.S. Supreme Court decisions and on enactment by the U.S. Congress of critically important civil rights laws. The long march has been advanced by the advocacy of groups that have arisen over the course of history of the United States to promote the rights and liberties of citizens characterized by age (both seniors and those under eighteen), sex, gender, and sexual orientation and characterized as Arab American and Muslim, Asian American, Black American, disabled, Hispanic and Latino/Latina (now designated by Latinx), Jewish, Native American, and so on.

The march forward has depended on laws and often complex jurisprudence concerning suffrage rights of those groups. Landmark Supreme Court decisions have been ruled on regarding every one of the first ten amendments with respect to the federal government and, after the adoption of the Fourteenth Amendment, many of them were applied to state and local governments through the judicial doctrine of incorporation of the due process and equal protection clauses. Several of the later amendments were interpreted by the Court to apply to state governments.

Supreme Court decisions have defined and expanded the meanings of constitutional protections regarding rights and liberties by answering or clarifying such issues as the following: (1) what exactly is understood to be the right to bear arms; (2) what is meant by reasonable search and seizure; (3) what constitutes a fair and speedy trial; 4) what rights to property are guaranteed by the Fifth Amendment, and, indeed, what constitutes "property"; (5) who can claim citizenship status and who can be labeled enemy combatants; (6) what is meant by "cruel and unusual punishment" and how that legal concept has changed over time as methods of execution changed over time; (7) what is protected by the "privilege and immunities" clause; (8) what states must do to protect the legal rights of indigent persons accused of a crime; (9) what constitutes "quartering in a time of peace"; (10) what constitutes "double jeopardy"; (11) what is protected by the prohibition against "self-incrimination"; and (12) what constitutes "excessive" bail.

In its various landmark decisions, the Supreme Court established various "tests" to guide judges and courts in making distinctions as to what is and what is not permissible behavior by government. Examples of such tests are (1) the "clear and present danger" test; (2) the "reasonableness" test; (3) the "exclusionary rule"; (4) the *Katz* test for search and seizures and what is a "reasonable expectation of privacy"; (5) what is a permissible stop and frisk if the police officer believes a person "is or may be armed and presently dangerous"; (6) the "in plain sight" test; (7) exceptions for automobiles and buses; and (8) the Lawrence test on the "right to privacy."

This chapter discussed in some detail the civil rights laws and Supreme Court decisions affected by the concepts and accepted social customs present during what historians have demarcated as seven significant periods in American history: (1) the Founding to Civil War era, (2) the Reconstruction era, (3) the post-Reconstruction era, (4) the Progressive Era, (5) the Great Depression and New Deal era, (6) the civil rights era, and (7) the Fortress America era.

The organizations and persons who have been critically important stakeholders in the long march to ensure fundamental civil rights and civil liberties are profiled in chapter 4. Their actions, advocacy, and agitation have driven the inexorable march toward greater civil rights and liberties over the more than two hundred years of U.S. history. It is best understood as a never-ceasing march in the struggle to achieve them. Civil rights and liberty are articulated in the U.S. Constitution, but their achievement requires constant vigilance and a willingness to fight for their rights and liberties by those groups that, at any given time in U.S. history, have been viewed as unpopular minorities. They are precisely those groups that lack, or in the view of some Americans should lack, such protections. Such groups are the "they" as opposed to the "we" understood to be included in "We, the People" as articulated in the Declaration of Independence.

References

Abrams, Paula. 2009. *Cross Purposes.* Ann Arbor: University of Michigan Press.

Ackerman, Bruce, ed. 2002. *Bush v. Gore: The Question of Legitimacy.* New Haven, CT: Yale University Press.

Alley, Robert. 1999. *The Constitution and Religion: Leading Supreme Court Cases on Church and State.* Amherst, NY: Prometheus Books.

Ball, Howard. 2000. *The Bakke Case.* Lawrence: University Press of Kansas.

Barsdolph, Richard. 1971. *The Civil Rights Record: Black Americans and the Law, 1849–1970.* New York: Thomas Crowell Company.

Berman, Art. 2015. *Give Us the Ballot: The Modern Struggle for Voting Rights in America.* New York: Farrar, Strauss, and Giroux.

Bernstein, David. 2012. *Rehabilitating Lochner: Defending Individual Rights against Progressive Reform.* Chicago, IL: University of Chicago Press.

Bogus, Carl T. 2000. *The Second Amendment in Law and History.* New York: New Press.

Brest, Paul, Sanford Levinson, Jack Baldwin, Akeel Amar, and Reval Siegal. 2018. *Processes of Constitutional Decision Making: Cases and Materials,* 7th ed. New York: Wolters Kluwer.

Brooks, Roy. 1996. *Integration or Separation? A Strategy for Racial Equality.* Cambridge, MA: Harvard University Press.

Bullock, Charles, Ron Gaddle, and Justin Wert, eds. 2016. *The Rise and Fall of the Civil Rights Act.* Norman: University of Oklahoma Press.

Carpenter, Dale. 2012. *Flagrant Conduct: The Story of Lawrence v. Texas.* New York: W. W. Norton.

Chemerinsky, Erwin. 2015. *The Case against the Supreme Court.* New York: Penguin Books.

Chemerinsky, Erwin. 2019. *Constitutional Law: Principles and Policies,* 6th ed. New York: Wolters and Kluwer.

Cornell, Saul. 2008. *A Well Ordered Militia: The Founding Fathers and the Origins of Gun Control.* New York and Oxford: Oxford University Press.

Cress, Lawrence. 1982. *Citizens in Arms: The Army and Militia in American Society to the War of 1812.* Chapel Hill: University of North Carolina Press.

Cushman, Clare. 2001. *Supreme Court Decisions and Women's Rights.* Washington, D.C.: Congressional Quarterly Press.

Epstein, Richard. 2014. *The Classical Liberal Constitution.* Cambridge, MA: Harvard University Press.

Eskridge, William. 2008. *Sodomy Laws in America, 1861–2003.* New York: Penguin.

Fehenbacher, Don E. 1981. *Slavery, Law and Politics: The Dred Scott Case in Historical Perspectives.* New York: Oxford University Press.

Finkelman, Paul, ed. 2013. *Encyclopedia of American Civil Liberties.* Oxfordshire, UK: Routledge Press.

Finley, Keith. 2008. *Delaying the Dream: Southern Senators and the Fight against Civil Rights, 1936–1965.* Baton Rouge: Louisiana State University Press.

Fireside, Harvey. 2003. *Separate and Unequal: Homer Plessy and the Supreme Court Decision That Legalized Racism.* Gretna, LA: Pelican Press.

Foner, Eric. 1990. *A Short History of Reconstruction, 1863–1877.* New York: HarperCollins.

Friedlander, Alan, and Richard Gerber. 2018. *Welcoming Ruin: The Civil Rights Act of 1875.* Leiden and Boston: Brill Publishing.

Graham, Hugh. 1990. *The Civil Rights Era: Origins and Development of National Policy, 1960–1972.* New York: Oxford University Press.

Gregory, Raymond. 2014. *The Civil Rights Act and the Battle to End Workplace Discrimination.* Lanham, MD: Rowman and Littlefield.

Gutzman, Kevin. 2007. *The Politically Incorrect Guide to the Constitution.* Washington, D.C.: Regnery Publishing.

Hannah-Jones, Nikole. 2012. *Living Apart: How the Government Betrayed a Landmark Civil Rights Law.* New York: Open Road Media.

Holbrook, Stephen. 1989. *A Right to Bear Arms.* New York: Greenwood Press.

Howard, John. 1999. *The Shifting Wind: The Supreme Court and Civil Rights from Reconstruction to Brown.* New York: New York State University Press.

Issacharoff, Samuel, Pamela Karlan, Richard Pildes, and Nathaniel Persily. 2016. *The Law of Democracy: Legal Structures of the Political Process,* 5th ed. New York: Foundation Press.

Johnson, John. 2005. *Griswold v. Connecticut: Birth Control and the Constitutional Right to Privacy.* Lawrence: University Press of Kansas.

Kens, Paul. 1998. *Lochner v. New York: Economic Regulation on Trial.* Lawrence: University Press of Kansas.

Keppel, Ben. 2016. *Brown v. Board and the Transformation of American Culture.* Baton Rouge: Louisiana State University Press.

Killian, Johnny, and George Costello, eds. 2000. *The Constitution of the United States of America: Analyses and Interpretation.* Washington, D.C.: U.S. Government Printing.

Labunski, Richard E. 2006. *James Madison and the Struggle for the Bill of Rights.* New York: Oxford University Press.

LaFave, Wayne. 2012. *Search and Seizure.* St. Paul, MN: Thomson/West.

LaFave, Wayne, Jerold H. Israel, Nancy King, and Orin Kerr. 2017. *Criminal Procedure,* 6th ed. St. Paul, MN: West Publishing.

Lasson, Nelson. 1937. *The History and Development of the Fourth Amendment to the United States Constitution.* Baltimore, MD: The Johns Hopkins University Press.

Lawson, Steven. 1976. *Black Ballots: Voting Rights in the South, 1946–1969.* New York: Columbia University Press.

LeMay, Michael. 2009. *The Perennial Struggle.* 3rd ed. Upper Saddle River, NJ: Prentice-Hall.

LeMay, Michael. 2018. *Religious Freedom in America: A Reference Handbook.* Santa Barbara, CA: ABC-CLIO.

LeMay, Michael. 2020. *First Amendment Freedoms: A Reference Guide.* Santa Barbara, CA: ABC-CLIO.

Levy, Leonard. 1986. *Origins of the Fifth Amendment.* New York: Macmillan.

Levy, Leonard W. 1995. *Seasoned Judgments: The American Constitution, Rights, and History.* New York: Transaction Publishers.

Levy, Leonard W. 1999. *Origins of the Bill of Rights.* New Haven, CT: Yale University Press.

Long, Carolyn. 2006. *Mapp v. Ohio: Guarding against Unreasonable Search and Seizure.* Lawrence: University Press of Kansas.

Malcolm, Joyce. 1994. *To Keep and Bear Arms.* Cambridge, MA: Harvard University Press.

Marlow, Joyce, ed. 2001. *Votes for Women.* London: Virago Books.

Miller, Mark. 2009. *The View of the Courts from the Hill: Interactions between Congress and the Federal Judiciary.* Charlottesville: University of Virginia Press.

Nowak, John, and Ronald Rotunda. 2012. *Treatise on Constitutional Law: Substance and Procedure,* 5th ed. Eagan, MN: Thomson/West.

Nussbaum, Martha. 2010. *From Disgust to Humanity: Sexual Orientation and Constitutional Law.* New York: Oxford University Press.

Ogletree, Charles. 2004. *All Deliberate Speed: Reflections on First Half Century of Brown v. Board of Education.* New York: W. W. Norton.

Pankhurst, Christabel. 1959. *Unshackled: The Story of How We Won the Vote.* London: Hutchinson.

Raeburn, Antonin. 1974. *The Militant Suffragette.* London: New English Library.

Reagan, Leslie J. 1996. *When Abortion Was a Crime.* Berkeley: University of California Press.

Ross, William G. 1994. *Forging New Freedoms: Nativism, Education, and the Constitution.* Lincoln: University of Nebraska Press.

Rutherglen, George. 2013. *Civil Rights in the Shadow of Slavery: The Constitution, Common Law, and the Civil Rights Act of 1865.* New York: Oxford University Press.

Shilts, Randy. 1993. *Conduct Unbecoming: Gay and Lesbians in the United States Military.* New York: St. Martin's Press.

Spitzer, Robert. 2008. *The Politics of Gun Control*, 4th ed. Washington, D.C.: Congressional Quarterly Press.

Squires, Gregory. 2017. *The Fight for Fair Housing: Causes, Consequences, and Future Implications of the 1968 Federal Fair Housing Act*. London and Philadelphia: Routledge Press.

Stuart, Gary L. 2004. *Miranda: The Story of America's Right to Remain Silent*. Tucson: University of Arizona Press.

Tushnet, Mark V. 2007. *Out of Range*. New York and Oxford: Oxford University Press.

Tushnet, Mark V. 2008. *Dissent: Great Opposing Opinions in Landmark Supreme Court Cases*. Boston, MA: Beacon Press.

Uviller, H. Richard, and William Merkel. 2002. *The Militia and the Right to Bear Arms*. Durham, NC: Duke University Press.

White, Deborah. 2012. *Freedom on My Mind*. Boston, MA: St. Martin's Press.

Wood, Gordon S. 2009. *Empire of Liberty: A History of the Early Republic, 1789–1815*. New York: Oxford University Press.

Woods, Randall. 2006. *LBJ: Architect of American Ambition*. New York: Free Press.

Wunder, John. 1996. *The Indian Bill of Rights: 1968*. Philadelphia, PA: Taylor and Francis.

Zotti, Priscilla H. Machado. 2005. *Injustice for All: Mapp v. Ohio and the Fourth Amendment*. New York: Peter Lang.

2 Problems, Controversies, and Solutions

Introduction

The effort in U.S. politics to live up to the guarantees and protections of civil rights and civil liberties as expressed in the Constitution and the Bill of Rights and subsequent amendments required actors in the political arena to cope with numerous problems. This chapter focuses on problems associated with ensuring the civil rights and liberties of all the American people. It shows how the struggle to do so was an enduring preoccupation of governmental and of many nongovernmental actors and organizations who fought the battles necessary to protect those rights and to redress failures to live up to the lofty goals expressed in the U.S. Constitution. To better understand the scope and nature of the problems and of efforts to craft resolutions, if not permanent solutions, to those civil liberties/rights problems, this chapter distinguishes two categories of problems in U.S. politics that emerged at various times throughout American history. The height or depth of concerns over civil rights and liberties waxed and waned during particular eras, but the struggle itself was perennial (LeMay 2009).

Man drinking cup of water from a "colored only" water fountain, July 1939. The 1896 court case *Plessy v. Ferguson* upheld the right of states to establish "separate but equal" facilities for African Americans. The fight against segregation began in earnest during the 1950s and was one of the first steps in the civil rights movement. *Plessy v. Ferguson* was overturned by *Brown v. Board of Education* in 1954. (Library of Congress)

The first category of problems discussed in this chapter is that of discrimination that denied or hindered the full enjoyment of civil rights for various minority persons. The second category concerns problems arising from the ever-changing environment of U.S. politics and how those changes required rethinking or redefining what was meant by the various concepts of civil rights guarantees within the changing context of politics. Such rethinking took place in both the halls of Congress and state legislatures, as well as in the solemn chambers of American courthouses. Solutions to problems raised in both categories involved enacting laws or using jurisprudence to redress grievances that, over time, expanded the understanding of those political rights. In the case of the Supreme Court, or other courts that addressed those grievances, the chapter discusses "resolutions" rather than "solutions" to the problems in order to better convey to the reader that solutions were never achieved with any degree of finality. As stated in chapter 1, the march towards civil rights often took steps backwards as well as forwards. The long arc of history may bend towards the expansion of civil rights and liberties, to paraphrase the use of the imagery of Dr. Martin Luther King Jr., but the arc was far from even and seldom continuous. The success in getting government, including the courts, to redress grievances experienced by individuals often depended on the political savvy and strength that organizations working for the civil rights and liberties of various minorities in the American political arena were able to muster to bring to the competition. In turn, that often depended on their ability to gain access to the vote and to exercise the franchise, or to have their standing to bring suit in courts of law be recognized.

The Denial of Rights to the "Other"

The struggle to achieve a degree of civil rights and liberties by racial and ethnic groups in U.S. politics and society has been a persistent one. Their struggle to be recognized as legitimately among "we, the people," rather than "they" who are not—or, in the view of many in majority society, should not be—included in the American polity and therefore do not, or should not, enjoy the privileges and immunities of citizenship, has been the ongoing struggle of the American experiment in self-governance (LeMay 2009). In founding the American polity out of a colonial experience, the White/Anglo-Saxon/Protestant (WASP) majority emerged to become the dominant group in U.S. society and politics. They established what has been distinguished as the first American regime, the Jeffersonian Democratic-Republican regime. The first electoral—or political party—regime comprised persons who held and defended certain regime principles: a view of the common good manifested in particular ruling beliefs, habits, and institutions broadly associated with a segment of society (Zentner and LeMay 2020). Regimes are governments that construct, or reconstruct, a changing set of prevailing commitment of ideology, interests, and political party coalitions. They establish party systems and realignments of party systems that control government by assembling a ruling majority party coalition. The coalition, in turn, determines who is and who is not accepted to legitimately take part in elections and the governing of society.

To better understand the politics of the struggle by various minorities to secure their right to be part of the American polity, it is helpful to distinguish between two basic concepts: prejudice and discrimination. *Prejudice* can be understood as a mindset whereby the individual or group accepts as valid the negative social definitions that the majority society forms in reference to some minority, and that predisposes members of the majority to apply those negative social definitions to all individuals who are viewed as belonging to the "out-group" simply on that basis—for example, their race, color, creed, previous condition of servitude, or national origin. *Discrimination*, by contrast, is applied prejudice. Negative social attitudes are translated into actions into laws, policies, regulations, or social customs that enforce the subordination of the basic rights of persons ascribed to minority status (LeMay 2009). Ascribed status is one assigned at birth or assumed involuntarily later in life, often based on biological factors that cannot be changed through individual effort or achievement. The first such "other" minority group discussed in this chapter is Black Americans.

Black Americans

Slavery was the "original sin" of the U.S. Constitution. Article 1, Section 2, states that representatives and direct taxes shall be apportioned according to the number of free persons, including those bound in service for a term of three years, and, excluding Indians not taxed, three-fifths of all other persons. Citizenship was limited to "free, white persons." The vast majority of Blacks present within the U.S. population prior to the U.S. Civil War were slaves, brought involuntarily to the United States. Non-whites, moreover, could not become naturalized citizens. The first naturalization act, the Act of March 26, 1790 (1 Stat. 103), stated that "any alien, being a free white person, who shall have resided within the limits and under the jurisdiction of the United States for a term of two years, may be admitted to become a citizen thereof. . . ." And Article IV, Section 2, stipulates "that citizens of each State shall be entitled to all privileges and immunities of citizens in the several states" and that "no person held in Service or Labor in one state, under the laws thereof, escaping into another, shall, in consequence of any law or regulation thereof, but shall be delivered up on claim of the party to whom such service or labor may be due" (LeMay and Barkan 1999). The Supreme Court, in *Dred Scott v. Sandford* (60 U.S. 393, 1857), ruled that no Black could claim U.S. citizenship. Indeed, citizenship of Blacks was denied until the Emancipation Proclamation of September 22, 1862, freed slaves living in the Confederacy. Congress finally abolished slavery itself in the Thirteenth Amendment, wherein Section 1 stipulates: "Neither slavery nor involuntary servitude . . .

shall exist within the United States, or any place subject to its jurisdiction." It was passed by Congress on January 31, 1865, and ratified on December 6, 1865. Three years later, the civil rights of all persons, born or naturalized, were declared in the Fourteenth Amendment, ratified on July 28, 1868, which specifically included former slaves who had been freed by the Thirteenth Amendment.

But effective participation, voting, and other civil rights of African Americans was greatly restricted, especially in the eleven former Confederate States, by the use of Black Codes and Jim Crow laws. Black Codes were laws governing the conduct of free Blacks passed in 1865 and 1866 in Southern states to restrict African Americans' freedom and to compel them to work for low wages. Jim Crow laws were post-Reconstruction Era state laws and state constitutional amendments that established a legalized system of discrimination against African Americans during the 1880s to 1920s. Jim Crowism was spurred by the Supreme Court's decision in *Plessy v. Ferguson* (163 U.S. 537, 1896) that established the "separate-but-equal" doctrine. Jim Crow laws called for the segregation of African Americans and white citizens. Those laws segregated public facilities like swimming pools, parks, and public transportation (buses, street cars, and trains) and allowed for the segregation of private facilities, such as hotels, motels, and restaurants. The disenfranchisement of African Americans was accomplished by suppressing their vote in state and national elections through such devices as the poll tax, the grandfather clause, the white primary, the use of literacy tests, and the use of residency and requirements for record keeping (Campbell 2003; Dailey, Gilmore, and Simon 2000; Davis 2011; Fireside 2004; Foner 2014; LeMay 2009; Woodward and McFeely 2001).

Black Americans reacted to this discrimination and disenfranchisement by forming civil rights organizations and following leaders who advocated one of three coping strategies: accommodation, separatism, or radicalism (LeMay 2009). The accommodation strategy stresses the minority group's acceptance of the dominant culture and advocates for inclusion following economic empowerment or by using education and the courts. There are two good examples of leaders and black groups employing the accommodation strategy. Arguably the most prominent American black leader from 1890 to 1915 was Booker T. Washington, founder of the National Negro Business League and prominent educator at the Tuskegee Institute (Hamilton 2017; Washington 1901; West 2006). A second good example is the Urban League. It was founded in 1906 by George Edmund Haynes, the first African American to earn a PhD from Columbia University, and Ruth Standish Baldwin, a white New York City philanthropist. It began with an emphasis on jobs for African Americans. The Urban League emerged as a force in the American civil rights struggle during the Urban League presidency of Whitney Young (1961–1971) and his successor, Vernon E. Jordan Jr. (1971–1981). In addition to its economic programs, it has been an amicus supporter of various lawsuits.

The separatist strategy involves leaders and groups who reject the value system of the majority society and advocate their own value system, voluntarily maintaining, as much as possible, the separation of its members from the majority. Again, there are two good examples of Black separatist leaders and groups. Marcus Garvey promoted Black nationalism through the Universal Negro Improvement Association, founded in 1919 (Brooks 1996; LeMay 2009). A more successful and longer-lasting use of that strategy was by the Nation of Islam (NOI, or more commonly known as the Black Muslims). NOI emerged in the 1930s and was built into a national movement by Elijah Muhammad (born Elijah Poole) and Malcolm X (born Malcolm Little). Shortly before his assassination in 1965, Malcolm X founded the Organization of Afro-American Unity (OAAU). Since the deaths of Elijah Muhammad and Malcolm X, NOI has been reinvigorated and led by Minister Louis Farrakhan (born Louis Walcott) (Curtis 2002; LeMay 2009; Marsh 2000; Sniderman and Piazza 2002).

By far, the strategy of new-style radicalism has been used by more Black civil rights organizations and advocated by the most prominent of Black leaders. Leaders and organizations using new-style radicalism emphasize nonviolent protest activism and advocate "Black Power" through group action. Protest politics of the Black civil rights movement has been used most successfully against de jure segregation, by ending Jim Crow laws. It has promoted desegregation of American society and politics. The Black Power movement has inspired Red, Brown, Grey, and Gay Power movements. Perhaps the best philosophical justification for civil disobedience to change discriminatory laws is the eloquent "Letter from a Birmingham Jail," written by Dr. Martin Luther King Jr. in 1963.

The "granddaddy" of the Black civil rights organizations is the National Association for the Advancement of Colored People (NAACP). It was founded on February 12, 1909, and quickly grew to become the foremost, largest, and most widely recognized civil rights organization. It established its national office in New York City in 1910. Among its founders were W.E.B. Du Bois, Ida B. Wells-Barnett, and Mary Church Terrell. It published *The Crisis* magazine as the premier crusading voice for civil rights, edited and published by Du Bois. Other prominent NAACP leaders include Julian Bond, Benjamin Chavis, Medger Evers, Josephine St. Pierre Ruggin, Roy Williams, and its pioneering legal counsel, Thurgood Marshall, who went on to be appointed Associate Justice of the U.S. Supreme Court. The NAACP most notably used federal and Supreme Court cases as its preferred tactic to promote Black civil rights.

The Congress of Racial Equality (CORE) was founded in 1942. Among its more prominent leaders were Floyd McKissick, James Farmer, and Roy Innis. In 1957, following the *Brown v. Board of Education* decision of 1954 and launched by the Montgomery Bus Boycott, the Southern Christian Leadership Conference (SCLC) was founded in Atlanta, Georgia. SCLC pioneered the Black direct action protests with marches, boycotts, freedom rides, sit-ins, and similar protest actions advocating peaceful civil disobedience of segregation laws. Among its prominent leaders were Ralph Abernathy, Jesse Jackson, Coretta Scott King, Martin Luther King Jr., Edgar Nixon, James Orange, Rosa Parks, Bayard Rustin, Charles Steele, Wyatt Walker, Hosea Williams, and Andrew Young.

There are two spin-off organizations of the SCLC: the Mississippi Movement (1960), with such leaders as Bob Moses, James Meredith, Medger Evers, and Fannie Lou Farmer; and the Student Nonviolent Coordinating Committee (SNCC), founded by Ella Barker in Raleigh, North Carolina in 1960. SNCC leaders included James Foreman, Prathin Hall, Bernard Lafayette, John Lewis, Diane Nash, Charles Sherrod, and Fred Shuttlesworth (LeMay 2009).

Notable laws and Supreme Court decisions won by the activism of the Black civil rights movement are exemplified by *Gunn v. United States* (1910); *Brown v. Board of Education* (1954); the Civil Rights Acts of 1957 the 1963 March on Washington (at which MLK delivered his famous "I Have a Dream" speech); and the 1964, 1965, and 1968 Civil Rights Acts. More discussion of the organization and civil rights activists follows in the profiles in chapter 4.

Asian Americans

Asian Americans make up one of the nation's smallest racial minorities, although it is rapidly growing. This section discusses three subgroups of Asian Americans: Chinese Americans, Japanese Americans, and Korean Americans (Lee 2020; LeMay 2009). Chinese Americans, at 23 percent of all Asian Americans, are the largest subgroup. Chinese began immigrating to the United States after discovery of gold in California in 1848, pulled by the sudden demand for labor created by the gold rush. Indeed, they referred to the United States as "the land of the golden hills." Anti-Chinese sentiment developed almost immediately. Pushed by groups like the Know Nothing Party, the Order of Caucasians, the Teamsters, and the Workingmen's Party, an effort to exclude them began by the 1850s and by the

1870s included violence, local ordinances, the use of the courts, and calls for exclusion by Congress. Chinese immigrants were the first group to face national legislation banning them and specifically barring them from naturalization. Attempts to ban them were led by the Chinese Exclusion League (1870s), which later became the Asiatic Exclusion League (1905). The United States negotiated an amended Burlingame treaty in October 1881 (22 Stat. 826, 1037–39) (LeMay and Barkan 1999: 49–50). It recognized the right of the United States to limit the immigration of Chinese laborers.

President Rutherford B. Hayes vetoed the first bill that imposed an exclusion of Chinese immigrant laborers. Another bill was vetoed by President Chester Arthur in April 1882. On May 6, 1882, Congress passed a "suspension" of immigration of Chinese laborers—more commonly known as the Chinese Exclusion Act (22 Stat. 58; LeMay and Barkan 1999: 51–54). Section 14 of the Act stipulated that "no State court or court of the United States shall admit Chinese to citizenship, and all laws in conflict with this act are hereby repealed." Anti-Chinese sentiment raged in California, and discriminatory local ordinances were enacted in San Francisco that prescribed what jobs or occupations—such as a laundry business, among other things—in which they could legally engage. The U.S. Supreme Court overturned the law in *Yick Wo v. Hopkins*, May 10, 1886 (118 U.S. 220).

The Supreme Court weighed in on several cases dealing with discrimination against Chinese immigrants that upheld the laws against them, in part because, as noncitizens, they lacked the civil rights protections afforded citizens (LeMay and Barkan 1999: 60–76). In 1888, Congress extended the ban on the immigration of Chinese laborers by the Scott Act (25 Stat. 476) and required Chinese leaving the United States with the intent to return to secure a "re-entry certificate" before doing so. Congress, ex-post-facto, rescinded the reentry certificates by the Act of October 1, 1888 (25 Stat. 540), a law upheld as constitutional despite its ex-post-facto nature, by the Supreme

Court in *Chae Chan Ping v. United States* (130 U.S. 581, May 13, 1889).

The Supreme Court considered the question of whether a native-born person of Chinese descent was a citizen. It held that such a person was a citizen in *Wong Kim Ark v. United States* (March 28, 1898, 169 U.S. 649). Organizations to advocate for their rights and to reject anti-Chinese laws passed at local, state, and even the national levels included the Six Companies and the Chinese American Citizens League (founded in 1895). In recognition of the alliance of China with the United States against Japan in World War II, Congress repealed all the various Chinese Exclusion Acts, authorized a small quota for immigration from China, and allowed for Chinese immigrants to naturalize by the Act of December 17, 1943 (57 Stat. 600; LeMay and Barkan 1999: 195–197).

The civil rights movement of the 1960s spurred the formation of the Asian American Political Alliance (comprising both Chinese and Japanese Americans) in 1968. Margaret Fung is a prominent Chinese American civil rights leader who founded the Asian American Legal Defense Education Fund (ASLDEF) in 1974 in New York City to promote and protect the civil rights of Asian Americans. Another such activist is Bill Chong, executive director of the Asian Americans for Equality (AAFE).

Japanese Americans make up about 8 percent of Asian Americans and are the sixth-largest Asian group in the United States. Japanese people first immigrated to what would become the United States via Hawaii in 1868, immigrating to the mainland, on the West Coast, in the early 1870s; and by the 1910 census, they numbered 72,000. Their numbers were stabilized because of the Act of May 26, 1924, known as the Johnson-Reed Immigration Act of 1924 (43 Stat. 153; LeMay and Barkan 1999: 148–153), which specifically barred Japanese immigration until it was rescinded in 1952 by the McCarran-Walter Act (Act of June 27, 1952, 66 Stat. 163; LeMay and Barkan 1999: 220–225).

On March 14, 1907, President Theodore Roosevelt implemented Executive Order 589 to regulate the entrance of Japanese and Chinese laborers to the United States. It is more commonly known as the "Gentleman's Agreement." It was an agreement by which Japan controlled the emigration from Japan and Korea (then under Japanese jurisdiction). It drastically cut immigration from Japan except for the immigration of Japanese picture brides. Picture brides were Japanese women who, by mail, were linked to marry Japanese immigrants residing in the United States. They did not meet their proposed spouse until they arrived in the United States. Because state laws forbade Asian men from marrying white women, the law allowed for the immigration of Japanese-born women to be their brides.

In 1921, the Supreme Court ruled, in *Ozawa v. United States* (November 13, 1922, 260 U.S. 195), that Japanese people were not Caucasians and were therefore subject to the Asian restriction laws. The first-generation Japanese immigrants, known as the "Issei," were barred from naturalization to citizenship (Kitano 1976; Salyer 1995). The effect was to develop an unusually pronounced generation gap among Japanese Americans. The issei were legally barred from becoming citizens until 1954. They were unable to legally own land for a time in California and in other Western states (for example, by Arizona, Washington, Texas, Louisiana, New Mexico, Idaho, Montana, Oregon, Arkansas, Minnesota, Nebraska, Utah, and Wyoming). They were banned from owning land by the Webb-Heney Alien Land Law of 1913, named after attorney Francis Heney and California state attorney general Ulysses Webb. The 1913 act was not invalidated until 1952, when the Supreme Court of California held that such alien land acts violated the equal protection clause of the Fourteenth Amendment by the decision of *Sei Fujii v. California* (38 Cal2nd 718) (McCain 1994).

The second generation of Japanese Americans, known as the "Nisei," were born between 1910 and 1940. As native-born citizens, they were able to vote, own land, and marry across racial lines (Hosokawa 1969). The third generation, known as the "Sansei," were born after World War II. The "Kibei" were a subset of the Nisei who, as young children, were sent to Japan to be raised in the traditional culture. By the time the war broke out in 1941, the Kibei were trying to return to the United States (Hosokawa 1969; Kitano 1976; LeMay 2009).

The Pearl Harbor attack on December 7, 1941, began a virtual civil rights nightmare for Japanese Issei and Japanese American Nisei living on the mainland. Nearly 120,000, included about 70,000 Nisei, were rounded up and interred in "relocation camps," supposedly out of "military necessity." The relocation camps were in fact concentration camps guarded by armed troops stationed around the perimeter, with spotlight towers and fifteen-foot barbed-wire fences. Residents lived in barracks where stalls a mere eighteen by twenty-one feet housed families of six or seven, partitioned off with seven-foot-high walls, and four-foot openings afforded them little privacy. Residents used outside latrines and ate at camp mess halls. There were ten camps located in seven states run by the War Relocation Authority. Executive order 9066 of February 19, 1942, authorizing the relocation, and the Act of March 21, 1942 (56 Stat. 173), were some of the darkest stains on the civil rights and civil liberties record of the United States (Daniels et al. 1991; Daniels 1993; Hosokawa 1969; Kitano 1976; Lee 2020, LeMay 2009; McCain 1994; Ng 2001; Takaki 1998). Their constitutionality was upheld by the Supreme Court in *Hirabayashi v. United States* (June 21, 1943, 320 U.S. 81) and *Korematsu v. United States* (December 18, 1944, 323 U.S. 214). The incarceration of Japanese American citizens in the camps was not ended until the ruling in *Ex Parte Mitsuye Endo* (December 18, 1944, 323 U.S. 283–310). In his opinion in the *Endo* decision, Justice Murphy stated that the "detention was another example of the unconstitutional resort to racism inherent in the entire evacuation program" (LeMay and Barkan 1999: 200).

The civil rights campaign to redress the civil rights violations against Japanese Americans and to secure the right to naturalization of the Issei was led by the Japanese American Citizens League (JACL). Notable JACL leaders and activists include: Richard Aoki, Mitsuye Endo, Gordon Hirabayashi, Yuri Kochiyama, Fred Korematsu, Karen Korematsu, Edison Uno, Dr. Thomas Yatabe, and Aiko Yoshinaga. The JACL was led by the Nisei, and Japanese Americans have achieved remarkable assimilation, even being referred to as "the model minority" (Marger 2003). The JACL played a role in the enactment of the McCarran-Walter Act of June 27, 1952 (66 Stat. 163), which repealed the "free white persons" language of the Naturalization Act of 1790, thereby permitting nonwhite immigrants to become naturalized citizens, including, importantly, the Issei. The JACL was the primary force behind the Civil Liberties Act of August 10, 1988 (102 Stat. 904), also known as the Japanese Reparations Act. It was sponsored by Senators Daniel Inouye and Spark Matsunaga (D-Hawaii) and Representatives Robert Matsui and Norman Mineta (D-CA). It was signed into law by President Ronald Reagan (Daniels et al. 1991; Takaki 1998).

Korean Americans make up about 10 percent of the Asian American population and rank in fifth place among them. They often play the role of "middleman minority," as a sort of buffer between the dominant society and other minority groups, like Blacks and Hispanics. Korean immigrants came in three waves. A short, small wave came between 1903 and 1905, who came as contract laborers to Hawaii to replace Chinese and Japanese agricultural workers there. A second wave of about 25,000 came between 1951 and 1965. They were mostly wives of American servicemen and Korean War orphans adopted by Americans, and some were international students who came after the Korean War to study in the United States and then remained. The third and largest wave, averaging more than 33,000 per year, came since 1965 (LeMay 2009). The third-wave Korean immigrants are highly educated, from middle-class backgrounds, and are skilled workers, professionals, or businessowners who often migrate in family units. They are highly concentrated in large cities but are fairly dispersed geographically (LeMay 2009; Marger 2003).

Prominent organizations for Korean American civil rights are the Korean American League for Civic Action (KALCA), headquartered in New York City, and the Korean American Citizens League (KACL), founded in 1990 and led by its executive director, Sam Hyun.

Hispanic Americans

In the Southwest, many Hispanics can trace their ancestry back to generations before Anglo Americans ever set foot in the area. They were nonetheless viewed as "Mexicans" and as Catholics, even though there are Hispanics who are Evangelical Protestants or simply nonpracticing. They were—and many still are—treated as racially different from Caucasians despite the fact that the majority of Hispanics are Caucasian. Many Chicanos became U.S. citizens by treaty rights—the Treaty of Guadalupe Hidalgo (which ended the Mexican American War in 1848). Hispanics have faced, and still do experience, discrimination in education, employment, housing, immigration, law enforcement, and political participation (voting rights denied or diluted through gerrymandering) (LeMay 2009: 336–377). Various Hispanic organizations and civil rights leaders have fought against that discrimination and for their civil rights using all three coping strategies (accommodation, separatism, and radicalism).

The League of United Latin American Citizens (LULAC) was founded in 1929 in Corpus Christi, Texas, by World War I veterans who sought to end rampant discrimination against all Latinos. It is the oldest and largest Hispanic organization in the United States and has offices in twenty-one states, with its headquarters in Washington, D.C., and a membership of about 120,000. Its founders included Maria Hernandez, Pedro Hernandez Barrera, Ben Garza, Manuel Gonzales, Rafael Galvan, and others. Its president is Domingo Garcia, and its CEO is

Sindy Marisol Benavides. In the late 1940s and 1950s, LULAC campaigned against the Bracero Program. Examples of its successful federal court school desegregation cases include *Mendez v. Westminster* (161 F2d 774, 9th Circuit, 1947) and *Minerval Delgado v. Bastrop Independent School District (1948-06-15)* in the Texas district court of the United States. LULAC also filed an amicus brief in *Brown v. Board of Education* (1954) (Marquez 2003; Orozco 2009; Strum 2010).

A California-based Hispanic organization using accommodation was the Community Service Organization (CSO), which began in 1947. CSO was founded by Fred Ross, Antonio Rios, and Eduardo Roybal and had links to Saul Alinsky. Fred Ross was the West Coast organizer for Alinsky's Chicago-based Industrial Area Foundation (LeMay 2009: 300). Middle-class Chicanos used CSO as a political organization to help elect Ed Roybal, who went on to serve in the U.S. Congress. CSO notably was the organization within which Cesar Chavez and Dolores Huerta began their civil rights work before they left to cofound and lead the United Farm Workers (UFW). By the 1960s, barrio youth looked on the CSO as too accommodationist, and CSO membership declined markedly during the 1960s as young members joined more militant groups. The younger generation of Hispanics began describing their movement using the term Chicano as a matter of self-pride, influenced by the Black Pride and Black Power development within the African American civil rights movement.

Cesar Chavez became the Chicano movement's best-known leader, and like Dr. Martin Luther King Jr., Chavez was a charismatic leader who understood and commanded the loyalty of those he led. He cofounded the United Farm Workers with Dolores Huerta. They led a movement often referred to as "La Causa." It began in Delano, California in 1965 with a strike—La Huelga by Filipino and Mexican workers harvesting grapes, and it became a social movement that used strikes and boycotts against lettuce and grape growers. Another notable UFW leader was Arturo Rodriquez. Like the SCLC, Chavez and the UFW were firmly committed to nonviolence (Chavez 1984).

Just as the SCLC inspired Chavez and the UFW, SNCC and the Black Panthers influenced Hispanic student and barrio-youth organizations. Los Angeles' barrios gave rise to the Brown Berets. The "Prime Minister" of the Brown Berets was David Sanchez, similar in the organization to "Chairman" Bobby Seale of the Black Panther Party, which was emulated by the Brown Berets. The Brown Berets manned picket lines with UMAS members protesting student conditions in East Los Angeles (LeMay 2009: 301–302).

University-based youth formed two groups: the United Mexican American Students (UMAS) in California, led by Phil Castruita, and the National Organization of Mexican American Students (NOMAS—which also means "no more" in Spanish), formed in Texas. San Antonio, Texas, was also the base of the Mexican American Youth Organization (MAYO) begun in 1967 by Jose Angel Gutierrez. In New Mexico, a militant protest leader, Reies Lopez Tijerina, known as "El Tigre," began a New Mexico land grant movement in 1962, the militant Alianza Federal de Mercedes. For decades, the Alianza fought in U.S. courts to reclaim land taken illegally from Mexicans in Texas and New Mexico after the Treaty of Guadalupe Hidalgo. "Brown Power" became a slogan in the Chicano movement like "Black Power" did in the Black civil rights movement. Tijerina argued that Chicanos had to demand their rights, to fight for them, to be willing, if need be, to die for them, and to strike out for freedom and to tear down the system that "enslaved" Chicanos (Steiner 1969).

A Los Angeles barrio-based newspaper, *La Raza*, voiced that militant sentiment, and its name soon became commonly used to refer to the Chicano movement. The La Raza Unida Conference was held in El Paso, Texas, in 1967 and inspired new leaders like Jose Angel Gutierrez, who led the Mexican American Youth Organization (MAYO) in San Antonio. Gutierrez helped organize La Raza Unida in Crystal City, Texas, in

1970. For a time, La Raza Unida Partido, ran candidates for local office, organized community co-ops, supported Chicano businesses, and led boycotts against hostile merchants. Also known as "the People's Party," La Raza Unida won numerous offices and essentially captured the Crystal City government. A National Council of La Raza was formed in 1968, led by its president Raul Humberto Yzaguirre and by activist Janet Murguia. Los Angeles became the "capital" of the La Raza movement, becoming to the Chicanos what Boston is to Irish Americans and New York City is to American Jews (LeMay 2009: 306–307; Steiner 1969).

Yet another Chicano leader was Rodolfo "Corky" Gonzales, who in 1965 founded the Crusade for Justice, a Chicano youth group centered in Denver, Colorado. Corky Gonzales helped organize the Poor People's March on Washington, D.C., in 1968. In 1967, the Crusade had a membership of 1,800. Corky Gonzales coined the term "Aztlan" to refer to the "Lost Lands" of Northern Mexico that are now the southwestern United States. From a national conference of Chicano youth held in Denver in 1969, various campus groups merged to form a more militant student group, Estudiantil Chicano de Aztlan, or MECHA, for the Chicano Student Movement of Aztlan. The Mexican American Political Association (MAPA) was led by Louis Valdez, a disciple of Cesar Chavez. When Valdez spoke to a rally in LA wearing an outfit style favored by Che Guevara, he showed a militancy more typical of the fiery Tijerina and the Brown Berets than that of the nonviolence advocate Cesar Chavez (LeMay 2009: 307–308; Steiner 1969: 116–117).

Finally, the Mexican American Legal Defense and Education Fund (MALDEF), founded in 1967, whose general counsel and president was Vilma Martinez, developed a strategy based on court cases and voter drives. MALDEF, along with the American Coordinating Council on Political Education (ACCPE), launched a nationwide Hispanic voter registration drive (McClain and Steward 1995: 204–205). MALDEF's political organization brought measurable electoral results. Hispanic elected officials increased from less than 800 in 1970 to more than 3,500 by 1988 (LeMay 2009: 150). By the time of President William Clinton's administration, Hispanic elected officials rose to national cabinet-level positions. Arguably the most prominent was Leon Panetta, who was President Clinton's White House Chief of Staff (1994–1997) after having served as the Director of the Office of Management and Budget (1993–1994) and a member of the U.S. House of Representatives, serving California, from 1997–1993. From the House, Panetta went on to serve as director of the Central Intelligence Agency (2009–2011) and secretary of defense (2011–2013) to President Barack Obama. Another Clinton Cabinet member was HUD secretary Henry Cisneros (1993–1997), who was the former mayor of San Antonio (1981–1989). There were two other notable Hispanic members of President Clinton's administration. Frederico Pena, former mayor of Denver (1984–1992), was President Clinton's secretary of transportation (1993–1997) and secretary of energy (1997–1998). Pena later served as the co-National Chair of Barack Obama's presidential committee in 2007–2008. Antonia Novella, the fourteenth surgeon general of the United States (1990–1993), was the first woman and first Hispanic (Puerto Rican) to serve as surgeon general. Other prominent Hispanic electoral leaders include Bill Richardson, governor of New Mexico, who for a brief time was a candidate for the Democratic nominee for president. Julian Castro, former mayor of San Antonio (2009–2014) and HUD secretary in President Obama's cabinet (2014–2017), was also, for a time, a candidate for the Democratic Party's nomination for president in 2020.

Hispanic voting power has been hindered by gerrymandering. The U.S. Supreme Court issued a landmark decision concerning partisan gerrymandering in *Rucho et al. v. Common Cause et al.* (588 U.S. ___, 2019). By a 5–4 decision, the Supreme Court ruled that partisan gerrymandering was a political question to be decided in the political arena, not in federal courts. Chief Justice John Roberts wrote the majority opinion, joined by the Court's four other conservative (and Republican-appointed) justices: Clarence Thomas, Samuel Alito, Neil Gorsuch, and Brett Kavanaugh. The dissenting opinions and votes were by the Court's four liberal justices: Elena Kagan, Ruth Bader Ginsburg, Stephen Breyer, and Sonia Sotomayor.

Native Americans

National policy toward Native Americans has taken many approaches over the years: from (1) avowed friendship (in 1875 the Continental Congress created the Committee on Indian Affairs headed by Benjamin Franklin) to (2) recognizing their independence and sovereignty (Act of March 3, 1819 [3 Stat. 516] and the Act of March 11, 1824), which created the Bureau of Indian Affairs (BIA) to negotiate treaties and to implement "forced assimilation" of Native Americans into the dominant white society, often at Indian boarding schools; to (3) expulsion and genocide (Indian Removal Act of May 28, 1830, 4 Stat. 411), which led to forced removal of 15,000 Indians in which 4,000 died on the "Trail of Tears"; to (4) forced geographic segregation on reservations by the General Allotment Act of 1887 (25 U.S. 331, aka the Dawes Act after Senator Henry Dawes (R-MA); to (5) attempts to allow for cultural pluralism as "limited or domestic dependent nations," or quasi-sovereigns (LeMay 2009: 183–193; Wilkins 2002: 48).

The decimation of the Native American population is well documented. Their population plunged from an estimated 2–10 million at first contact with European colonizers to about 150,000 by 1850, due to diseases, the ravages of malnutrition, forced expulsion, and a government policy of genocide. Since that low point in 1850, their population has slowly climbed upward to about 5.2 million in the 2010 census.

In 1819, Congress established the Indian Civilization Fund, and some tribes, like the Cherokee of North Carolina, became bicultural. The U.S. Supreme Court heard two cases involving the Cherokee in 1831 and 1832. In *Cherokee Nation v. Georgia* (30 U.S. 1, 1831), in a suit brought by Cherokee Chief John Ross, the Supreme Court ruled that it had no jurisdiction in the matter, as the Cherokees were not an independent nation and thus had no standing. Just one year later, in *Worcester v. Georgia* (31 U.S. 515, 1832), the Court ruled that the Cherokee nation was sovereign and that Georgia had no right to enforce its laws against them. President Andrew Jackson simply ignored the ruling, however, and proceeded with his policy of Indian removal. President Jackson allegedly remarked, "John Marshall has made his decision. Now let him enforce it" (cited in LeMay 2009: 185).

The first reservations were created in 1820 in the Oklahoma territory, and between then and 1880, more were established in Oklahoma, Arizona, and New Mexico. In 1879, the policy of forced assimilation began, and between 1887, with the General Allotment Act, and 1934, when Congress enacted the Indian Reorganization Act (aka the Wheeler-Howard Act, the Act of June 18, 1934, 48 Stat. 984), Indian lands decreased from 138 million acres to 90 million acres. The Indian Reorganization Act has been called the "Indian New Deal." It was enacted under President Franklin Roosevelt, and it reversed the policy of forced cultural assimilation. Since the end of the "trust funds," Indian tribal lands are located in thirty-five states and total just over 56 million acres (LeMay 2009: 187–189). The most recent Supreme Court case of note is that of *McGirt v. Oklahoma* (July 9, 2020). In a 5–4 decision in which the majority opinion was written by Justice Neil Gorsuch, the Court held that for purposes of the Major Crimes Act, land throughout much of eastern Oklahoma reserved for the Creek Nation since the nineteenth century remains a Native American territory. The McGirt decision is likely to have an impact of Native American opposition to the planned route of an oil pipeline project through Oklahoma. In dissent in the McGirt ruling were Chief Justice John Roberts and Justices Alito, Kavanaugh, and Thomas (Scotusblog.com 2020). Greater acceptance and tolerance of Native Americans began after World War I, when some 17,000 enlisted in U.S. armed forces voluntarily. That number was then about 30 percent of their adult males and was about twice the national average of enlistees. Congress passed the Indian Citizens Act of June 2, 1924 (43 Stat. 253). It granted U.S. citizenship to "indigenous peoples" of the United States. And again, in World War II, some 25,000 Native American men and 1,000 women served in uniform, including the famous "code talkers" (Thompson 1996). Some 45,000 served off-reservation in war-related industry jobs.

In 1944, the National Congress of American Indians (NCAI) was founded in Denver, Colorado, lobbying for changes in law. In 1946, Congress created the Indian Claims Commission, which operated until 1978. In 1952, the BIA began to assist off-reservation Native Americans with an employment-assistance program. In August 1954, the National Termination Policy was passed. It called for the termination of federal supervision over trust and restricted property of Native American bands and small tribes. In 1975, Congress passed the Indian Self-Determination and Education Assistance Act (88 Stat. 2203) during the Presidency of Gerald Ford. It was the culmination of fifteen years of activism by the Native American civil rights movement.

The highest ranking Native American national elected politician is Ben Nighthorse Campbell, a Cheyenne American who served in the Colorado House of Representatives from 1983 to 1987. He was then elected as a Democrat to the U.S. House of Representatives from Colorado, serving from 1987 to 1993. Campbell served in the United States Senate from 1993 to 2005, changing his party affiliation to Republican in 1995. He is one of forty-four members of the Council of Chiefs of the Northern Cheyenne Tribes. Senator Nighthorse helped enact laws to settle disputes over water rights and, in 1991, to change the name of the Custer Battlefield Monument (in Montana) to the Little Bighorn Battlefield Monument. He was instrumental in establishing the National Museum of the American Indian within the Smithsonian Institution and for getting national recognition of the contributions made by the Code Talkers to World War II (Viola 1993; Nez 2012).

Approximately 60 percent of the Native American population lives off-reservation, and the increased urbanization of the Native American population contributed to the pan-Indian movement, which led to the development of three organizations: the National Indian Youth Council (NIYC), founded in 1961; the American Indian Movement (AIM), founded in Minneapolis in 1968; and the Council of Energy Resource Tribes (CERT), founded in 1975.

As did the Hispanic movement, the Native American civil rights movement turned to a more radical and militant strategy using a variation of the tactics developed within the Black civil rights movement. Like Hispanic "Brown Power," Native American "Red Power" began in the early 1960s as part of a pan-Indian movement, which created organizations that crossed or spanned tribal boundaries. Again like with the Hispanic movement, World War II played a key role in the organizational development of the pan-Indian movement. In 1944, the NCAI was organized in Denver, Colorado, as the first truly viable national pan-Indian organization. NCAI was integrationist rather than radical; it was more akin to the NAACP in that it used the courts and lobbied for legislation. Napoleon Johnson was its president, and he also served as a justice on the Oklahoma State Supreme Court. The National Indian Youth Council (NIYC) began in 1961. Among its leaders was Dr. Kyle Powys Whyte, its president and a professor of philosophy at Michigan State University. CERT was founded in 1974, with the five largest tribes, and by 1998, over forty-five tribes had joined. CERT fought court cases to protect Indian lands from energy company exploitation, including winning a $330 million award to Sioux tribes over Black Hills land. The Sioux, however, refused the award, insisting on control of the land rather than a cash settlement. CERT has notably sponsored and funded a large scholarship program (LeMay 2009: 314).

These pan-Indian movement activists and organizations secured a number of legislative victories: the Indian Civil Rights Act of 1968, the Indian Education Act of 1972, the Indian Self-Determination and Education Assistance Act of 1975, the Indian Child Welfare Act of 1978, and the Indian Religious Freedom Act of 1978 (Thompson 1996; Wilkins 2002).

The most activist of the pan-Indian groups was the American Indian Movement. Among its leaders were Dennis Banks, Ada Deer, Vine Deloria, and Russell Means. They used direct protest tactics, including "fish-ins," and the siege of Wounded Knee on the Pine Ridge Reservation (LeMay 2009: 313). Other pan-Indian groups are the National Indian Youth Council, founded in 1961, the Alaska Federation of Natives (1966), the Indians of All Tribes (1969), the Native American Rights Fund (1970), the Women of All Red Nations (1975), and the Indian Law Resource Center (1977) (Wilkins 2002: 208–213).

Other Native American activists who pursued a variety of civil rights objectives include Barbara May Cameron, a lesbian and woman's rights activist; Deborah Parker, an indigenous rights activist who helped secure passage of the Violence against Women Reauthorization Act in 2013; and Elizabeth Peratrovich, an Alaskan activist for native people's rights.

Muslim and Arab Americans

"Arab American" is a term used by the U.S. Census Bureau to describe individuals who trace their ancestry to the Arabic-speaking regions of Africa, West Asia, and Southwest Asia. Countries of origin that would therefore be included in the category of Arab American are, for example, Lebanon, Egypt, Syria, Palestine, Jordan, Morocco, Iraq, Yemen, Kurdistan, Algeria, Saudi Arabia, Tunisia, Kuwait, United Arab Emirates, Oman, Qatar, and Bahrain. Arab Americans have a variety of skin tones and hair types and live a variety of lifestyles. In their formal religious affiliations, they are Christian (Eastern Orthodox, Roman Catholic, or Protestant), Muslim (Sunni, Shi'a, or Druze), or even Jewish or atheist. They hold a wide range of political or ideological beliefs. In terms of civil rights and liberties problems, however, overt forms of discrimination, hatred, and outright violence against the Arab American community increased dramatically after the September 11, 2001, attacks, the rise of international terrorism, and the launching of the "War on Terror" during the administration of President George W. Bush (Alden 2008; Mittelstadt, Speaker, Meissner, and Chisti 2011; Salehyan 2009).

Arab immigration can be distinguished as arriving in three waves. The first wave has been called the Great Migration (1880–1924). Of the roughly 20 million immigrants who came to the United States during that era, some 200,000 were Arabs, most from greater Syria (LeMay 2009: 112–113). They faced discrimination largely based on skin tone, and that discrimination was typically manifested in negative stereotyping, particularly in the media. All immigration to the United States declined dramatically after 1924 and the enactment of the quota system. A second mini-wave came after World War II, mostly Palestinians who emigrated after the establishment of the state of Israel.

The third and largest wave came after the passing of the 1965 immigration act. The 1965 law enabled the arrival of some 400,000 new Middle Eastern immigrants between 1965 and 1992, mostly from Lebanon, Palestine, and Egypt. The post-1965 wave was nearly 60 percent Muslim. Middle Eastern immigrants are often lumped together by politicians and the general public simply as "Arabs." They have faced widespread prejudice, and Middle Easterners have been the targets of repeated FBI investigation and subjected to occasions of random violence. Each confrontation between the United States and a Middle Eastern country has preceded an outbreak of hatred and anti-Arab actions. After the 1991 Gulf War, for example, there were incidents of arson, bombings, assaults, and attempted murders across the country. The American-Arab Anti-Discrimination Committee (ADC) has been an outspoken critic of American foreign and domestic policy. Following the September 11, 2001, attacks, Arab Americans and persons simply assumed to be "Muslims" were subjected to harassment and discrimination, including arbitrary detention, racial profiling, and aggressive checks and summary detentions for questioning at U.S. airports and border crossings and in "sweeps" by ICE and the FBI (LeMay 2006). The number of such detainees has been estimated at more than 2,000 people, and the Equal Employment Opportunity Commission (EEOC) and state fair-employment agencies have documented significant increases in alleged workplace discrimination based on religion or national origin since the 2001 attacks (LeMay 2006, 2013b: 81–103). The most dramatic policy enactments that came directly from the 9/11 attacks were the USA Patriot Acts I and II (2001 and 2006, respectively), the establishment of the Department of Homeland Security Act (2002), and the Intelligence Reform and Terrorism Prevention Act of 2004 (LeMay 2006: 205–238).

A number of Arab American civil rights organizations formed to cope with that discrimination and to advocate for policy and program changes. The oldest is the American-Arab Anti-Discrimination League (ADL), founded in 1980 by James Abourezk, a member of the U.S. House of Representatives (1971–1973) and former U.S. Senator (1973–1979, D-SD). The National Council of American-Islamic Relations (NCU-SAR) was founded in 1983. It is headquartered in Washington, D.C., and its president is Dr. John Duke Anthony. Another important Arab American civil rights advocacy organization is the Council of American-Islamic Relations (CAIR), founded in 1994 by Nihad Awad and Omar Ahmad. The Arab-American Political Action Committee (AAPAC) was begun in 1998 in Detroit, Michigan, which has one of the nation's largest Arab-American communities. AAPAC is a political action committee that endorses and electioneers for numerous candidates for local, state, and national-level offices and is headed by its president, Mona Fadallah. She also served as Secretary of the Arab-American Civil Rights League (ACRL). ACRL is a 501(c)(3) nonprofit committed to protecting the civil rights of Arab Americans. It builds coalitions to promote understanding and to combat discrimination and negative stereotyping. It is led by prominent civil rights attorneys and advocates. Its founder is Nabih Ayad, and its board chairman is Nasser Beydoun. Finally, in 2001, U.S. Marine Corps Gunnery Sergeant Jamal S. Baadani founded the Association of Patriotic Arab Americans in Military (APAAM). There are currently 3,500 Arab Americans serving in the various branches of the U.S. military.

Four ways to better reconcile U.S. security policy with human civil rights policy protocols have been suggested: (1) separate U.S. immigration enforcement from its counterterrorism practices (Alden 2008: 292); (2) maintaining the United States as a desirable destination for the world's immigration in order to ensure U.S. global competitiveness (Alden 2008: 24); (3) prioritize the deportation of unauthorized individuals with criminal records as opposed to those caught up in sweeps and who commit nonviolent criminal or simple civil offenses (LeMay 2013b: 101); and (4) continue U.S. efforts to capture and record the entry and exit of foreign individuals to and from the United States, as was the policy goal of the NSEERS program (Mittelstadt, Speaker, Meissner, and Chisti 2011). A significant portion of those arrested and detained under the Secure Communities program were caught on minor violations like traffic offenses. Secure Communities was a program that attempted to identify dangerous criminals through local-federal law enforcement partnerships, administered by Immigration and Customs Enforcement (ICE) within the Department of Homeland Security from 2008 to 2013. It was suspended by President Barack Obama from 2014 to 2017 and was reactivated by President Donald Trump by Executive Order 13768, titled Enhancing Public Safety in the Interior of the United States, issued in 2017. The program removed more than 43,300 convicted criminal aliens, although as noted, many were for minor criminal offenses. It has been widely criticized for racial or ethnic targeting, particularly of Arab Americans and Muslims. The American-Arab Anti-Discrimination Committee (ADC) received 800 reports of employment discrimination in the months following the 9/11 attacks (LeMay 2013b: 94–95). ADC also found ample evidence of anti-Muslim backlash against Muslim-run businesses.

Another example of such bias was the Trump administration's travel ban. The ban was first issued on January 25, 2017, executive order 13767, titled "Border Security and Immigration Enhancement Enforcement Improvements," more commonly known as the Muslim travel ban. The first iteration of the ban targeted restrictions on immigration from eight Muslim-dominant countries. The first two iterations of the ban were put on hold by U.S. district court actions. The Muslim dominant countries covered by the ban even in its third iteration were Iran, Iraq, Libya, Somalia, Sudan, Syria, and Yemen. The third version of the travel ban was brought to the U.S. Supreme Court by the state of Hawaii, supported by amicus briefs by the ACLU and several American Arab and Muslim organizations. The final version of the ban was partially upheld by the U.S. Supreme Court in *Trump v. Hawaii* (585 U.S. _____, June 26, 2018). Chief Justice John Roberts delivered the majority opinion of the Court. He was joined by Justices Anthony Kennedy, Clarence Thomas, Samuel Alito, and Neil Gorsuch. In dissent were all the liberal justices on the Supreme Court: Justices Stephen Breyer, Elena Kagan, Ruth Bader Ginsburg, and Sonia Sotomayor (LeMay 2019: 250–255).

Political Ideological Minorities

Socialists, communists, and fascists exemplify organizations that pursued "old-style radicalism" to advocate for their civil rights (LeMay 2009). Old-style radicals reject the value system of the majority society and seek to replace it with their own value system, thereby radically altering government, politics, and society. Three such "isms" represented the approach. Each was a minor or third party advocating a radical political ideology. They sought to win office and through the electoral process to control government, law, and policy in order to remake U.S. society. Political ideologies of the radical left were socialism and communism. A political ideology of the radical right was fascism (also known as American Nazism).

The earliest *ism* to develop in America was socialism. It first emerged among the 1848 German immigrant followers of German Socialist Ferdinand Lassalle and advocated reform rather than revolution. American socialism never became widely popular, but it attracted a following among immigrant groups of naturalized Americans: Germans, Russians, Scandinavians, Slavs, and some Eastern European Jews. Socialist movements developed in a half-dozen large American cities, for example, New York, Philadelphia, St. Louis, Milwaukee, Cincinnati, and Chicago (Judd 1989; LeMay 2009). German workers in those cities and Jewish workers in New York provided the "shock troops" of the Socialist Party of America. Some of the socialist groups' party leaders were Eugene Debs (the party's four-time nominee for the presidency), Morris Hillquit, and Victor Berger (George and Wilcox 1992). The socialist party's inner diversity developed schismatic factionalism that led to its electoral demise after 1912. A fundamentalist and radical faction of American socialism was the Western Syndicalists, who formed the Industrial Workers of the World (commonly known as the Wobblies) in Chicago, Illinois, on June 27, 1905. Prominent leaders of the IWW were William Haywood, Charles Ruthenberg, William Foster, and Ben Fletcher, all of whom later became avowed communists. Eugene Debs and many of the Wobblies were arrested, and many of the movement's leaders were imprisoned following the Palmer Raids during the Red Scare in the summer of 1919. They were suppressed using the Espionage Act of June 15, 1917 (40 Stat. 217). In 1919, many foreign-born Wobblies and socialists were deported to Russia aboard the *Buford*, at the time dubbed "the Soviet Ark." The Espionage Act and its amendment, the Sedition Act of 1918, were used against the socialists, and the laws were upheld as constitutional by the Supreme Court in *Schenck v. United States* (249 U.S. 47, 1919) and *Abrams v. United States* (250 U.S. 616, 1919) (Kohn 1994; Preston 1994; Thomas 2008).

When the United States declared war on Germany on April 7, 1917, it also waged war on the German language, pursuing the battle on two fronts: one legal, the other in schools. The Trading with the Enemy Act (49 Stat. 411, October 6, 1917) suppressed the American foreign language press and declared non-English printed matter unmailable without a certified English translation. In less than a decade, the number of foreign language newspapers, magazines, and related press declined from the hundreds to the dozens. In Iowa, Governor William Harding banned the use of any foreign language in public schools, on the streets, in trains, and even over the telephone (his executive order was referred to as the Babel Proclamation). In the Midwest, thousands were charged with violating the various English-only statutes. As to the education front, by 1918, twenty-five states had removed the teaching of the German language from their curriculum. After the World War I–induced hysteria subsided, the U.S. Supreme Court threw out laws in Nebraska and Ohio that banned foreign-language education (*Meyer v. Nebraska*, 262 U.S. 390, 1923).

Communism in the United States, as evidenced by the American Communist Party, grew out of the socialist party movement. The American Communist Party has always been small, typically fewer than 100,000 members (Buhle 1987; LeMay 2009). Two communist party organizations formed in 1919: the Communist Labor Party, and the Communist Party of America. Their members were driven underground by Attorney General A. Mitchell Palmer's raids during the summer of 1919. Prominent American communist leaders were William Foster, Eugene Dennis, Harry Haywood, Richard Moore, Grace Campbell, Otto Hall, and S. V. Philips. The party's outreach to Black Americans was led by James Ford, of the American Negro Labor Congress, who became the party's vice-presidential nominee on the Foster/Ford ticket in 1932

(LeMay 2009). Another outreach organization of communists to Blacks was the African Blood Brotherhood, founded in 1919 by Cyril Briggs, and involving also Claude McKay, editor of *The Liberator*, Otto Huiswood, and Harry Haywood of the IWW. American communist and socialist party leadership was suppressed using the Alien Registration Act (8 U.S. 10, 1940; also known as the Smith Act; Foner and Shapiro 1991). Twelve members were indicted and their convictions were upheld in 1951. Another law used to suppress the party was the McCarren Walter Act (Act of June 27, 1952, 66 Stat. 163). It was also used to deport foreign-born communists (LeMay and Barkan 1999).

In the United States, fascism arose after World War I in response to postwar economic dislocations, particularly the Great Depression, and after the fascist dictators came to power in Italy (Benito Mussolini in 1922) and Germany (Adolf Hitler in 1933). American fascists developed in and were recruited from among such Italian American organizations as the Order of the Sons of Italy, and in 1925 the Fascist League of North America was formed. Its members soon infiltrated the Italian War Veterans Federation, the Italian Chamber of Commerce, the Dante Alighieri Society, the Italy-America Society, and the Black Shirts. American-born fascist organizations developed, such as the Black Legion, the White Legion, the White Crusaders, and the Knights of the White Camelia. Others supporting the fascist line were the Liberty League, the Friends of New Germany, the Southern Council to Uphold the Constitution, the Silver Shirts (led by Reverend William Dudley Pelley), and the Sentinels of the Republic (LeMay 2009; MacDonnell 1995; Lipset and Marks 2000; Schonbach 1985; Solomon 1998).

Lawrence Dennis became the theoretician of American fascism, and Father Charles Coughlin, sometimes characterized as the American version of Paul Goebbels, Hitler's propagandist, preached a fascist message and established the National Union for Social Justice. Joseph McWilliams led the small ultra-reactionary Christian Front and the Christian Mobilizers, an extreme anti-Semitic group; Walter Winchell colorfully labeled him "Joe McNazi." Another such leader was the Reverend Gerald Winrod, who led the Defenders of the Christian Faith in 1922 and began their paramilitary organization, the Khaki Shirts (MacDonnell 1995). By 1930, German and Italian Fascists movements linked and formed such groups as the American National Socialist League, the Friends of New Germany, and U.S. Fascists.

An antifascist movement, led most notably by the Mazzini Society, campaigned against American fascism and formed the Anti-Fascist Alliance of North America. American fascism began to decline when Mussolini invaded Ethiopia and after the 1936 presidential election, when Father Charles Coughlin, and William Hearst's Liberty League, were rejected. American Nazism declined dramatically in 1939, after Germany's invasion of Poland. In the 1960s, a brief neo-Nazi movement was led by George Lincoln Rockwell, known as the "sixties Fuhrer." The rise of neo-Nazi fascism was a reaction to the civil rights movement, as exemplified more currently by the neo-Nazi skinheads, officially known as the National Socialist Movement, led by Commander Jeff Schoep (LeMay 2009). The right of such fascist groups to protest in U.S. society and politics was upheld in the aforementioned Supreme Court decision *Nationalist Socialist Party of America v. Village of Skokie* (432 U.S. 43, 1977). The *Skokie* decision echoed the Ku Klux Klan (KKK)'s right to do so under the "clear and present danger" test established as judicial doctrine by the U.S. Supreme Court in *Brandenburg v. Ohio* (395 U.S. 444, 1969).

Quite a number of current neo-Nazi and white supremacist organizations have arisen or have increased their visibility since 2016. They are exemplified by such organizations as the following: American Renaissance, American Freedom Party, American Nazi Party, Aryan Brotherhood of Texas, Aryan Nation, Council of Conservative Citizens, Creativity Alliance, EURO, Hammerskin Nation, the revived KKK, National Alliance, National Association for the Advancement of White

People, National Policy Institute, National Vanguard, and the Order of the Bruder Schweigen (Silent Brotherhood). The white supremacist movement is also aided and abetted by shite separatist organizations such as Ethnopluralism, Ethnocentrism, Neo-Confederate, and the Northwest Territorial Imperative. They have been politically emboldened by the Trump administration, for example, by the Proud Boys.

Women's Rights—the Suffragettes and NOW

Immigrant women's citizenship status was often tied to that of their husbands. White, native-born women were recognized as citizens, but for well over a century, their right to vote in national elections was denied them. The franchise had to be won through their advocacy and struggle. The women's suffrage movement can be traced to 1790, but it began in earnest in the 1840s and was often associated with the abolition and temperance social movements.

Women had won the right to vote, mostly in western states, in the 1890s (Mead 2004). Suffrage organizations, which had been fighting for the right to vote on a state-by-state basis, began to refocus on a national amendment in the 1890s, led by Lucy Burns and Alice Paul. The National Woman's Party staged marches, demonstrations, and hunger strikes, and joined with the National American Woman Suffrage Association to sway public opinion. The Nineteenth Amendment, which prohibits the federal government from denying the right to vote to citizens on the basis of sex, was first introduced to Congress in 1878. President Woodrow Wilson endorsed the amendment in 1918. After several failed attempts, it was passed in the House of Representatives on May 21, 1919, in the Senate on June 4, 1919, and ratified on August 18, 1920. Tennessee was the last of the thirty-six states to secure its ratification.

After it was passed and ratified, in 1920, it was upheld in two U.S. Supreme Court decisions: *Leser v. Garnett* (258 U.S. 130, 1922), and *Fairchild v. Hughes* (258 U.S. 126, 1922). Thirty-six million women were enfranchised by the Nineteenth

Amendment and made eligible to vote in the 1920 presidential election.

Gender rights were fought for by leaders such as Jane Addams, the Hull House leader and Nobel prize laureate who also advocated children's rights. Another leader was Carrie Chapman Catt, who was a leading suffragette and president of the National American Women's Suffrage Association and cofounder, in 1920, of the League of Women Voters. Another early suffragette was Lucretia Mott. Emma DeVoe was a leader of the League of Women Voters. Famous suffragettes include Susan B. Anthony, Antoinette Brown Blackwell, Julia Ward Howe, Abbey Kelley, Elizabeth Cady Stanton, Lucy Stone, Ida B. Wells and Josephine Ruffin (both suffragettes and cofounders of the NAACP), and Victoria Woodhall.

After 1920, the National Woman's Party, founded in 1912 to advocate for women's right to vote, led by Alice Paul, worked to ensure that women were treated equally to men by campaigning to enact an Equal Rights Amendment (ERA), written by Crystal Eastman. The ERA was introduced into Congress in the 1950s and reintroduced in 1971. In 1971, the ERA passed the House of Representatives, and it passed the U.S. Senate in 1972. It went to the states for ratification but failed to reach the necessary thirty-eight states by its ratification deadline of 1982. Proposed legislation to remove the deadline to ratify the ERA was introduced by Representative Jackie Speier (D-CA) in 2019 (Baker 2009; DuBois 1998; Keyssar 2000; Mead 2004).

During the 1960s and 1970s, women's rights leaders include Bella Abzug, who in 1971 was a cofounder of the National Women's Political Caucus (NWPC), as were Fannie Lou Hamer, of the Freedom Democratic Party, and Gloria Steinem. Shirley Chisholm (D-NY) was the first black woman elected to the U.S. House of Representatives, where she served for seven terms. In 1972, she was the first black woman to seek the nomination for president from a major party. Chisholm was also a cofounder of the NWPC. A women's civil rights/ Latina rights and labor leader was Corona "Bert" Humberto

(1918–2001). Jill Ruckelshaus was another leader of the National Women's Political Caucus and was active throughout the late 1960s and 1970s. Winfred Stanley was the first member of Congress to introduce a bill to prohibit discrimination based on sex. Janette Rankin (D-MT, 1880–1973) was the first female elected to the U.S. Congress (in 1916), even before women had achieved the right to vote in national elections (Hagedorn and LeMay 2019). Willa Brown (1906–1992) was a civil rights activist and the first African American woman to run for the United States Congress. Representative Barbara Jordan (D-TX, 1936–1996) was a noted civil rights activist and chair of the Jordan Commission. Harriette Moore, along with her husband Harry Moore, was a civil rights activist. They are both considered "martyrs" of the civil rights movement, killed by a KKK bombing of their Mims, Florida, home in December 1951. Jo Ann Robinson helped launch the Montgomery bus boycott in the mid-1950s. First Lady Eleanor Roosevelt was a lifelong advocate of women's rights and helped found the UN and form its Universal Declaration of Human Rights. Delores Huerta was cofounder of the UFW (1930–).

There is an ongoing effort to enact the ERA. On January 27, 2020, Virginia became the thirty-eighth state to ratify the ERA. On February 13, 2020, the U.S. House of Representatives voted 232 to 182 to pass HJ Res. 79, to remove the original time limit assigned to the ERA (Equal Rights Amendment.org 2020). Today, the grassroots arm of the women's civil rights movement is the National Organization for Women (NOW). NOW was founded in 1966. It advocates on many issues and employs several strategies to secure women's rights. NOW is the largest organization of feminist activists in the United States and comprises hundreds of chapters and thousands of members and is organized in all fifty states and the District of Columbia. It promotes feminist ideals, leads societal change, advocates for legislation at all levels of government, seeks to eliminate discrimination, and works to achieve and to protect the equal rights of all women and girls in all aspects of social, political, and economic life. At its founding meeting in June 1966, twenty-eight women were cofounders. In October, 1966, at a national conference, twenty-one more women and men joined as cofounders. Its first president was Betty Friedan. Its second president was the civil rights activist Aileen Hernandez.

In 1992, the label "Year of the Woman" was coined for the election resulting in a record number of U.S. Senators. In 2018, the label was again popularly used for the record number of women candidates running for office at all levels of government, and in which five women were newly elected to the U.S. Senate and twenty-four women were elected to the U.S. House of Representatives. The 2018 election brought the totals in Congress to 103 women in the U.S. House and 25 women in the U.S. Senate. Representative Nancy Pelosi (D-CA) was elected for a second time as the U.S. Speaker of the House, the third most powerful position in the national government and third in line for assumption of the presidency, making her arguably the most powerful woman in American electoral politics (Hagedorn and LeMay 2019). Former first lady, Michelle Obama, is often cited as the most admired woman in America.

Religious Minorities

Factions within the WASP majority often targeted the civil rights and liberties of religious minorities based on religious animosity, bias, or bigotry, leading to religious discrimination not only in social customs and norms but also in laws and policies, particularly at the local and state levels of government. Religious discrimination involves treating a person or group differently based simply on what they do or do not believe. It arises when different religious denominations are treated unequally in laws, education, employment, or housing. It has been present in American society from colonial times to today (Barnes 2016; Curran 2014; Farrelly 2017; La Beau 2017;

Kinzer 1964; LeMay 2009). Among its earliest, ugliest, and often most violent manifestations was the anti-Catholicism and anti-Irish movement during the 1840s and 1850s, exemplified by the rise of the Secret Order of the Star Spangled Banner and its political party development, the American Party (better known as the Know Nothing Party). A spin-off group of the Know Nothing Party, called the Plug Uglies, led a riot in Baltimore, Maryland, that left eight dead and one in Newark, New Jersey, that left twenty dead (LeMay 2013a: 42). Anti-Catholicism was exemplified by Lyman Beecher, the Presbyterian minister and leader of the American Temperance Society, who preached against "Rum and Romanism." The Temperance Society was cofounded in Boston in 1826 by the evangelical preacher Dr. Justin Edwards. By 1830, it had grown to more than 8,000 local groups and claimed 1.5 million members who had "taken the pledge." The Temperance Movement members, and especially its leadership, saw Catholics, and particularly Irish Catholics, as a major source of the "sin" of alcoholism (Young 2007).

Anti-Catholicism was also a prominent part of the KKK (Barnes 2016). It was the explicit motivation behind the founding of the American Protective Association (APA) (Kinzer 1964). The APA was an anti-Catholic, anti-immigrant social movement that arose during the 1890s and grew to an estimated membership of two million. The APA worked in coalition with the KKK to promote restriction of immigration, especially of people from southern and eastern Europe who adhered to Catholicism, Greek Orthodoxy, and Judaism. In spirit, the APA was the successor of the Know Nothing Party and a precursor to President Donald Trump's Muslim travel ban. The APA was founded in Clinton, Iowa, in 1887 by Henry Bowers. Lasting about a decade, the APA played on xenophobic fears among the population in rural America over the growth and political power of the immigrant-populated cities with their "evil and corrupt" urban political machines, like Tammany Hall in New York City. The APA's membership declined with the Progressive Era, ushered in by the election of William McKinley in 1896 (Zentner and LeMay 2020). By 1910, the APA exerted little political power, and it disappeared by 1912.

Irish Catholics

At 34.7 million residents claiming Irish ancestry in the 2010 census, Irish Americans rank second only to German Americans in their percentage of the total population. They were about 2 percent of the population in 1790. They began arriving in significant numbers after 1830, particularly with the potato famine after 1850. Between 1840 and 1860, nearly 1.7 million Irish immigrants came to the United States, and they made up nearly 43 percent of the foreign-born population in the 1850 census (LeMay 2013a: 106). The famine-induced wave activated anti-Catholicism in Eastern seaboard cities, where Irish Catholics faced developing class consciousness and were seen as a particular threat. Catholicism was seen as a dangerous and alien religion; "Popery" (as many called Catholicism at the time) was thought to be opposed in its very nature to Democratic Republicanism (Gjerde 1998: 137; LeMay 2013a: 106; Zentner and LeMay 2020).

Anti-Catholic and anti-Irish riots in Boston in 1837 presaged later riots over public school curriculum. Their influx launched the "great school debate" between Catholic and Protestant school leaders over curriculum and led to the creation of the nationwide Catholic school system (Ravitch 1974). Their right to have and maintain a private Catholic school system was upheld by the U.S. Supreme Court in *Pierce v. Society of Sisters* (258 U.S. 10, 1925). Reverend Theodore Parker (1810–1860), an American Transcendentalist and Unitarian minister, called the Irish people "inferior in nature . . . behind us in development . . . a lower form" (in Spring 2008). The Irish population were the first group to face overt job discrimination when cities like New York, Boston, and Philadelphia sported "No Irish Need Apply" signs for some years (LeMay 2009:

124). The jobs in which they did concentrate were often seasonal, lower paying, and periodic. Fleeing political, religious, and social persecution by the Protestant ruling class in Ireland, many became trapped in enclaves and the tenement slums of big cities, and some "escaped" their grim conditions through alcohol, earning them the stereotypical image of excessive drinkers. It was an all-too-typical reaction of blaming the victims of discrimination for the evils or disparities brought about by discrimination.

In the 1850s, unions were mainly local, but after the Civil War they began to appear at the national level—such as the American Miners Association, led by Irish immigrant Martin Burke. By the late 1870s, second-generation Irish American Terrence Powderly led the first effective national-level labor union, the Knights of Labor. In 1886, Peter McGuire, sometimes called the "Father of Labor Day," founded and led the American Federation of Labor (AFL).

The rapid industrialization and urbanization during and after the Civil War provided the Irish population with opportunities to get work in city governments, and by 1870 they began to take leadership in big-city politics and local bureaucracies, like the cities' police and streets departments, giving them a degree of success with the growing urban machines. Irish immigrants became the mainstay of many ward and district organizations of the Democratic political party (Fuchs 1990; LeMay 2013a; Zentner and LeMay 2020). By the 1870s and 1880s, they began to serve as mayors of the nation's major cities, and "bosses" like "Dick" Connolly, "Brains" Sweeny, Richard Croker, John Purroy Mitchel, John Francis "Iron Mike" Hylan, James Pendergast, and Thomas Platt shared power and machine-style politics with the likes of William Magear Tweed and George Washington Plunkitt. Machines soon controlled big-city politics in Boston, Chicago, Cleveland, Kansas City, New York City, Philadelphia, and St. Louis (Gosnell and Merriam 2007; Fuchs 1990). That very success brought them opposition from Progressive-Era reformers, such as Fiorello La

Guardia in New York, political cartoonist Thomas Nast, and the previously discussed American Protective Association.

Jewish Americans

An estimated 30 to 40 percent of Eastern Europeans entering the United States from 1870 to 1930 were Jewish (LeMay 2009). The American Jewish population was about 200,000 by 1860 (American Jewish Historical Society 1999: 35), with most of them arriving from southwestern Germany between 1830 and 1860. They spoke German, and most settled in New York City, although Cincinnati had about 10,000 Jews in 1860 (Daniels 2002: 155). They constructed a Jewish hospital, build several synagogues, and started a Jewish newspaper published in English and German (Toltzman 2005: 47).

During the midnineteenth century, German Jewish immigrants were Ashkenazis, better educated and more politically progressive than most immigrants at the time. In Hebrew, "Ashkenazi" refers to Germany, and Ashkenazi Jews are those from Eastern Europe, in contrast with Sephardic Jews from the Mediterranean Sea area—such as Spain, Portugal, the Middle East, and Northern Africa. In New York, Jewish children attended public schools as well as their Saturday religious schools. There were some anti-Semitic attitudes among the majority Protestant population and occasional flare ups of violence, but the overwhelmingly urban Jewish immigrants were not highly visible and had open access to public schooling (LeMay 2013a: 106).

By the 1890s, Jewish immigrants increasingly came from Eastern Europe, particularly Russia and the Baltics, from where they fled religious persecution and pogroms (violent outbreaks of anti-Semitism involving looting, pillaging, riots, murders, and, in some cases, total destruction of Jewish ghettos). Government troops would sit idly by or even join in the anti-Semitic violence (LeMay 2009: 142).

Jewish immigrants prior to 1910 were active in unionization, especially in the garment industry. The Amalgamated

Clothing Workers and International Ladies Garment Workers Union (ILGWU) was predominantly Jewish; by World War II, over 60 percent of the ILGWU was Jewish, and the Dressmakers Local 22 of New York City was 75 percent Jewish (LeMay 2009: 143). They were also heavily employed in cigar manufacturing, bookbinding, distilling, printing, and skilled carpentry. In unskilled trades, they tended toward pushcart peddling and sales. A 1900 census by the U.S. Immigration Service found the proportion of Jewish immigrants in the professions to be the highest among non-English-speaking immigrants.

In the United States, they experienced anti-Semitism, but nothing like the pogroms of Europe. In the 1870s, largely latent anti-Semitism broke out into the open. In 1877, for example, Jews were blackballed from the New York Bar Association, and in 1878, New York college fraternities followed suit. The KKK revived in the late nineteenth century and became the leading nativist group that was specifically anti-Semitic.

Fighting for their civil rights were such organizations as the American Jewish Committee. In 1913, B'nai B'rith's Anti-Defamation League (ADL) was formed. B'nai B'rith (in Hebrew, meaning Children of the Covenant) is a Jewish service organization that combats anti-Semitism and bigotry (Wilhelm 2011). It was founded in October 1843 and is headquartered in Washington, D.C. It was founded by Henry Jones and Isaac Rosenberg in Aaron Sinsheimer's café. B'nai B'rith soon established numerous hospitals, orphanages, and homes for the aged. In 1903, its president was Simon Wolf, and in the 1950s, it was led by Frank Goldman. B'nai B'rith founded two related organizations: the Anti-Defamation League (ADL), in NYC in 1913 by Sigmund Livingston; and the Hillel Foundation in 1923, founded by Benjamin Frankel. The ADL supports numerous amicus briefs to combat anti-Semitism and promote freedom of religion. During the 1960s, its national director was Benjamin Epstein. Its current president is Charles Kaufman, and its CEO is Jonathan Greenblatt. The ADL's national director is Abraham Foxman (Foxman 2003).

The conservative Jewish Theological Seminary trains rabbis. It was founded in NYC in 1886 by Dr. Sabato Marais and Dr. H. Pereira Mendes. Another way of fighting anti-Semitism and promoting Jewish life and their civil rights in America occurred between 1883 and 1915, when some 150 Yiddish-language newspapers began to publish, including the highly influential *Jewish Daily Forward* (LeMay 2009: 144). The Jewish/Yiddish language press promoted unionism and opposed reforms in immigration law that would restrict Jewish immigrants from Eastern Europe.

In terms of policy differences between Jews and local laws (known as Sabbatarian or Sunday Blue Laws or Sunday closing laws), the Supreme Court handed down four decisions in 1961, all of which upheld the constitutionality of Sunday blue laws: *McGowan v. Maryland* (366 U.S. 420), decided by a 6–3 ruling; *Braunfeld v.Brown* (366 U.S. 599), decided by a 5–4 vote; *Gallagher v. Crown Kosher Super Market of Massachusetts* (366 U.S. 617), decided 5–4; and *Two Guys from Harrison-Allentown, PA v. McGinley* (361 U.S. 582, 8–1). In his dissent in the Braunfeld case, Justice William Brennan, joined by Justice Potter Stewart, argued against the state of Pennsylvania and stated in his minority opinion: "Pennsylvania has passed a law which compels an Orthodox Jew to choose between his religious faith and his economic survival." The majority of the Court disagreed and upheld the Pennsylvania law. In 1963, the Court ruled on another Sunday closing law, *Thorton v. Caldor* (472 U.S. 703).

The Supreme Court case of *National Socialist Party of America v. Village of Skokie* (432 U.S. 43, 1977) pitted several Jewish lawyers arguing on the two sides of the case. The ACLU challenged the injunction by the Circuit Court of Cook County, Illinois. Two ACLU lawyers arguing their case, both Jewish, were David Goldberg and Burton Joseph. Goldberg was the legal director for the Illinois chapter of the ACLU, and Burton Joseph was a Jewish attorney with the firm of Joseph, Lichtenstein, and Levinson. Burton's parents ran a caretaking business for Skokie's Jewish cemetery. Goldberg and Joseph successfully argued the case for the neo-Nazi, Frank Collin. Arguing the case for the Village of Skokie was village attorney Harvey Schwartz. The Court upheld the Nazi organization's right to march and to protest on First Amendment grounds (Strum 1999).

Another significant source of Jewish immigration, and another example of a group using a separatist strategy for coping with discrimination, are the various sects of Hasidic Jews. Like Black Muslims, they use the psychological approach to separatism and have successfully maintained, for over a century, a religious/ethnic subculture amid a majority culture. Hasidic Jews (also known as Chasidic, from the Hebrew word meaning pious) have a population of about 180,000, or about 3 percent of approximately 6 million Jews in the United States (Hoffman 1991; LeMay 2009: 231). They are an ultra-Orthodox sect among Jews who live in close neighborhoods within walking distance of their synagogue. They wear distinctive, traditional garb and exhibit communal tightness, with high degrees of ritual religious observance that permeates every aspect of their lives. Hasidism is mystical and enthusiastic, transformative, and communitarian. The center of their communal life is their synagogue, led by a "rebbe," a distinctive Yiddish word for rabbi or teacher. Historically, each rebbe comes from a town in which their court was located in Eastern Europe: the Lubavitch from Lubavitch in Russia, the Satmar from Satu Mare in Hungary, the Bobover from the Polish town of Bobova, and so on. They came to the United States fleeing persecution of Nazi Germany and Communist Soviet Russia. Today, there are 3,270 synagogues in the United States, among which 1,500 are Orthodox, 975 are Reform, and 865 are conservative; and among the Orthodox, 346 are Hasidic or mixed synagogues (Singer and Grossman 2002: 128–129).

Among Jews in the United States, the Hasidic Jews face the most negative stereotyping, the most pronounced form of anti-Semitism in America. Anti-Semitism ebbs and flows depending on social conditions, and discrimination against

Hasidic Jews rose most notably after they came to the United States in 1940, settling in Brooklyn, New York, led by Rebbe Yosef Schneersohn. He established the headquarters of the Lubavitch Hasidic court in Crown Heights, Brooklyn. He was succeeded by his son, Rebbe Menachem Schneersohn. Since the 1960s, they have established incorporated villages, but whether in the midst of Brooklyn, New York, or a small village of 1,000 in Ramapo, New York, they live in a world apart. They are generally self-employed in various trades, attend schools in a *yeshiva* (a Jewish religious school), and live and marry within the Hasidic culture. They do participate in local elections, and some are employed in jobs outside their ethnic enclave, but like the Old Order Amish and Old Order Mennonites, they maintain a high degree of culture identity. Hasidism has been remarkably successful in using psychological separatism while maintaining a degree of involvement in the majority society (LeMay 2009: 230–237).

Hasidic Jews clashed with the majority society and lost their case in the Supreme Court decision in *Board of Education of Kiryas Joel Village School District v. Grumet* (512 U.S. 687, 1994). The case was brought on behalf of the Satmar Hasidic Jews seeking to have state funding to support their village public school and bear the cost of special education for Hasidic special-needs children. The Hasidic community lost the case in a 5–4 decision decided on Establishment Clause grounds.

Other Jewish civil rights activists who are leaders in other fields of civil rights include Sandra Froman, a past president of the National Rifle Association; Franklin Kamey, a noted gay rights activist; and Rebecca Walker, a feminist writer. Two famous Holocaust survivors and writers were Eli Wiesel (1928–2016), the Romanian-born, American writer, professor, political activist, 1986 Nobel laureate, Holocaust survivor, and author of fifty-seven books; and Simon Wiesenthal (1908–2005), the Holocaust survivor, writer, and relentless pursuer of Nazis and Nazi collaborators. An example of a fully assimilated Jewish American political leader is former senator

(D-CT, I-CT) and former Democratic vice-presidential candidate Joseph Lieberman (2000) (LeMay 2009: 146).

Minority Christian Denominations

Jews are not the only religious groups that were affected by Sabbatarian laws and the four 1961 Supreme Court decisions cited above. A number of Christian denominations or sects also observe Saturday as their Sabbath, including, for example, Jehovah's Witnesses, Seventh-day Adventists, Seventh-day Baptists, Church of God, Seventh Day, and two sects of the Church of Jesus Christ of the Latter-day Saints—the Strangites and the Fettingites (LeMay 2009: 170–183). None won cases that challenged the Blue Laws, but the Sunday Blue Laws problem essentially went away as U.S. society became more secularized, and most local ordinances concerning Sunday closing laws were simply repealed, rescinded, or no longer enforced.

The Supreme Court has ruled on religious institutions functioning as a government agency (e.g., having virtual veto power over a liquor licensing board) in *Larkin v. Grendel's Den* (459 U.S. 116, 1982). And the Supreme Court held that a religious institution could have its tax exempt status taken away in *Bob Jones University v. United States* (461 U.S. 574, 1983).

Minority Christian faiths such as the Jehovah's Witnesses and the Seventh-day Adventists have aggressively proselytized. Their evangelism has led them to clash with government over local ordinances regarding door-to-door canvassing or selling religious tracts without first getting a license or permit. They have won some and lost some cases challenging state and local laws on the matter. The Seventh-day Adventists, founded in 1863 by Joseph Bates, James White, Ellen White, and J. N. Andrews, run primary and secondary private schools, and Adventists have been parties to cases or have supported First Amendment challenges through amicus briefs. They have been aggressive and successful advocates for the separation of church and state, as have the Jehovah's Witnesses (Cox and Jones 2019; LeMay 2009: 237–241).

Yet another public policy area in which problems arose with religious minorities is exemplified by pacifists during times of war. Conscientious objectors oppose military service involving combat based on grounds of their religious beliefs. They have been involved in or backed challenges to conscription laws based on the First Amendment's freedom of religion clause. Objection to conscription on pacifist grounds in U.S. history went back to the Quakers during the Civil War.

Pacifists objected to the draft in World Wars I and II, the Korean War, and the Vietnam War. Serving in combat in these wars for which the draft, or compulsory military service, was used raised problems for such religious groups as the Amish and Mennonites, Christadelphians, Black Muslims (NOI), Seventh-day Adventists, Jehovah's Witnesses, and Unitarian Universalists. These religious groups had official pacifist doctrines. Although the Roman Catholic Church is not, and never was, a pacifist denomination, during World War I, a noted conscientious objector was Ben Salmon, who wrote on the theology of a "just war." He was denied conscientious objection status, refused to serve, was indicted and convicted, but his arguments about a "just war" versus an "immoral war" influenced subsequent jurisprudence on the matter. The problem for religious conscientious objectors generally arises only in times of war when the draft is used extensively.

Pacifist religious groups have advocated and secured some rights for alternative service to military service or for noncombatant roles in the military. One of the most notable examples of the latter, Desmond Doss, was a Seventh-day Adventist and conscientious objector whose heroism as a medic during World War II earned him posthumously the U.S. Congressional Medal of Honor, the nation's highest award for valor. Since World War I, the United States has enacted legal provisions for conscientious objectors within regulations of the Selective Service System and the Department of Defense. Exemptions are given on a case-by-case basis, usually to adherents of formal religious organizations that have been recognized by the U.S. government as "pacifist." Those individuals who are accorded conscientious objector (CO) status are allowed to either perform alternative civilian service in lieu of combatant military service or to serve in noncombatant roles while in the military, such as serving as unarmed medics like Desmond Doss.

Two U.S. Supreme Court decisions ruled on the issue of *selective conscientious objection* status wherein the litigant refused a draft order of the Selective Service. Both cases involved objections to service in the Vietnam War raised by individuals not belonging to an officially recognized denomination or religion with acknowledged pacifist doctrine. *Sisson v. United States* (399 U.S. 257, 1970) was the first important case won by a selective CO who objected to service in a particular war but not all war, in which the objector believed that a particular war (Vietnam) was immoral. In *Sisson*, the defendant had been acquitted of draft evasion in a jury trial after which the national government appealed. The Supreme Court ruled 6–3 that the government had no power to appeal a verdict of acquittal no matter how wrong the legal basis was for the acquittal. The majority opinion was written by Justice John Marshall Harlan, with dissents from Justice Byron White, Chief Justice Earl Warren, and Justice William Douglas. *Gillette v. United States* (401 U.S. 437, 1971) upheld a lower court ruling denying a draft exemption to a man who, on the basis of *humanist principles*, refused to participate in the Vietnam War, but who acknowledged that he would have fought in a war of self-defense. The 8–1 decision added constraints on the terms of CO status from draftees in the selective service system.

Guy Gillette was a Roman Catholic who objected to the Vietnam War on the basis of "unjust killing" doctrine. Justice Thurgood Marshall wrote the majority opinion for the Court. The issue or problem has not been officially "solved," but it has declined in importance as the United States began using an all-volunteer military rather than conscription into military service by means of the draft.

Other laws create problems for religious minorities. For years the Old Order Amish and Mennonites objected to state compulsory secondary school attendance laws. They won their status for exemptions to such laws in *Wisconsin v. Yoder* (406 U.S. 205, 1972), whereby the Supreme Court held that Amish children could not be placed under compulsory education past the eighth grade, ruling that freedom of religion outweighed the state's interest in educating their children. The *Yoder* decision was 6–1, with the majority opinion written by Chief Justice Warren Burger. Two justices, Lewis Powell and William Rehnquist, took no part in the *Yoder* case.

Other religious denominations that have significant to extensive private religious school systems have been litigants to or have supported cases with amicus briefs over various aspects of financial support to private religious or secular schools. Exemplary Supreme Court rulings across nearly a century of such jurisprudence include *Pierce v. Society of Sisters* (268 U.S. 510, 1925), *Everson v. Board of Education* (330 U.S. 1, 1947), *Abington School District v. Schempp* (373 U.S. 203, 1963), *Lemon v. Kurtzman* (403 U.S. 602, 1971—in which the Court issued its three-part Lemon test), *Committee for Public Education and Religious Liberty v. Nyquist* (413 U.S. 756, 1971), *Roemer v. Board of Public Works of Maryland* (426 U.S. 736, 1976), *Committee for Public Education and Religious Liberty v. Regan* (413 U.S. 402, 1980), *Aguilar v. Felton* (473 U.S. 402, 1985), *Zobrest v. Catalina Foothills School District* (509 U.S. 1, 1993), and *Arizona Christian School Tuition Organization v. Winn* (563 U.S. 125, 2011).

Other Minorities

Minorities based on three other characteristics—age, sexual orientation, and disabilities—are discussed briefly in this section. Each demographic group has faced discrimination in the law and by social custom, and each developed civil rights organizations focused on their group that were designed to protest that discrimination by lobbying for changes in the law and by seeking redress through federal courts.

The Young

Discrimination based on the individual's age cohort affected both ends of the age spectrum. Persons under the age of twenty-one were denied the vote until enactment of the Twenty-Sixth Amendment, which was ratified on July 1, 1971, in direct response to the Vietnam War. Anti–Vietnam War protestors argued that if eighteen- to twenty-one-year-olds were subject to the draft to serve in Vietnam, they should be given the right to vote at age eighteen. Various student/youth organizations protested the Vietnam War and lobbied for enactment of the Twenty-Sixth Amendment, for example, the SNCC. SNCC's antiwar position was emphasized by its leader at the time, Stokely Carmichael. Writing under his assumed Muslim name, Kwame Ture, Stokely Carmichael coauthored with Charles Hamilton, the book *Black Power* (1992). He is also noted for coining or popularizing the phrase "Black Is Beautiful" as a motto for the Black Power movement.

Another group advocating for the Twenty-Sixth Amendment was the Students for a Democratic Society (SDS, 1960–1964). SDS was a principle representative of the New Left and notable critic and opponent of the Vietnam War. SDS leaders were active in starting the youth movement and the Berkeley Free Speech Movement. SDS's founders were Tom Hayden, Bill Ayers, Aryeh Neier, and Alan Haber. They coined and popularized the youth movement's chants: "Make love—not war," and "Hell no, we won't go." SDS activists inspired the youth rights movement, the youth voice movement, and the youth media movement, and fought to end all discrimination against youth (Hefner 1979).

Protections against warrantless search and seizure under the Fourth Amendment were age-limited for minors, particularly with regard to searching a student's purse, a public school locker, the body of a student under the age of eighteen (a strip search), or the use of random urinalysis tests for students participating in interscholastic athletics. Four federal court cases illustrate those limits on the rights of minors. In *New Jersey v. T.T.O.* (469 U.S. 325, 1985), the Court held that an assistant principal, believing a female high school student was high on marijuana, could search her purse without a warrant. The Court issued a two-pronged test: (1) the search must be justified in its inception; and (2) as conducted, the search must be reasonably related in scope to the circumstances. In *Veronia School District 471 v. Acton* (515 U.S. 646, 1995), the Court held that random urinalysis testing of students in order to participate in interscholastic athletics did not violate the privacy rights guaranteed by the Fourth Amendment. In *Jenkins v. Talladega City Board of Education* (115 F3d 821, 11th Cir., 1997), the Circuit Court held that an eighth-grade student could be strip-searched (in a bathroom) for stolen money. In the case *In re: S.S.C.* (2011), a federal court, applying the test established in *New Jersey v. T.L.O.*, held that a student does not have a reasonable expectation of privacy in his public school locker and ruled that school officials were justified in searching the locker for drugs and did not violate the Fourth Amendment's right to privacy.

The Elderly

The elderly face discrimination primarily in the workplace regarding programs or policies requiring mandatory retirement or alleged discrimination in hiring for persons in the over-fifty-year-old range. By far the largest and most powerful advocate for seniors—and indeed, one of the most powerful lobbying organizations in Washington, D.C., overall—is the American Association of Retired Persons (AARP). The AARP has 38 million members. Its official name now is AARP (the initials), as it changed its name to the initials given that membership is now no longer only for persons who are retired. Indeed, anyone age fifty years old or older may join AARP, whose motto is "to empower people to choose how they live as they age." AARP was founded in 1958 by Ethel Percy Andrus and Leonard Davis. AARP effectively lobbies for the elderly on a number of issues deemed important to that age cohort. They have been especially active in securing increased benefits or protecting benefits for health care under Medicare. AARP was critically important in securing enactment of the Medicare Prescription Drug Improvement and Modernization Act in 2003 and in changes to the Social Security System in 2005. They strongly and successfully opposed the American Health Care Act of 2017, which would have decreased benefits. Their chief lobbyist is John Rother (Lynch 2011; Morris 1996).

Sexual Orientation

The lesbian, gay, bisexual, and transgender community (LGBT) has used many of the tactics and the protest politics discussed above as the approach of the new-style radicalism developed by the Black and Hispanic political movements. These share in common the promoting of identity politics. Identity politics is a tendency for people of a particular religion, race, sexual orientation, or social background to form exclusive political alliances, moving away from broad-based party politics. Identity politics uses that shared identity for political empowerment, to mobilize a constituency, to seek recognition of that identity as a political goal, and as a strategy to achieve that political goal. Since the 1970s, the LGBT movement has emerged and increasingly used the identity politics approach, although in recent years, as in the case of Black and Hispanic politics, it has increasingly turned to standard electoral politics, as a number of openly lesbian and gay politicians have sought and been elected to national political office. The most recent example is the strong showing of Pete Buttigieg seeking the Democratic Party's presidential nomination in 2020. A number of members of Congress, again all from the Democratic Party, are serving and have won office despite being openly lesbian or gay. Electoral success has followed the movement for "coming out of the closet." The estimate of the size of the same-sex preference population is about eight percent of the total U.S. population (estimated at ten percent of males and six percent of females) (Anderson and Adley 1997; Fisher 1975; LeMay 2009).

The Stonewall Riots of 1969 are often noted as the "birth" of the gay rights movement (Tarrow 1994). Indeed, it was the extensive discrimination in jobs, housing, public accommodation and services, and mass-media stereotyping that drove the gay and lesbian movement out of the closet and into political activism (LeMay 2009: 159–162). Since 2000, the LGBT movement's advocacy for same-sex marriage rights has defined the movement's focus and exemplified its political success. Same-sex marriage is much more than just about the right to marry whomever one loves. Legal marriage status affects Social Security benefits, veterans' benefits, health insurance, Medicaid, hospital visitation rights, estate taxes, retirement savings, pensions, family leave, and immigration law, among other rights and protections conferred to U.S. citizens upon a legally recognized marriage (Cathcart and Gabel-Brett 2016; Frank 2017).

A number of organizations and activists led developments within the gay rights movement. The Mattachine Foundation began in Los Angeles in 1950, founded by Harry Hay, and is considered the first homosexual political movement. New York's Mattachine organization spun off an action committee whose members were the nucleus of the New Gay Liberation Front, begun in 1969. The Gay Liberation Front's founder was Morris Kight. In December, 1969, the Gay Activist Alliance also began in New York as a spin-off by dissident members of the Gay Liberation Alliance. The Gay Activist Alliance was founded by Arthur Evans. The Alliance sought to end overt gay discrimination in jobs, housing, and public accommodation; the repeal of local or state sodomy laws; and the ending of law enforcement procedures employed by police against openly gay persons and gay-oriented business establishments (LeMay 2009: 161).

Several lesbian and women's rights organizations are notable advocates of the LGBT movement. The first lesbian organization was the Daughters of Bilitis. It was formed in San Francisco in 1955 by Del Martin and Phyllis Lyon to promote social alternatives to lesbian bars which at the time were so subject to raids and police harassment. San Francisco was the city where the first openly gay official, San Francisco Board of Supervisors member Harvey Milk, was elected in 1978. Milk was tragically assassinated later that same year.

The Human Rights Campaign was begun in 1980 by Steve Endean and is headquartered in Washington, D.C. It is the largest LGBT advocacy group and lobbying organization in the United States, and was a major player in getting the same-sex marriage act passed in Congress. Its president in 2019 is Alphonso David.

The Aids Coalition to Unleash Power (ACT UP) was formed in 1987 in New York City as a grassroots political group aimed at ending the AIDS pandemic that was devastating the gay community, and improving the lives of people with AIDs through direct action, medical research, treatment and advocacy to change legislation and public policies. ACT UP is headquartered in New York City. Its founders were Larry Kramer, Didier Lestrade, Marsha Johnson, and Vito Russo.

Same-sex marriage expanded from one state allowing it in 2004 to all fifty states doing so by 2015, won through various state court rulings, the enactment of state laws, direct popular votes (referenda), and federal court rulings. Same-sex, or gay, marriage and the marriage of opposite-sex couples are now recognized as equal in the law as marriage equality, the fundamental right guaranteed by the due process clause and by the equal protection clause of the Fourteenth Amendment.

Marriage equality was first established in the 1967 landmark civil rights case of *Loving v. Virginia* (398 U.S. 1), in which the Supreme Court applied the equality of marriage right for opposite-race couples. The push to apply it to same-sex couples began in 1972 with the now overturned *Baker v. Nelson* decision in which the Supreme Court declined to hear the constitutional argument. The Supreme Court of

Hawaii ruled that it was unconstitutional under Hawaii's constitution to abridge marriage on the basis of sex. The precedent set by Hawaii led the opposition to same-sex marriage to the push for enactment of the Defense of Marriage Act (DOMA), which was passed in 1996. DOMA stated that no state needs to recognize the legal validity of same-sex marriage even if recognized by another state. Following enactment of DOMA, an increasing number of noted civil rights movement leaders, such as Coretta Scott King, Julian Bond, and Mildred Loving, advocated for same-sex marriage rights. In June 2013, the Supreme Court struck down DOMA as a violation of the Fifth Amendment by the decision in *United States v. Windsor* (570 U.S. 744), which led to federal recognition of same-sex marriage with federal benefits for married couples connected to any state in which marriage was solemnized.

By 2015, public opinion support for same-sex marriage reached 60 percent. In June 2015, the Supreme Court ruled that it is a fundamental right of same-sex couples to marry on the same conditions as opposite-sex couples, with all the accompanying rights and responsibilities by the landmark decision, *Obergefell v. Hodges* (576 U.S. 644). The 5–4 decision struck down all state bans on same-sex marriage and required states to honor out-of-state same-sex marriage licenses. The majority opinion in *Obergefell* was written by Justice Anthony Kennedy, with consent by Justices Ruth Bader Ginsburg, Stephen Breyer, Elena Kagan, and Sonia Sotomayor. The four dissenting justices in the decision were Justice Clarence Thomas, with Chief Justice John Roberts, Antonin Scalia, and Samuel Alito. Remarkably, the *Obergefell* case had 148 amicus briefs filed with it, the most of any Supreme Court case (Cathcart and Gabel-Brett 2016; Frank 2017).

People with Disabilities

The disability rights movement began in the 1970s to redress injustices faced by people with disabilities and by seeking to reverse a long history of ignoring and segregating the disabled. The disability rights movement used tactics of the Black civil rights movement and sought action in federal courts and in the U.S. Congress. Much as the Black civil rights movement was given legal impetus by *Brown v. Board of Education* (1954), a historic shift in disability public policy began in 1973 with enactment of the Rehabilitation Act of 1973 (87 Stat. 355). Section 504 of the 1973 Act banned discrimination on the basis of disability for programs of federal agencies, in programs receiving federal assistance, in federal employment, and in the employment practices of federal contractors. For the first time the law viewed as discrimination the exclusion and segregation of people with disabilities, rejecting the view that problems faced by people with disabilities, such as unemployment and a lack of education, were simply the inevitable consequences of the physical or mental limitations imposed by the disability itself. For the first time in American history, people with disabilities were viewed as a class, entitled to the protection of their rights by law.

The disability rights movement pressured the administrations of Presidents Reagan and Bush regarding their "deregulation" of what those administrations considered unduly burdensome. The disability movement urged the government to not deregulate Section 504 of the Rehabilitation Act. During the 1980s the movement also focused on reinstating civil rights protections stripped away by negative Supreme Court decisions, such as *Southeastern Community College v. Davis* (442 U.S. 397, 1979), and *Grove City College v. Bell* (465 U.S. 555, 1984). Disability movement activists fought to secure enactment of the Civil Rights Restoration Act (CRRA) (465 U.S. 555, 1984). In 1988, they fought to amend the Fair Housing Act to improve enforcement provisions to include disability antidiscrimination in a traditional civil rights law banning racial discrimination. In subsequent jurisprudence, the Disability Rights Education and Defense Fund (DREDF) of Berkeley, California, filed an amicus brief on behalf of sixty-three national, state, and local organizations aimed at securing civil rights for persons with disabilities, educating the courts on discriminatory employment practices and showing those concerns were supported by millions of Americans affiliated with those disability-rights organizations.

Movement to enact the Americans with Disabilities Act (ADA) was spurred by a draft bill prepared by the National Council on Disability appointed by President Ronald Reagan. An ADA bill was introduced as a bipartisan bill by Senator Lowell Weicker (R-CT) and Representative Tony Coelho (D-CA). Support for the bill was generated by Justin Dart, chair of the Congressional Task Force on the Rights and Empowerment of People with Disabilities and sometimes referred to as the "Father of the ADA." In 1988, a new ADA bill was introduced in the U.S. Senate by Senator Tom Harkin (D-Iowa) and Senator David Durrenberger (R-MN). The companion House bill was introduced by Representatives Coelho and Hamilton Fish (R-NY). The ADA was finally passed on July 26, 1990 (42 U.S.C. 126).

Another disability rights national organization is the American Association of People with Disabilities (AAPD), of which Justin Dart was a cofounder. It is headquartered in Washington, D.C., and its current President and CEO is Marian Town. AAPD is a cross-disability rights organization that convenes national meetings, connects organizations of the disability community, and serves as a catalyst for change.

Finally, mention should be made of the international Paralympic Games that have done much to change the image of the abilities of people with disabilities by competition in a host of sporting events that parallel the winter and summer Olympic Games competitions. Paralympics was developed in England by Sir Ludwig Guttermann for British World War II veterans with spinal cord injuries in 1948. Their first quadrennial Olympic-style games were held in 1960 in Rome, and the size and diversity of sports competing in the Paralympic Games has grown ever since. In the 2012 games, held in London, more than 4,200 athletes representing 164 countries competed in twenty sports. In the 2016 summer games, 4,342 athletes from 159 nations competed in 528 events in twenty-two different sports. (The 2020 games, like the 2020 Olympics, were delayed until 2021 due to the coronavirus pandemic.)

Conclusion

As this chapter has demonstrated, the civil rights and liberties of various minorities had to be won by decades-long struggles to overcome problems faced by a host of minority groups of individuals in American society. They had to overcome negative stereotyping about persons who were seen as the "other" by members of the dominant majority society on the basis of race, political ideology, gender, minority religious affiliation, ethnicity, national origin, age, sexual orientation, and disability. They had to use a variety of strategies and tactics to secure their rights to be included in "we, the people"—using accommodation, separatism, or radicalism.

Their struggle to achieve civil rights denied them or limited with respect to them had to be won in the U.S. courts and in state legislatures and the halls of the U.S. Congress. They had to influence federal administrations and the entrenched regulations and practices of federal, state, and local government bureaucracies. They had to launch and win a great number of landmark Supreme Court decisions that set precedents and sometimes established "judicial tests" to guide lower court and subsequent court jurisprudence on civil rights. The chapter demonstrated that "solutions" to the problems arising from prejudice and discrimination are typically better understood as "resolutions," somewhat temporary fixes to those problems, rather than a once-and-for-all solution. Resolutions to the problems and concerns over civil rights and liberties were sometimes won in the courts, by contentious jurisprudence, and sometimes in the legislatures by enacting or amending laws, or indeed, the federal or state constitution. Sometimes, solutions were won in the arena of public opinion, by changing the attitudes, customs, and norms of the majority society.

A host of organizations led by civil rights activists developed and modified tactics while pursuing one of three overall coping strategies to deal with prejudice and discrimination: accommodation, separatism, or new or old-style radicalism. They marched in the streets, boycotted, demonstrated, preached, and challenged stereotypes to change the images and attitudes prevalent in the majority society. In many cases, as the chapter has discussed, those activists and organizations had to secure constitutional amendments to secure their rights or to extend those rights to individual citizens denied those rights. They had to change society's perception of who is included in the "we." They sometimes had to secure enactment of national legislation to overturn negative court decisions. Sometimes they used jurisprudence to change the hearts and minds of the justices by convincing them through suits, and by *amicus curiae* briefs, to overturn previous Supreme Court decisions by new landmark decisions. Many such activist groups eventually saw some of their members succeed in being elected to high level state and federal offices.

In securing their civil rights and civil liberties, these civil rights and liberties organizations of minority groups protected, extended and expanded the rights of *all* American citizens. This chapter also demonstrated that civil rights must be won by such struggle; that the majority never gives up political power. Such power—black power, red power, brown power, gray power, gay power—must be seized. This chapter has demonstrated that the struggle for civil rights is, indeed, a perennial one. It is both the right and the duty of all citizens who wish to preserve and protect the fundamental rights guaranteed them by the Bill of Rights.

References

Alden, Edward. 2008. *The Closing of the American Border: Terrorism, Immigration, and Security since 9/11.* New York: Harper Perennial.

American Jewish Historical Society. 1999. *American Jewish Desk Reference.* New York: Random House.

Anderson, C. W., and Adley, A. R. 1997. *Gay and Lesbian Issues: Abstracts of the Psychological and Behavioral Issues, 1985–1996.* Washington, D.C.: American Psychological Association.

Baker, Jean. 2009. *Women and the U.S. Constitution, 1771–1920.* Washington, D.C.: American Historical Association Press.

Barnes, Kenneth. 2016. *Anti-Catholicism in Arkansas: How Politicians, the Press, the Klan, and Religious Leaders Imagined an Enemy.* Fayetteville: University of Arkansas Press.

Brooks, Roy. 1996. *Integration or Separation?: A Strategy for Racial Equality.* Cambridge, MA: Harvard University Press.

Buhle, Paul. 1987. *Marxism in the United States.* London: Verso.

Campbell, Nadia. 2003. *More Justice, More Peace: The Black Person's Guide to the American Legal System.* Chicago, IL: Chicago Review Press.

Cathcart, Kevin, and Leslie Gabel-Brett, eds. 2016. *Love Unifies Us: Winning the Freedom to Marry in America.* New York: The New Press.

Chavez, John. 1984. *The Lost Land: The Chicano Image of the Southwest.* Albuquerque: University of New Mexico Press.

Cox, Daniel, and Robert Jones, eds. 2019. *America's Changing Religious Identity.* Washington, D.C.: Public Religion Research Institute.

Curran, Robert. 2014. *Papist Devils: Catholics in British America, 1574–1783.* Washington, D.C.: Catholic University Press of America.

Curtis, Edward. 2002. *Islam in Black America.* Albany: State University of New York Press.

Dailey, Jane, Glenda Gilmore, and Bryant Simon, eds. 2000. *Jumpin' Jim Crow: Southern Politics from Civil War to Civil Rights*. Princeton, NJ: Princeton University Press.

Daniels, Roger. 1993. *Concentration Camps, North America: Japanese in the United States and Canada during World War II*. Malabar, FL: Krieger Publishing.

Daniels, Roger. 2002. *Coming to America: A History of Immigration and Ethnicity in American Life*. 2nd ed. New York: Perennial.

Daniels, Roger, Sandra Taylor, and Harry H. L. Kitano, eds. 1991. *Japanese Americans: From Relocation to Redress*. Seattle: University of Washington Press.

Davis, Hugh. 2011. *We Will Be Satisfied with Nothing Less: The African American Struggle for Equal Rights in the North during Reconstruction*. Ithaca, NY: Cornell University Press.

DuBois, Ellen Carol. 1998. *Woman Suffrage and Women's Rights*. New York: New York University Press.

Equal Rights Amendment.org. 2020. "Virginia Becomes the 38th State to Ratify the ERA." https://www.equalrightsamendment.org.

Farrelly, Maura Jane. 2017. *Anti-Catholicism in America, 1620–1860*. Cambridge, UK: Cambridge University Press.

Fireside, Harvey. 2003. *Separate and Unequal: Homer Plessy and the Supreme Court Decision That Legalized Racism*. Gretna, LA: Pelican Press.

Fisher, Peter. 1975. *The Gay Mystique*. New York: Stein and Day.

Foner, Eric. 2014. *Reconstruction: America's Unfinished Revolution, 1863–1877*. New York: HarperCollins.

Foner, Philip, and Herbert Shapiro, eds. 1991. *American Communism and Black Americans: A Documentary History, 1930–1934*. Philadelphia, PA: Temple University Press.

Foxman, Abraham. 2003. *Never Again? The Threat of the New Anti-Semitism.* New York: HarperOne.

Frank, Nathaniel. 2017. *Awakening: How Gays and Lesbians Brought Marriage Equality to America.* Cambridge, MA: Belknap Press of Harvard University Press.

Fuchs, Lawrence. 1990. *The American Kaleidoscope: Race, Ethnicity, and Civil Culture.* Hanover, NH: University Press of New England.

George, John, and Laird Wilcox. 1992. *Nazis, Communists, Klansmen and Others on the Fringe: Political Extremism in America.* New York: Prometheus Books.

Gjerde, Jon, ed. 1998. *Major Problems in American Immigration and Ethnic History.* Boston, MA: Houghton Mifflin.

Gosnell, Harold, and Charles Merriam. 2007. *Boss Platt and His New York Machine: A Study of the Leadership of Thomas C. Platt, Theodore Roosevelt, and Others.* LaVergne, TN: Lightning Sources.

Hagedorn, Sara, and Michael LeMay. 2019. *The American Congress: A Reference Handbook.* Santa Barbara, CA: ABC-CLIO.

Hamilton, Kenneth. 2017. *Booker T. Washington in American Memory.* Champaign: University of Illinois Press.

Hefner, Keith. 1979. *Children's Rights Handbook.* Ann Arbor, MI: Youth Liberation Press.

Hoffman, Edward. 1991. *Despite All Odds: The Story of the Lubavitch.* New York: Simon and Schuster.

Hosokawa, William. 1969. *Nisei: The Quiet Americans.* New York: William Morrow.

Judd, Richard. 1989. *Socialist Cities: Municipal Politics and the Grass Roots of American Socialism.* New York: State University of New York Press.

Keyssar, Alexander. 2000. *The Right to Vote: The Contested History of Democracy in the United States.* New York: Basic Books.

Kinzer, Donald. 1964. *An Episode in Anti-Catholicism: The American Protective Association*. Seattle: University of Washington Press.

Kitano, Harry. 1976. *Japanese Americans: the Evolution of a Subculture*. Englewood Cliffs, NJ: Prentice-Hall.

Kohn, Stephen. 1994. *American Political Prisoners: Prosecutions under the Espionage and Sedition Act*. Westport, CT: Praeger Press.

La Beau, Bryan. 2017. *A History of Religion in America: From the First Settlement through the Civil War*. Abington, UK: Routledge.

Lee, Erika. 2020. *The Making of Asian America: A History*. New York: Simon and Schuster.

LeMay, Michael. 2006. *Guarding the Gates: Immigration and National Security*. Santa Barbara, CA: Praeger Press.

LeMay, Michael. 2009. *The Perennial Struggle*. 3rd ed. Upper Saddle River, NJ: Prentice-Hall.

LeMay, Michael, ed. 2013a. *Transforming America: Perspectives on U.S. Immigration, Vol. 1. The Founding to 1865*. Santa Barbara, CA: Praeger Press.

LeMay, Michael, ed. 2013b. *Transforming America: Perspectives on U.S. Immigration, Vol. 3, Immigration and Superpower Status, 1945 to Present*. Santa Barbara, CA: Praeger Press.

LeMay, Michael. 2019. *Immigration Reform: A Reference Handbook*. Santa Barbara, CA: ABC-CLIO.

LeMay, Michael, and Elliott Barkan, eds. 1999. *U.S. Immigration and Naturalization Laws and Issues: A Documentary History*. Westport, CT: Greenwood Press.

Lipset, Seymour Martin, and Gary Marks. 2000. *It Didn't Happen Here: Why Socialism Failed in the United States*. New York: W. W. Norton.

Lynch, Frederick. 2011. *One Nation under AARP: The Fight over Medicare, Social Security, and America's Future*. Berkeley: University of California Press.

MacDonnell, Francis. 1995. *Insidious Foes.* New York: Oxford University Press.

Marger, Martin. 2003. *Race and Ethnic Relations,* 6th ed. Belmont, CA: Wadsworth.

Marquez, Benjamin. 2003. *Constructing Identities in Mexican American Political Organizations: Choosing Sides, Taking Sides.* Austin: University of Texas Press.

Marsh, Clifton. 2000. *The Lost-Found Nation of Islam in America.* Lanham, MD: Scarecrow Press.

McCain, Charles. 1994. *Japanese Immigrants and American Law: the Alien Land Laws and Other Issues.* London: Routledge.

McClain, Paula, and Joseph Steward, Jr. 1995. *Can We All Get Along? Racial and Ethnic Minorities in American Politics.* Boulder: Westview Press.

Mead, Rebecca. 2004. *How the Vote Was Won: Woman Suffrage in the Western United States, 1868–1919.* New York: New York University Press.

Mittelstadt, Michelle, Bureka Speaker, Doris Meissner, and Muzaffe Chisti. 2011. *Through the Prism of National Security: Major Immigration Policy and Program Changes in the Decade since 9/11.* Washington, D.C.: Migration Policy Institute.

Morris, Charles. 1996. *The AARP: America's Most Powerful Lobby and the Clash of Generations.* New York: Crown/Penguin Random House.

Nez, Chester. 2012. *Code Talkers: The First and Only Memoir by One of the Original Navajo Code Talkers of World War II.* New York: Dutton Caliber/Penguin Random House.

Ng, Wendy. 2001. *Japanese American Internment during World War II.* Westport, CT: Greenwood Press.

Orozco, Cynthia. 2009. *No Mexicans, Women, or Dogs Allowed: The Rise of the Mexican Civil Rights Movement*. Austin: University of Texas Press.

Preston, William. 1994. *Aliens and Dissenters: Federal Suppression of Radicals, 1903–1933*. 2nd ed. Urbana: University of Illinois Press.

Ravitch, Dianne. 1974. *The Great School Wars: A History of New York Public Schools as Battlefield of Social Change*. Baltimore, MD: Johns Hopkins University Press.

Salehyan, Idean. 2009. "U.S. Asylum and Refugee Policy toward Muslim Nations since 9/11." In *Immigration Policy and Security*, edited by Terry Givens, Gary Freeman, and David Lean, 52–65. New York: Routledge.

Salyer, Lucy. 1995. *Laws Harsh as Tigers: Chinese Immigrants and the Shaping of Modern Immigration Law*. Chapel Hill: University of North Carolina Press.

Schonbach, Morris. 1985. *Native American Fascism during the 1930s and 1940s: A Study of Its Roots, Its Growth and Its Decline*. New York: Garland Press.

SCOTUSblog.com. 2020. "McGirt v. Oklahoma." https://www.scotusblog.com/case-files/mcgirt-v-oklahoma.

Singer, David, and Lawrence Grossman, eds. 2002. *American Jewish Yearbook*. Basel, Switzerland: Springer Nature.

Sniderman, Paul, and Thomas Piazza. 2002. *Black Pride and Black Prejudice*. Princeton, NJ: Princeton University Press.

Solomon, Mark. 1998. *The Cry was Unity: Communism and African American, 1917–1936*. Jackson: University Press of Mississippi.

Spring, Joel. 2008. *The American School: From the Puritans to No Child Left Behind*, 7th ed. New York: McGraw-Hill.

Steiner, Stan. 1969. *La Raza*. New York: Harper and Row.

Strum, Philippa. 1999. *When the Nazis Came to Skokie: Freedom of Speech We Hate.* Lawrence: University Press of Kansas.

Strum, Philippa. 2010. *Mendez v. Westminster: School Desegregation and Mexican American Rights.* Lawrence: University Press of Kansas.

Takaki, Ronald. 1998. *Strangers from a Different Shore: A History of Asian Americans.* Boston, MA: Little, Brown.

Tarrow, Sidney. 1994. *Power in Movement: Social Movements, Collective Action, and Politics.* New York: Stein and Day.

Thomas, William H., Jr. 2008. *Unsafe for Democracy: World War I and the U.S. Justice Department's Covert Campaign to Suppress Dissent.* Madison: University of Wisconsin Press.

Thompson, William. 1996. *Native American Issues: A Reference Handbook.* Santa Barbara, CA: ABC-CLIO.

Toltzman, Don. 2005. *Images of America: German Cincinnati.* Charleston, SC: Arcadia Publishing.

Ture, Kwame, and Charles V. Hamilton. 1992. *Black Power: The Politics of Liberation.* New York: Vintage Press.

Viola, Herman. 1993. *Ben Nighthorse Campbell: An American Warrior.* Lanham, MD: Rowman and Littlefield.

Washington, Booker T. 1901. *Up from Slavery: An Autobiography.* Garden City, NY: Doubleday.

West, Michael. 2006. *The Education of Booker T. Washington: American Democracy and the Idea of Race Relations.* New York: Columbia University Press.

Wilhelm, Cornelia. 2011. *The Independent Order of B'nai B'rith and True Sisters Pioneers of a New Jewish Identity, 1843–1914.* Detroit, MI: Wayne State University Press.

Wilkins, David. 2002. *American Indian Politics and the American Political System.* Lanham, MD: Rowman and Littlefield.

Woodward, C. Vann, and William McFeely. 2001. *The Strange Career of Jim Crow.* New York: Oxford University Press.

Young, Michael. 2007. *Bearing Witness against Sin: The Evangelical Birth of the American Social Movement.* Chicago, IL: University of Chicago Press.

Zentner, Scot, and Michael LeMay. 2020. *Party and Nation: Immigration and Regime Politics in American History.* Lanham, MD: Lexington Books.

Introduction

This chapter presents nine original essays on topics important for the reader to better understand the extension of civil rights and civil liberties in the United States during the long march of the nation's history. They are written by scholars and activists of civil rights and liberties from various academic disciplinary backgrounds and experiences. Collectively, these essays provide insights and a perspective beyond and different from that of this author. The essays are presented here in alphabetical order of the contributors' surnames.

The COVID-19 Pandemic and Lessons for Civil Rights Coping Strategies
Ken Bedell

In early 2020, COVID-19 spread from city to city and then into rural areas across the United States. Health officials and researchers rushed to figure out what groups of people were the most vulnerable and how to protect them. At first, doctors and health departments noticed that many of those hospitalized and dying were older Americans. On April 30, the White House published a "Fact Sheet" that announced: "PROTECTING

Goran Miletic, International Grand Marshal of the Pride Parade, partakes in the closing activity of the 2012 Toronto Pride Festival, which celebrates the history, courage, diversity, and future of LGBTQ+ individuals. (Manuel Machado/Dreamstime.com)

OUR OLDER PEOPLE: President Donald J. Trump is ensuring the safety and well-being of America's seniors during the coronavirus disease (COVID-19) outbreak." The fact sheet lists resources that the federal government directed to nursing homes, including money for inspections and medical supplies. The fact sheet also reports that the President is "instructing States to take additional measures to protect the safety of senior citizens and other vulnerable populations."

By April 30, 2020, "other vulnerable populations" were identified by health officials and journalists. African Americans and Hispanics of all ages were dying at about twice the rate of whites. There was little data collected about the impact of the disease on other minority populations. However, estimates of death rates for American Indians were two to three times the death rates for whites. This racial gap made the response to COVID-19 a civil rights issue. Though the federal government and states did not rush to address the racial gap, public health experts provided explanations.

Experts pointed out that the racial gap is the result of long-standing structural inequalities. Whites are more likely to have the luxury of following stay-at-home advice, which is the best way to avoid the virus. Blacks and Hispanics are overrepresented in service and other jobs that cannot be done from home. This puts nonwhites at risk at work as well as on public transportation. Across the country, whites live in less densely populated areas than Blacks and Hispanics. About one in four African Americans and Hispanics live in poverty. For whites, only one in ten live in poverty. This gives whites options to deal with the impact of the virus. Also, the delivery of health care in past decades has favored better general health for whites. The result is that serious underlying medical conditions are more prevalent in minority populations.

It is easy to understand why President Trump and governors took action to "ensuring the safety and well-being of America's seniors," but they did not address the safety and well-being of people of color. The safety of seniors could be addressed by encouraging them to say home without causing much inconvenience or economic disruption.

Addressing the racial gap is much more complicated. How can you undo the racist laws, policies, practices, customs, and white racism that have resulted in nonwhites being more vulnerable? What law or executive order from the president or a governor would address the racial gap? Yet, from the perspective of civil rights, the question must be raised. It is impossible to avoid the logic that if the civil rights dream of an equitable society were a reality, the COVID-19 racial gap would not exist or would be much smaller.

In all of U.S. history, those who desired civil rights advances and an equitable society have used two strategies. The first strategy is to eliminate barriers that keep some people from full participation. An excellent example is the 1870 Fifteenth Amendment to the Constitution. It was intended to ensure that African American men could vote and could no longer be barred from participating in the political process. Eliminating barriers is a favorite civil rights strategy because laws or Supreme Court decisions can identify a specific activity that can be prohibited. Practices like giving preference to hiring white people or refusing to rent a hotel room to an African American can be outlawed.

The second strategy to create an equitable society has been to focus on generating opportunity. This strategy is based on the observation that whites dominate political life, the arts and culture, and the economy. It is then argued that nonwhites do not participate equally because they do not have opportunity. An example of this approach is the "No Child Left Behind" act passed by Congress during the George W. Bush administration in 2001. The law opens with the claim that it is "[a]n act to close the achievement gap with accountability, flexibility, and choice so that no child is left behind."

Educational reform is a common strategy to increase opportunity. In 1954 the Supreme Court's unanimous decision to apply the Fourteenth Amendment to the Constitution in

Brown v. Board of Education of Topeka is a good example. The Court said that equal protection of the law required school districts to provide the same education to every child. Because, they argued, separate schools for Blacks and whites are inherently unequal, schools must be integrated so that equal opportunity is guaranteed.

The COVID-19 pandemic in 2020 with a racial gap is a reminder that even fifty years after the civil rights movement inspired by Rev. Dr. Martin Luther King Jr., there remain vast differences in the experience of white Americans and other Americans. The strategies of eliminating barriers and increasing opportunity for nonwhites have not been successful.

An even more important lesson is that white leadership and most whites did not even see the needs of minority communities. There is a racial blindness that recognizes that seniors are at risk and thinks of ways that the risks could be reduced. But when the risks experienced by Blacks, Hispanics, and other minorities are known, the same process is not used to investigate ways to make minority groups safer. Even though statistics documenting the racial gap were available by the end of the second month of the pandemic, neither the federal government nor any state government created a strategy or a program to "protect the safety" of vulnerable minority groups.

In short, COVID-19 exposed a deeply embedded racism. This white racial blindness, based on an ideology of white superiority, sustains an unequal society. In the examples given above of reducing barriers and increasing opportunity, we see that racism and racial blindness have prevented the creation of an equitable society.

Within ten years of the enactment of the Fourteenth Amendment, most African Americans in the former Confederate States were disenfranchised. White politicians wrestled political power from the Blacks. The Supreme Court decision in *Brown vs. Board of Education* in 1954 resulted in a little school integration, but today most school districts are as segregated by race as they were before 1954. And the education gap is about as great today as it was when the "No Child Left Behind" act was passed in 2001.

The COVID-19 racial gap could have been eliminated or substantially decreased if federal and state officials had worked with minority communities to keep them safe. There may have been ways to isolate infected individuals away from crowded urban neighborhoods. Delivering masks to people riding public transportation could have become a priority like it was a priority for seniors in nursing homes. Departments of health could have been directed to discover and implement strategies to protect Blacks, Hispanics, Native Americans, and other vulnerable minorities.

Because of the example of America's response to COVID-19, we can see the way forward in building an equitable society. Removing racial barriers and creating opportunity need to be supported by white people overcoming their racial blindness. Only then can whites and nonwhites work together to create a nation with full civil rights for all.

Ken Bedell, PhD, is a long-time civil rights activist. In the Obama Administration, he served as a senior advisor in the Faith-Based and Neighborhood Partnership Center. Ken is author of Different Ships—Same Boat *(2000) and* Realizing the Civil Rights Dream *(2017).*

Two Courts: State Courts of Last Resort and Civil Rights Adjudication
Taraleigh Davis

The United States has a dual system of judicial power. Each state has a system of courts that operates within each state's constitution, while the federal system stems from the provisions of Article III of the U.S. Constitution. All states have a state court of last resort; most are referred to as a state Supreme Court. Procedures vary, but most courts of last resort decide whether or not to hear a case. The Court of last resort in a state is the highest judicial body within that state, and its rulings are not subject to further review by another court. The power of state courts of last resort should be wielded with an eye toward impartial justice in civil rights adjudication.

Examples of civil rights include the right to a fair trial and the right to vote. Though the U.S. Constitution did not initially establish voting rights, several amendments, including the Fifteenth, Nineteenth, and Twenty-Sixth Amendments, guarantee that voting rights cannot be denied based on race, sex, or age. The Twenty-Fourth Amendment forbids having a poll tax as a voting condition, and the equal protection clause of the Fourteenth Amendment provides for equal voting rights. The U.S. Constitution in Article I Section 4 gives the authority to regulate the time, place, and manner of elections up to each state, unless Congress legislates otherwise (U.S. Constitution, Art. I, Sec. 8). State courts of last resort are under the jurisdiction to make sure that voting rights in their states are upheld. Recently, state courts have issued opinions that many see as disenfranchising voters.

On March 13, 2020, President Donald Trump proclaimed a national emergency due to the spread of COVID-19 throughout the United States. By March 23, 2020, there was an increase in cases nationwide—and in the state of Wisconsin, there was an increase of over 100 percent every seventy-two hours. The Secretary of the Department of Health in Wisconsin issued a stay-at-home mandate via Emergency Order #12, ordering individuals within the state of Wisconsin to stay at home except for essential activities. Nonessential businesses and operations were also ordered to cease, and schools were closed (Palm 2020). The Wisconsin Supreme Court suspended all jury trials and mandated remote hearing for other matters (Wisconsin State Supreme Court 2020). As the states' spring elections in April approached, many states postponed their elections to June. Governor Tony Evers sought to have the Wisconsin spring election delayed to June 9, due to rising concerns over the spread of COVID-19. Wisconsin's election was not just the presidential primary but also included many local races, including the mayor of Milwaukee and a State Supreme Court justice. Wisconsinites were scrambling to request absentee ballots, but the system was overloaded. After unsuccessfully calling a special session with the Republican-controlled legislature, Governor Tony Evers issued Executive Order #[74] postponing the Spring Election until June 9 or another date if the state legislature decided. The Supreme Court of Wisconsin ruled remotely to block Governor Evers's order in *Wisconsin Legislature v. Evers* (2020AP608-OA) just fourteen hours before polls were scheduled to open.

> This action [EO #74] has the practical effect of suspending or rewriting numerous election-related statutes, including mandatory election dates, election procedures, and terms of office for local officials. While the Governor's emergency powers are vast, they are not unlimited. This court acknowledges the public health emergency plaguing our state, country, and world, but any action taken by the Governor, no matter how well-intentioned, must be authorized by law. . . . Even if the Governor's policy judgments reflected in the order are well-founded, and even if we agreed with those policy judgments, none of the authorities cited in the order support this broad sweep of power.

The impact of this ruling cannot be understated. There was a severe shortage of poll workers. For example, in Milwaukee, the largest city in Wisconsin, a half million residents only had five polling places open for the April 7 election instead of the usual 180 polling places. Voter disenfranchisement occurred across the state as voters had to choose between their safety and having their vote count. As noted in the dissent in *Wisconsin Legislature v. Evers* (2020AP608-OA):

> The majority gives Wisconsinites an untenable choice: endanger your safety and potentially your life by voting

or give up your right to vote by heeding the recent and urgent warnings about the fast growing pandemic. These orders are but another example of this court's unmitigated support of efforts to disenfranchise voters.

In 2018, Florida Amendment 4 passed by a ballot initiative passed by 65 percent of the vote. The Voting Rights Restoration for Felons Initiative "automatically" restored the voting rights of Floridians who had been convicted of a felony, except those convicted of murder or a felony sexual offense, upon completing their sentences "including prison, parole, and probation" (Florida Division of Elections 2018). After the amendment to Florida's Constitution was approved by a supermajority vote of over 5 million Floridians, the State legislature broadened the plain language of Amendment 4. Legislation was implemented defining the term "all terms of the sentence" to include "full payment of restitution, or any fines, fees, or costs resulting from the conviction." Senate Bill 7066 had created what some describe as a modern-day poll tax.

In January 2020, the State Supreme Court agreed with Florida state lawmakers' definition of "all terms." In the *per curiam* advisory opinion, the justices wrote, "We conclude that the phrase, when read and understood in context, plainly refers to obligations and includes 'all'—not some—LFOs (legal financial obligations) imposed in conjunction with an adjudication of guilt" (Supreme Court of Florida SC19-1341).

The ruling on Amendment 4 should be doubly concerning with regard to voting rights. In essence, the Florida Supreme Court ruling in January 2020 created a roadblock to voting based on wealth. This requirement punishes poor felons, whereas felons who could pay their fines are not denied the right to vote. This punishment is not based on the individual's culpability but rather on an unrelated factor of their wealth.

The 5 million voters who supported Amendment 4 in the November 2018 elections are experiencing voter disenfranchisement. The Florida Supreme Court ruled that Amendment 4 had an ordinary meaning to voters that meant not only incarceration but also fines and fees. By changing the meaning of what was clearly stated on the ballot, the legislature and the Supreme Court in Florida ignored the voter's intent when the voters approved Amendment 4.

Both of these examples highlight a concerning trend. Voting rights are no longer being attacked by Jim Crow laws or poll taxes but rather by the institution meant to protect civil rights: state courts of last resort. No longer does it seem that State Supreme Courts are using their power to execute blind justice, but justice through a partisan or ideological lens.

References

Florida Division of Elections. 2018. "Voting Restoration Amendment 14-01." Division of Elections Florida Department of State. https://dos.elections.myflorida.com /initiatives/initdetail.asp?account=64388&seqnum=1.

Palm, Andrea. 2020. "Emergency Order #12 Safer at Home Order." State of Wisconsin Department of Health Services. https://evers.wi.gov/Documents/COVID19 /EMO12-SaferAtHome.pdf.

The State of Wisconsin Office of the Governor. 2020. "EXECUTIVE ORDER #74 Relating to Suspending In-Person Voting on April 7, 2020, Due to the COVID-19 Pandemic." Official Site of Governor Tony Evers. Last modified April 2020. https://evers.wi.gov/Documents /COVID19/EO074-SuspendingInPersonVotingAndSpecia lSession.pdf.

Supreme Court of Florida. 2020. "Advisory Opinion to the Governor RE: Implementation of Amendment 4, the Voting Restoration Amendment." Supreme Court. Last modified January 16, 2020. https://law.justia.com/cases /florida/supreme-court/2020/sc19-1341.html.

Wisconsin State Supreme Court. 2020. "In RE the Matter
    of the Extension of Orders and Interim Rule Concerning
    Continuation of Jury Trials, Suspension of Statutory
    Deadlines for Non-Criminal Jury Trials, and Remote
    Hearings during the Covid-19 Pandemic." https://wicourts
    .gov/news/docs/jurytrials.pdf.

*Taraleigh Davis is a teaching assistant and PhD candidate, and
she is a Graduate Fellowship recipient in the Department of Political Science at the University of Wisconsin-Milwaukee.*

Defining Equality: Civil Rights Act of 1964 and the Americans with Disabilities Act
Michelle D. Deardorff

During an intermission for a concert or sports event—particularly
in an older venue—have you noticed that the line for the wom-
en's restroom snakes around the lobby, while men march in
and out of the facilities and return to their seats? While women
make new acquaintances during the shared twenty-minute
interval and grouse about the inequity of the wait, men are
only aware of this disparity when a few women commandeer
the empty men's restroom in order to disperse the feminine
crowd before the next act or inning.

Formal equality is the reason for the described difference
in the queues. Historically, men and women's restrooms were
legally mandated to be identical. If the women's restrooms had
five stalls, the men's restroom had to have five toilet fixtures (for
men, a combination of stalls and urinals) or occupy the same
size space in the building. Equality or "potty parity" was measured and ensured by laws requiring the identical treatment of
men and women. This is formal equality in which all people
must be treated the same in order to be equal. For biological
and sociological reasons (such as for any accompanying children), women spend on average seventy-nine seconds per visit
to a public restroom compared to men's forty-seven seconds on

a typical trip (Washington State Department of Transportation 1989). Because of the differences in their circumstances, architectural designs that treat men and women identically have resulted in disparate consequences to the detriment of women.

How would we protect equality if we were more interested in processing the same number of men and women through a public restroom in, say, five minutes and less interested in counting the number of toilet fixtures or square footage? What would equality look like if we worried less about treating people identically and more about making their experiences or opportunities to succeed be comparable? This is particularly an issue when the two groups being equated are different in significant ways—such as biological (e.g., reproductive characteristics) or sociological (e.g., income earned, child-rearing obligations, and educational opportunities).

The *substantive equality* answer to the problem of potty-parity was a simple one: cities passed legislation to rewrite building codes, requiring greater female-to-male ratios in toilet fixtures for new construction and ensuring wait times for all restrooms are similar or nonexistent. The substantive goal is processing through people at the same rate, not constructing identical, parallel restrooms facilities. In the United States, two of our key federal civil rights protections reflect these competing understandings of equality: the Civil Rights Act of 1964 (formal) and the Americans with Disabilities Act of 1990 (substantive).

Formal Equality—The Civil Rights Act of 1964

Formal equality defines equality as parallel treatment, in which two people who are similar in their essential situations should be treated as similarly as possible to each other. This is the traditional understanding of equality in America: we are equal when we are treated the same under law or policy. This is true for all protected characteristics like gender, race, national origin, and religion. The Civil Rights Act (CRA) of 1964 is one of the most important federal statutes for protecting citizenship rights. This law provided the United States Department of Justice with extensive investigatory rights and empowered it to prosecute cases of public and private discrimination.

The CRA of 1964 prohibits segregation of schools and public facilities (transportation, stores, and restaurants) and discrimination in federally supported programs. It made illegal the practice of Jim Crow—state laws prohibiting African Americans from sharing public and private spaces with whites. Although African Americans were taxed, they were prohibited from using the same public (restrooms, schools, libraries, and government offices) and private (stores, hotels, and restaurants) facilities as whites. The result was that Black Americans were separated and provided significantly diminished alternatives to whites. A remnant of the state slave codes, these laws were most visible in the Southern states, although the practices were evident throughout the nation, applied to other races and ethnicities, and impacted federal laws and policies.

Title VII of the Civil Rights Act of 1964 prohibits discrimination by employers on the basis of race, color, religion, sex, or national origin and created the Equal Employment Opportunity Commission (EEOC) to provide for enforcement of the law. Since 1964, women and minority groups have been able to use Title VII as their primary statutory support in challenging discriminatory employment practices in the federal courts. Although this approach to equality requires similarly situated employees to be treated identically, there are concerns that such formal equality is inadequate to provide a fair working environment. Formal equality assumes that treating people identically results in the same outcome. But is a pregnant woman the same as a man who had a heart attack? If a hearing person and a deaf person are treated the same, are they equal? Formal equality also ignores differences within groups. Should the only woman of Asian descent in an office be compared with the white women or the Asian man to determine if she is being treated fairly? Are there differences that affect discrimination in the workplace that are not protected under Title VII, such as employees with young children and those who are child-free? What about employees who are transgender?

Formal equality is easy to measure and demonstrate in organizational policies and decision making, so judges are comfortable with this approach. It limits the discretionary decision making of employers and judges who are provided clear rules to follow. This approach is consistent with the traditional American understanding of equality, although as more individuals in our nation claim their own civil rights (regardless of physical, mental, and developmental disabilities, weight, gender orientation or identity, and trans status), the limitations of formal equality become more apparent.

Substantive Equality—Americans with Disabilities Act of 1990

In response to these equality issues and to political pressure raised by the Americans with Disabilities movement, Congress passed the Americans with Disabilities Act (ADA). The ADA relies on the *substantive model of equality*. The ADA requires that qualified disabled employees are not only protected from discrimination (treated differently), but also are accommodated in the workplace to ensure they have the same potential for success on the job as other employees. For instance, a blind person could be provided computer software to assist in meeting the requirements of employment. In contrast, formal equality would require that blind and sighted people be treated identically to one another, with the typical result of the blind person being penalized for the disability.

The ADA defines as disabled "any individual who (i) has a physical or mental impairment which substantially limits one or more of such person's major life activities, (ii) has a record of such an impairment, or (iii) is regarded as having such an impairment." This definition extends discrimination protection not only to people with disabilities but also to people who were previously disabled or who might be assumed to be disabled.

The law recognizes that the stereotypes regarding disabilities could handicap workers as much as an actual disability. The ADA rejects the formal equality assumed by the Civil Rights Act of 1964, requiring that disabled individuals be treated no worse than similarly situated able-bodied individuals. Under certain circumstances, the disabled must be provided accommodations or be treated differently from other employees in order to achieve an equal outcome. This approach to equality focuses on assuring an outcome that is equitable as opposed to parallel. Judges and employers find this law much harder to implement in the courtroom because standards of accommodation and reasonable cost require them to exercise more discretion.

As groups continue to challenge traditional understandings of equality, only time will tell whether we will continue to employ multiple definitions of equality in protecting civil rights, move entirely to a substantive model, or create a new one.

References

The Civil Rights Act of 1964, Public Law 88-352 (78 Stat. 241).

Deardorff, Michelle D. 2005. "Title VII," *Encyclopedia of the Supreme Court*. Edited by David Schultz. New York: Facts on Files, Inc., 468–469.

Deardorff, Michelle D., and James Dahl. 2016. *Pregnancy Discrimination and the American Worker*. London: Palgrave MacMillan.

The Rehabilitation Act of 1973, Public Law: 93-112 (9/26/73) (29 U.S.C. 791 et seq.).

Washington State Department of Transportation. 1989. "Rest Area Usage Design Criteria Update." www.wsdot.wa.gov /publications/manuals/fulltext/M220-01/1710.pdf.

Michelle D. Deardorff is the Adolph S. Ochs Professor of Government and Department Head, University of Tennessee at Chattanooga.

She is co-author of Pregnancy Discrimination and the American Worker *(2016).*

Warrants for Me but Not for Thee: Students' Fourth Amendment Rights in Public Schools
Joshua Dunn

Perhaps nursed on a diet of television legal dramas, many Americans likely believe that in order to search your property, the government must have a warrant. But what many believe turns out to be different from reality. If there are exigent searches (*Warden v. Hayden*, 387 U.S. 294, 1967), or police are conducting a search incident to a lawful arrest (*Chimel v. California*, 395 U.S. 752, 1969), or a suspect has consented to a search (*Schneckloth v. Bustamonte*, 412 U.S. 218, 1973), or if evidence is in plain view, no warrant is required (*Coolidge v. New Hampshire*, 403 U.S. 443, 1971). And those are just some of the official exceptions crafted by the Supreme Court. Anyone who has flown in the past twenty years, or gone to a courthouse, or visited the U.S. Capitol building should also recall being searched without a warrant. Much to the consternation of public-school students, included among the exceptions to the warrant requirement are searches in K–12 schools.

The Supreme Court first considered the application of the Fourth Amendment to schools in 1984's *New Jersey v. T.L.O.* (469 U.S. 325). A teacher had discovered two students, including T.L.O. (her name was not used because she was a minor), smoking cigarettes in a bathroom at the Piscataway High School. The students were taken to the principal's office, where they were questioned by the vice principal. After questioning, the vice principal demanded to see T.L.O.'s purse and quickly discovered cigarette rolling papers, which he associated with marijuana use. He believed a more thorough search of her purse would yield more evidence of drug use. It did. He found marijuana, a pipe, empty plastic bags, a large sum of money, an index card listing T.L.O.'s clients who owed her money, and two letters implicating her in drug dealing.

T.L.O. was charged as a delinquent. She argued, however, that the evidence from her purse should be suppressed, claiming that the search was unconstitutional. New Jersey argued that the Fourth Amendment did not apply, claiming that students had no need to bring purely personal items to school and therefore should have no reasonable expectation of privacy on school grounds. The Court rejected New Jersey's argument but held that the search of T.L.O.'s purse was reasonable. Schools have a legitimate interest in "maintaining discipline" but students also have "legitimate expectations of privacy." Thus, the Fourth Amendment applies but in a much-reduced form compared to searches outside of school. Specifically, the Court held that school officials "need not obtain a warrant" and their searches do not have to be based on "probable cause" that the student being searched has violated the law. Instead, it held that the totality of the circumstances would determine whether or not a search was reasonable. The Court then created a two-pronged test to determine a reasonable search: (1) it must be "justified in its inception," and (2) it must be "permissible in its scope." For the first part of the test, officials only had to have reasonable grounds to believe that a student had violated the law or school rules. For the second part, the measures taken by school authorities had to be "reasonably related to the objectives of the search" and, importantly, "not excessively intrusive in light of the age and sex of the student and the nature of the infraction."

Though *T.L.O.* was a landmark decision, it left two significant unresolved questions, which would arise in later cases. First, are searches without "individualized suspicion," such as random drug tests, constitutional? And second, what constitutes "excessively intrusive" under *T.L.O.*'s second prong?

The Court addressed the first question in two cases, *Vernonia School District v. Acton* (515 U.S. 646, 1995) and *Pottawatomie Board of Education v. Earls* (536 U.S. 822, 2002). In

Vernonia, an Oregon school district had adopted random drug tests of student athletes. The district believed that athletes were often "leaders of the drug culture," were role models for other students, and that drug use created a high risk of injury for student athletes. Under the district's policy, all student athletes were tested at the beginning of their sport's season, followed by random testing each week of 10 percent of the team's members. James Acton, then a seventh-grader, objected to having to provide a urine sample and was thus prohibited from playing football.

Relying on its "special needs" doctrine, the Court ruled that the testing program did not violate the Fourth Amendment. Under this doctrine, the Court had previously approved suspicionless searches, such as sobriety checkpoints, where obtaining a warrant or having probable cause were "impracticable." The Court said the doctrine applied in this case and ruled that courts must balance the student's privacy interest against the legitimacy of the school's interests and the "efficacy" of the school's policy. Engaging in its own balancing of these considerations, the Court approved the district's program. Students, and particularly athletes, the Court said, have a diminished expectation of privacy as they have communal showers and undress in front of each other. The program was also minimally intrusive into privacy because monitor procuring the urine samples stood behind the urinal for male athletes and outside the stall for female athletes. Also, drug use, particularly among athletes, was a significant problem at the school.

The Court further expanded the authority of schools to engage in suspicionless testing in *Pottawatomie v. Earls*. In this case, an Oklahoma school district had mandated drug testing of all students participating in any extracurricular activity, not just athletics. Lindsay Earls wanted to sing in the school choir but objected to having to take a drug test, claiming that the program was more intrusive than the one in *Vernonia*, making it a Fourth Amendment violation. As well, the school district adopted the program as a preventative measure, not because, as in *Vernonia*, it had documented that drug use was a serious existing problem. The Court disagreed, ruling that as in *Vernonia*, the search was minimally intrusive. Further, it held that it could not "articulate a threshold level of drug use that would suffice to justify a drug testing program for schoolchildren," and, thus, school districts should be afforded latitude in determining when to adopt programs aimed at limiting drug use.

The Court addressed the second question, the meaning of "excessively intrusive," in *Safford Unified School District v. Redding* (557 U.S. 364, 2009). This case involved Savana Redding, a middle-school student in Arizona. Another student had been found with painkillers, and she claimed that Savana had given them to her. After Savana was pulled out of class, an assistant principal searched Savana's backpack and found no pills. She was then taken to the school nurse, who was female. The nurse had to remove all her clothes except her bra and underwear and then pull out and shake both, partially exposing her breasts and pubic area. Once again, no pills were found. Savana sued, claiming a violation of her Fourth Amendment rights. The Supreme Court agreed. It held that the search of her backpack satisfied the first prong of the *T.L.O.* test and was "justified in its inception." But the near strip search was overly intrusive because of Savana's age and sex and because her alleged infraction only involved pain killers, not illegal narcotics. The Court held that such a search requires school officials to show that either the alleged conduct constituted a danger to other students or had reason to believe that a student was hiding contraband in their underwear.

While perhaps unsatisfying to those who would prefer the Court to apply full Fourth Amendment protections to students or to those who would like the Court to remove any constitutional limits on school officials, the Court's approach to searches in schools fits the same pattern it established with other constitutional rights such as freedom of speech and due process. The Court famously declared that students do not shed their First Amendment rights at the "schoolhouse gate" in *Tinker v. Des*

Moines (393 U.S. 503, 1969); however, it also ruled that those rights have limits that only apply in the school setting. Also in *Goss v. Lopez*, the Court ruled that students are entitled to due process when facing punishment, but those rights need only be "rudimentary" for short suspensions. In other words, the Court wants to protect the constitutional rights but also allow schools the necessary flexibility to maintain order and accomplish their educational mission. As it said *Vernonia*, "Fourth Amendment rights, no less than First and Fourteenth Amendment rights, are different in public schools than elsewhere; the 'reasonableness' inquiry cannot disregard the schools' custodial and tutelary responsibility for children."

Joshua Dunn is Professor and Chair of the Department of Political Science and Director of the Center for the Study of Government and the Individual at the University of Colorado-Colorado Springs. He is the author of Complex Justice: The Case of Missouri v. Jenkins *(2008),* From Schoolhouse to Courthouse: The Judiciary's Role in American Education *(2009), and* Passing on the Right: Conservative Professors in the Progressive University *(2016).*

When Secular and Religious Interests Collide
Scott Merriman

It is sometimes argued that freedom of religion is absolute. However, this is not possible even if only the First Amendment is concerned. If freedom of religion trumped all, the other freedoms listed in the Bill or Rights would need to have asterisks, as in "Freedom to bear arms, except when it conflicts with another person's freedom of religion, etc." There are no such asterisks in the various amendments in the Bill of Rights.

Secular interests often collide with religious interests. It is obvious that they do; otherwise, the First Amendment would be unnecessary. If religion was off in its own bubble, not worried about or active in the world, there would be no need to give it the freedom it is given. Religious activities also move into the world and become involved with secular interests. This essay argues that some secular interests, including the interest of equality, must be balanced with the freedom of religion.

It should also be noted what is not at stake. No one is suggesting that any government should be allowed to dictate the beliefs of a house of worship. We just need to consider when those beliefs move into practice. Most freedom of religion cases also do not deal with practices inside a house of worship. The conduct of most religious figures has even been beyond the reach of the law, except in egregious cases and some cases of fraud. However, even then, few have tried to cover up those cases with freedom of religion. To put it another way, no one is arguing that sexually abusive behavior by clergy should be allowed because religious freedom is absolute.

In most modern cases where religious freedom is argued to be at stake, individuals (not houses of worship) have taken religious liberty far beyond the bounds of the religious building. One of the most notable cases in that area is *Hobby Lobby v. Burwell*, wherein a CEO argued that his corporation was a person, and the company had religious rights and could not be forced to provide contraceptive insurance coverage. In an interesting twist, Hobby Lobby had covered two of the four challenged contraceptives until an advocacy group pointed out their inclusion. One must wonder, if an opposed drug is voluntarily and unknowingly offered, how much of a true religious concern is it how the company treats his or her company employees?

If one's religious ideas are allowed to circumvent legally enacted laws, like the Affordable Care Act, then what laws could not be circumvented? While some religious groups take a day off of work, strictly based on religious texts, the other half of that religious text often is that one should labor for six days and then take one day off. Could a corporation mandate a six-day, twelve-hour workday per week with no overtime? There is no mention of time and a half in the Torah, Bible, or Koran.

Neither are there any mentions of health and safety regulations or environmental regulations in these sacred scriptures. All of these imply, of course, a literal reading of those texts. Though some might say that interpretation is needed and material in the holy texts would require a protection of the earth, the texts could also be read the other way. These interpretations of scripture, rather than narrowing these questions and solving these issues in fact in many ways do just the opposite.

Some religious texts have also been read as excluding those of other religions, and some religious organizations have used their belief systems to avoid hiring persons who are adherents to other religions. Expanded to the workplace, this would mean that a company could use a religious test before hiring their workers. In such cases, freedom of religion would then be used to deny another person's freedom of religion, as one cannot worship on the seventh day of the week (or whenever one's Sabbath day is) if one cannot eat on the other six.

I would argue that freedom of religion must be restricted at least when it interferes with people being equal. The bedrock of the Fourteenth Amendment is that all people should be treated equally and provided due process before the law. When unequal treatment is compelled by a person's religion, the state should have the right to get involved. Although a religion that believes men are inferior should not have to treat men equally in a religious building, a woman running a flower shop should not be allowed to ban men from her shop. It is a long road from a pulpit to a pay toilet.

I would also suggest that when claims of religious freedom interfere with a secular freedom, the Court should examine whether the claimed belief is required by one's religion. For instance, let's examine the baker who claims that his religious freedom is infringed because he has to serve people involved in a same-sex wedding. Does that baker's religion require a person to have no interaction with a same-sex wedding while allowing other interactions with same-sex couples and married same-sex couples, as the baker holds, or does it simply prohibit same-sex marriage? Many religions, to give a comparison, ban adultery, but few say that one needs to start handing out the modern equivalent of the scarlet letter. This would, at the very least, give some element of limitation. Otherwise, any personal discrimination allowed by a religion would, in effect, overturn any equal opportunity laws against bias or discriminatory behavior based on ethnicity, race, religion, gender, age, or sexual orientation.

One must also wonder why marriage equality and the use of contraceptives are among the few areas where this argument is being made. One might think that in cases of gender equality, it is because this is the newest legal battleground, and people are not willing to accept such change. One might also think that some bakers (and florists and so on) have decided that the loss of 5 percent of their business (if 5% of marriages are same-sex marriages) is worth it to take a stand, but it would be too much if the loss is 50 percent of their business, if bakers or florists did not sell to divorced couples who remarried. After all, the same sacred scripture persons use to deny same-sex marriage also states "Therefore, what God has joined together let no man rend asunder."

Scott Merriman is professor of history at Troy University. He is the author of twelve books, including several with ABC-CLIO: Religion and the State *(2009),* Religion and the Law in America *(2009), and* When Religious and Secular Interests Collide *(2017).*

Transgender Rights
Chuck Stewart

Transgender rights have become a hot topic in U.S. politics. The public and courts have often confused the issue by conflating gender, sex, sex roles, and other characteristics under the umbrella word sex. For example, Title VII of the U.S. Civil Rights Act of 1964 prohibited discrimination in employment based upon race, color, religion, sex, and national origin. Unfortunately, sex was not defined. For more than fifty years, legal arguments have been made for and against gay, lesbians, bisexual, and transgender (LGBT) rights under the wording of Title VII. Some attorneys have argued that sex simply meant women and men. This argument conflates sex with gender. Other attorneys have argued that Title VII prohibits employment decisions when the sex of the person involved is taken under consideration while making an employment decision. But what is sex? What is gender? What does it mean to be a woman or a man? And the prefix for transgender is trans, meaning beyond. What does it mean to be beyond gender?

Gender identity is a person's conviction of being female or male. The public display of acting masculine or feminine and engaging in behaviors deemed acceptable for those characteristics is identified as the social sex-role (sexologist John Money in 1955 used the term gender role). Clothing, hairstyles, and type of employment are some of the major sources of establishing a feminine or masculine persona. A person's sex (better called biological sex) is a concept based on *primary* sexual characteristics determined by chromosomes factors (XX—female, XY—male) as expressed in internal and external genitalia (breasts, clitoris, penis) and hormonal states; and *secondary* sexual characteristics (body hair, height, weight, voice). Sexual orientation is the sexual attraction for the other sex (*heterosexual*), the same sex (*homosexual*), both sexes (*bisexual*), or neither sexes (*nonsexual*). Often, affectional orientation (who one is attracted to for affection) is confused with sexual orientation because sexual attraction is strongly linked to who one wants affection from. Sexual attraction also ranges from those strongly desiring sex to those who are *asexual* (sometimes referred to as *graysexual*) and are not overly interested in engaging in sex. All of these characteristics fall on a spectrum and should not be viewed as exclusively binary.

For example, a *cis*gender woman is born with the internal and external genitalia, hormonal states, and secondary sexual characteristics of a woman (sex); feels like a female (gender identity); acts feminine by wearing the clothing and hair, using mannerisms, and working a job society dictates as appropriate for women (social sex-role); has a sexual attraction for men (sexual orientation being heterosexual); and seeks affection and emotional support from men (affectional orientation). The woman is concordant on all measures for defining a woman by most cultural standards. However, very few people meet all these requirements; most may vary in one or more characteristic. There is a range of expressions for each of these characteristics. The binary model is not accurate and should be discarded. For example, if this same cisgender woman simply worked in heavy construction and wore more manly clothing and no makeup, she would no longer be considered fully a woman by many people in the culture. She would be something else. Further, if she felt like she was not a woman but rather a man, he would be transgender regardless if he made efforts to make the transition through medical intervention. He would be classified as female-to-male transgender (FTM) and, respectably, be addressed by the male pronoun he.

Transgender people do not conform to the societal definition of gender but rather transcend gender norms. Some people completely reject gender norms and may identify as gender queer (or Genderqueer). Intersex (previously labeled hermaphrodite) people have a mixed set of biological sex characteristics—for example, a baby born with both an enlarged clitoris (often mistaken for a penis) and vaginal opening. The political term for opposing binary thinking on gender and sexual orientation is the word queer. The word queer has academic application and is widely used by younger lesbian, gay, bisexual, transgender, intersex, and queer people (LGBTIQ or LGBTQ+) but historically was used as a pejorative to denigrate nonheterosexual people.

Transgender people challenge the U.S. legal system and reveal a deep confusion in the courts and legislatures about the construction of gender. Several cases of employment discrimination based on sexual orientation and transgender status worked their way through the courts to the U.S. Supreme Court. They claimed that Title VII inclusion of sex as a protected class applied to their situation. The U.S. Supreme Court issued a landmark ruling in June 2020 interpreting Title VII to provide employment protection for LGBT (*Bostock v. Clayton County* 2020). In the 5—4 ruling, the conservative jurist Justice Gorsuch took a literalist approach to the decision and delivered the opinion of the court. He summarized:

> An employer violates Title VII when it intentionally fires an individual employee based in part on sex. It makes no difference if other factors besides the plaintiff's sex contributed to the decision or that the employer treated women as a group the same when compared to men as a group. A statutory violation occurs if an employer intentionally relies in part on an individual employee's sex when deciding to discharge the employee. Because discrimination on the basis of homosexuality or transgender status requires an employer to intentionally treat individual employees differently because of their sex, an employer who intentionally penalizes an employee for being homosexual or transgender also violates Title VII. . . . An employer who fires an individual for being homosexual or transgender fires that person for traits or actions it would not have questioned in members of a different sex. Sex plays a necessary and undisguisable role in the decision, exactly what Title VII forbids. . . . For an employer to discriminate against employees for being homosexual or transgender, the employer must intentionally discriminate against individual men and women in part because of sex. That has always been prohibited by Title VII's plain terms. (page 2)

The decision was surprising because Justice Gorsuch was chosen by President Trump for his conservative views. Instead, his literalist approach to the text proved to clearly recognize that discrimination against LGBT people is discrimination based on cultural sexual roles. Still, the ruling leaves gaps in LGBT rights. The ruling does not apply to businesses with fewer than fifteen workers, doesn't address the bathroom issue or dress code challenges faced by transgender workers, doesn't address the disparity in health plans provided by employers, and doesn't clarify whether or not employers and service providers can deny LGBTQ persons based on religious convictions.

The presidency of Donald Trump has been difficult for lesbians, gays, bisexual, and, in particular, transgender people. Although he was the first Republican candidate running for the presidency to openly state support for the LGBTQ community, his actions have indicated the opposite. Since taking office, his administration has taken more than thirty-five actions against the community (Acosta 2020). These included banning transgender service members from the military, creating Religious Discrimination Division of the HHS to defend physicians and other medical professionals who decide to refuse service to LGBTQ patients, allowing emergency shelters to deny access to transgender and gender-nonconforming people, refusing LGBTQ asylum seekers fleeing violence, and much more.

Further Reading

Acosta, Lucas. 2020. "The Real List of Trump's 'Unprecedented Steps' for the LGBTQ Community." *Human Rights Campaign*, June 11, 2020. https://www.hrc .org/blog/the-list-of-trumps-unprecedented-steps-for-the -lgbtq-community.

Bostock v. Clayton County, Georgia, No. 17-1618, Certiorari for the Eleventh Circuit, June 15, 2020.

Chuck Stewart, PhD, is an independent researcher and writer on LGBT topics. He is author of several books on the topic: Proud Heritage: People, Issues, and Documents of the LGBT

Experience; The Greenwood Encyclopedia of LGBT Issues
Worldwide; Gay and Lesbian Issues: A Reference Handbook;
and Homosexuality and the Law: A Dictionary. *His doctorate is
in education. Chuck currently teaches math and statistics courses
for National University.*

The Free Press in the Age of Trump
John R. Vile

The First Amendment to the U.S. Constitution places freedom
of the press in the hallowed company of freedom of speech,
religion, peaceable assembly, and petition. Courts have increasingly interpreted press freedoms liberally. In *New York Times
Company v. Sullivan*, 376 U.S. 254 (1964), the Court protected the press against inadvertent mistakes in reports about
public figures that reporters did not make with malice or with
reckless disregard for the truth. In *New York Times Company v.
United States*, 403 U.S. 713 (1971), the Court further allowed
for the release of the Pentagon Papers on the basis that the
First Amendment required a strong presumption against prior
restraint of publication.

Freedom of the press is critically important to a
democratic-republican form of government that relies on an
informed public to select its leaders. The foundations of this
freedom, however, have arguably been weakened during the
Trump administration.

Freedom of the press is at odds with the idea that "the king
[or national leader] can do no wrong." In the Hebrew Scriptures that Christians recognize as the Old Testament, one often
reads that it was common for kings to persecute or execute
prophets for prognostications that were contrary to their own.
In later European monarchies, court jesters often had the difficult task of couching hard truths or criticisms in inoffensive
comedic language.

For centuries Great Britain operated on the principle of "the
greater the truth, the greater the libel." Upholding laws against

seditious libel, British courts reasoned that unflattering truthful information about a monarch could pose a greater threat than information that was so obviously false that no one would believe it.

From an early point in U.S. history, often traced to the trial of Peter Zenger in New York in 1735, Americans allowed truth as a defense in libel cases, and newspapers often skated on the fine line between truth and calumny. As the early American republic divided into partisan rivalries between Democratic-Republicans and Federalists, each party sponsored its own publications with what we today would call partisan "spin." They often skewered the opposition. The criticism was so intense that the Federalist-dominated Congress during the administration of John Adams enacted the Sedition Acts of 1798 designed to criminalize criticisms of the U.S. government or its leaders.

In his First Inaugural Address in 1801, Adam's successor, Thomas Jefferson, pronounced, "If there be any among us who would wish to dissolve this Union, or to change its republican form, let them stand undisturbed as monuments of the safety with which error of opinion may be tolerated, where reason is left free to combat it." In his Second Inaugural Address, although Jefferson acknowledged how "the artillery of the press" had been directed against him, and held out the possibility of *state prosecutions* for actual libel, he still argued that the primary weapon against false reports was "their punishment in the public indignation."

As mass circulation newspapers later developed, many depended on sensationalism ("if it bleeds, it leads"), often labeled as "yellow journalism," to promote sales. Newspaper publisher Randolph Hearst's articles are believed to have played a major part in inflaming public passions leading up to the Spanish American War in 1898. In time, standards of journalistic professionalism increased, and the nation looked especially to such papers as *The New York Times, The Washington Post, The Chicago Tribune,* and the *San Francisco*

Examiner for balanced coverage. For many years, most Americans got their primary news from one of the three major television networks (ABC, CBS, and NBC), which generally avoided explicit ideological biases. Although they sometimes deviated from the ideal, newspapers generally sought to distinguish news stories from editorials, with the former directed to presenting facts and the latter to interpretations and opinions.

Because the great majority of news sources are neither owned nor supported by the government (National Public Radio and Television are exceptions), they have no obligation to support the government's line, and they often call presidents and other public officials to account both for perceived mistakes in policy and misstatements of fact.

Because of their role in promoting accountability, political scientists sometimes refer to the media as a fourth branch of government that aid the legislative, executive, and judicial branches. Although no government officials have been bold enough to suggest that the government has the power to close them down, some politicians have sought political gain by attacking the neutrality of the press. After losing the California gubernatorial race in 1962, Richard Nixon self-pityingly opined that the press would no longer be able to kick him around. Nixon's vice president Spiro Agnew sought, like Nixon, to appeal to "the silent majority" by denigrating his opponents, including those in the press, as "nattering nabobs of negativism."

Despite such precedents, it is doubtful that any modern U.S. president has attacked the press (or his political opponents) with the ferocity and consistency of Donald J. Trump. Just as he had called for criminal prosecutions of his Democratic rival Hillary Clinton (chants of "Lock her up!" were common at his rallies), he labeled reports by those who challenged his own factual assertions as "fake news," openly pointed them out and criticized them at his mass rallies, and even referred to the members of the press as "enemies of the people."

On January 17, 2018, outgoing Republican Senator Jeff Flake of Arizona delivered a speech on the Senate floor in which he repeated one-time Senator Daniel Patrick Moynihan's observation that "everyone is entitled to his own opinion, but not to his own facts." Flake likened the president's remarks about the press and public civil servants to those of foreign dictators like Russia's Joseph Stalin and said that they had a tendency "to undermine confidence in the federal courts, federal law enforcement, the intelligence community, and the free press." Fellow Republican John McCain, whom Trump had also denigrated, affirmed many of these same criticisms.

If anything, Trump's attacks on the press and on political opponents heated up during Special Counsel Robert Mueller's investigations of his possible ties to Russians who tried to influence the 2016 president elections and during the later Senate impeachment trial for abuse of power. At press briefings on the coronavirus pandemic, Trump personally demeaned members of the press and suggested that their pointed questions were stupid or ill-informed. Moreover, Trump has largely removed from his cabinet, his White House staff, the Justice Department, and other government agencies individuals who challenged his assertions and his policies, arguably leaving the press under even greater obligation to do so.

At least as of early April 2020, Trump's domestic approval ratings remain about where they have always been. Republicans supporters continue to watch sympathetic networks like Fox News or get information primarily from online sources and tweets from their friends. Opponents, who are more likely to watch CNN or MSNBC, and who have their own internet sources, have become even more critical of the president and have almost completely lost confidence in what he says. Networks on both sides of this ideological divide devote more and more time to commentary and less to objective reporting.

The nation, the First Amendment, and, indeed, the Bill of Rights are arguably undergoing a type of constitutional stress test. There is a continuing danger that presidential accusations of fake news will not only undercut the credibility of the press and prompt further counter editorializing by the president's political opponents but that voters will come to distrust them all, leaving people even more vulnerable to highly emotional political appeals than to sound decision making.

Fortunately, there are a variety of credible news sources to which interested voters can still turn, some of which, like the British Broadcasting Network (BBC), for example, provide foreign perspectives. One can only hope that thoughtful citizens will continue to weigh the credibility of claims and accusations by all political candidates and that Jefferson's faith that truth will be drive out errors from all directions will be vindicated. Parchment guarantees, like those of the Bill of Rights, may ultimately rest upon larger cultural norms that are cultivated by the civility of political discourse, public trust, and political education and discernment. The guarantees of the Bill or Rights are only as good as the will of the public and the press to challenge government based on them, and the courts to uphold them.

John R. Vile is a professor of political science and dean of the University Honors College at Middle Tennessee State University. He continues to contribute to the online First Amendment Encyclopedia, *of which he is a coauthor.*

Religious Opposition to Abortion Rights: Another Attempt at Establishment of Religion
David Weddle

This essay argues that opposition to abortion based on sectarian religious belief should not be enacted because such law would deny a civil right of women (to privacy) and violate the clause prohibiting the establishment of religion in the First Amendment of the Constitution.

The Supreme Court ruling in *Roe v. Wade* (1973) confirmed a civil right of privacy that permits abortion on a sliding scale of increasing government regulation. The justices correlated that regulation with the division of pregnancy into three trimesters. The Court concluded that a pregnant woman could choose abortion in the first trimester as having an abortion was less dangerous to her than carrying the fetus to term. Therefore, the compelling state interest is in the woman's health. As the embryo develops, however, so does the state's interest in its welfare as a potential citizen. Therefore, the Court allowed states to pass laws restricting abortion during the second trimester. In the third trimester, when the fetus reaches the point of viability, with a substantial chance of survival outside the womb sustained by neonatal technology, the state interest shifts from the woman's health to the fetus as a potential citizen under the state's protection.

By this reasoning, abortion is prohibited after the fetus reaches the point of viability, itself a shifting line determined by the current state of medical technology. In theory, the creation of an artificial womb would allow extracting a fertilized egg and sustaining its gestation to term. The embryo would then be "viable" moments after conception, effectively outlawing all abortions. By allowing technology to determine the legal question, the Court in *Roe v. Wade* opened the way for a future in which an embryo at conception would be viable and constitute a *potential* member of society accorded the protection of the Fourteenth Amendment, guaranteeing that its life cannot be taken without "due process."

The state, however, has an even greater interest in protecting the pregnant woman as an *actual* citizen. As "health" became more broadly defined as mental or emotional well-being, as well as physical survival, abortion has become more generally allowed. State legislatures continue to pass laws restricting access to abortion during the second trimester, but most have been declared unconstitutional by the courts. Often the grounds for nullification is that the law is not intended to protect the pregnant woman but rather to limit her access to abortion for the sake of the fetus, typically identified as the "unborn child."

One example is the recent effort to outlaw abortion after a fetal heartbeat is detected. Here the interest in protecting the fetus extends beyond the *Roe v. Wade* window to as early as six weeks, before many women even know they are pregnant and in the first trimester, the point in time in the pregnancy cycle when *Roe v. Wade* determined the state's interest was in protecting the woman's health. These laws often claim that a fetus is a person with a right to life that overrides a woman's right to privacy. This claim has no support in the Constitution and is exclusively based on religious belief; it played no role at all in the *Roe v. Wade* decision.

"Person" is a designation that bestows legal and moral rights on an individual, apart from one's age or physical condition. Once having defined what a *person* is, including corporations, courts have then determined what rights that person is entitled to hold. In *Roe v. Wade*, however, the Court found no legal precedent for regarding the fetus as a person. Instead, the justices argued that the right to abortion was limited by state interest: the entire body politic stands to lose the future contribution of a citizen-in-the-making.

State legislative bills to prevent late-stage abortions reinforce the Court's view that in the last three months of pregnancy, the state has a compelling interest in the survival of a potential citizen. So, the fetus requires protection—*not due to any intrinsic value in and of itself*—but because of the state's interest in its future value to society. The legal arguments about the regulation of the civil right to abortion, then, are utilitarian; they depend upon the state of medical technology, and they make no judgment about the metaphysical status of the fetus.

By contrast, conservative Christian opponents of abortion, mainly Protestant evangelicals and Roman Catholics, insist that the embryo has God-given dignity from conception, with the same right to life as its would-be mother. The Catholic position is that it is impossible to choose between the value of one life and another; therefore, abortion is not allowable even to save the life of the pregnant woman. This view derives not from law or science but solely from religious belief. When religious opponents of abortion speak of the "sanctity of life" bestowed by God at conception, they are referring to a divine act that cannot be verified by any legal analysis or empirical investigation. When the psalmist, for example, declared that God formed him in his "mother's womb" and already foresaw the entire span of his life (Psalm 139), he was offering a theological interpretation, not a biological description, of human existence.

The claim that "children yet unborn" (Psalm 78) are divine gifts is a religious conviction supported by appeal to the Bible—or more precisely, to a sectarian interpretation of the scriptural text. In his 1995 encyclical, *Evangelium Vitae* (*Gospel of Life*), Pope John Paul II stated that fetuses "when they are still in their mothers' womb—as many passages of the Bible bear witness . . . are the personal objects of God's loving and fatherly providence." The only explicit reference to the fetus, however, is in the Mosaic legal code, where its death can be compensated for by paying a fine, whereas the death of a pregnant woman must be atoned by the death of the one responsible, even if her death was accidental (Exodus 21). This provision states that the fetus carries less moral and legal weight than that of a human person. For that reason, Jewish tradition favors the view that a human comes into being when it takes its first breath (Psalm 104), not at conception. The Catholic view of the absolute inviolability of life from conception on is, then, a sectarian reading of the Bible that is not shared by other religious groups and is rejected by nonbelievers.

In that sense, the evangelical and Catholic opposition to abortion falls under the same constitutional ban as reading the Bible in public schools. In *Abington v. Schempp* (1963), the Court struck down a Pennsylvania law requiring reading from the Bible as constituting a "religious observance," even without comment, because the inclusion of passages from the New Testament were specifically Christian and offensive to Jewish students. The Court found that the intention of the law was to establish specifically Christian beliefs and practices in violation of the First Amendment. Proposed state laws to prohibit abortion, based on the religious belief that the fetus is a person with the right to protection, are, similarly, attempts to establish sectarian religious belief as the law of the land. These laws should for that reason, and in every case, be struck down as unconstitutional.

David Weddle (PhD, Harvard) is Professor Emeritus of Religion at Colorado College, where he taught courses on philosophy of religion, ethics, theology, and comparative religion. He is the author of Miracles: Wonder and Meaning in World Religions *(2011) and* Sacrifice in Judaism, Christianity, and Islam *(2017).*

"Fish-Ins" and the Indian Civil Rights Movement
David Zeh

During the late nineteenth century, the federal government began attempts to force assimilation of Native Americans into U.S. society through the Dawes Act, also known as the Severality Act of February 8, 1887 (25 U.S.C. 9), or the General Allotment Act. It sought to replace communal ownership of land on reservations with private ownership similar to the nonreservation land in the rest of the United States. However, the act did little to help Native Americans, as many lost their land due to the extreme poverty that plagued many reservations. After World War I, the federal government continued its pursuit in assimilating tribes by granting citizenship to every Native American (Act of November 6, 1919, 41 Stat. 350). One of the main goals of the Indian Citizenship Act was to also rescind the unique legal position held by Native Americans at the time.

By 1953, Congress began taking a more aggressive approach by enacting the House concurrent resolution 108, which sought to put an end to reservations as well as to tribal sovereignty. This would ultimately force Native Americans to integrate into

U.S. society without their consent. Throughout the 1980s, state governments also began adopting Public Law 280, which gave them power over reservations. Essentially, tribes no longer had legal jurisdiction over their own citizens.

During the early 1960s, Native American fishermen began a long series of heated battles with the state of Washington when state officials began making arrests as well as confiscating boats and fishing gear. Despite Washington having jurisdiction over reservations, the state was actually violating treaties between the tribes of the Pacific Northwest and Governor Isaac Stevens that had been negotiated and signed between 1853 and 1854. Article VI of the U.S. Constitution states that "all treaties made, or which shall be made, under the authority of the United States, shall be the supreme law of the land."

In 1964, tensions between Washington and the people of the Puget Sound area were reaching a critical point. After countless arrests and illegal actions by state officials, the Survival of the American Indian Association (SAIA) was formed to resolve the fishing rights issue through "direct and uncompromising civil disobedience" (Brown 2020). The group opposed assimilation and fought back through education and cultural activities. Throughout the late 1960s, the group demonstrated their disobedience by conducting multiple "fish-ins" (Chrisman 2007). The goal of the fish-ins was to get arrested in order to bring to the general public attention what was occurring. During these protests, men, women, and children were met with violence. Most were arrested for their actions. These demonstrations also gained national attention when celebrities like Marlon Brando were arrested alongside the Native Americans of Puget Sound.

The tide began to turn when President Lyndon Johnson provided Community Action Programs to alleviate the poverty that most tribes were experiencing around the country. These programs also allowed individual tribes to receive grants for economic projects on their respective reservations. In 1968, President Johnson's administration supported enactment by Congress of the Indian Civil Rights Act (Northwest

Justice Project 2018). This act provided Native Americans with personal freedoms against federal government actions and repealed Public Law 280, allowing tribes to remain sovereign once again.

However, the battle over fishing rights was still being fought in the state of Washington. In 1970, the SAIA continued protesting, resulting in a lawsuit filed with the Supreme Court of Washington. The state's high court ruled in favor of the Native Americans, allowing them to fish with nets for fifteen days at the Puyallup River during the fall. Despite this being an important victory for the SAIA, law enforcement attacked a fishing camp on the river on September 9 of that year. Violence erupted on both sides, leading the police to arrest fifty-five adults and five children. However, the situation proved to be effective for the SAIA as public opinion favored the Native Americans protesting their right to fish. The events that happened on September 9 also raised questions about police conspiring to cause violence in order to help the commercial fishing industry. Nine days later, U.S. Attorney Stanley Pitkin filed *United States v. Washington*. That case eventually led to the most important win for the SAIA (Chrisman 2007).

On May 23, 1977, U.S. District Court judge George Boldt made the historic ruling in *United States v. Washington* (431 U.S. 181, 1977) by favoring the fishing rights of Native Americans. This meant that Native Americans had full access to their ancestral fishing grounds as promised to them in treaties dating back to the 1850s. This led to a similar fish-in campaign in Wisconsin by the Chippewa tribe. While the SAIA had achieved its intended goals, there was significant backlash from the white commercial and sporting fishing industries. White sport fishermen soon began sporting signs that proclaimed "Save a Walleye, Spear an Indian" and "Spear a Pregnant Squaw, Save a Walleye," and bumper stickers that read "Indian Nigger" and "Red Nigger." The Chippewa waged a nine-year legal battle to ensure their treaty rights to fish and hunt (LeMay 2009: 311–312). They won those rights by the decision in *Lac Courte*

Oreiles Band of Lake Superior Chippewa Indians v. State of Wisconsin (740 F. Supp. 1400, W.D. Wis., 1990), ruled on May 9, 1990.

Despite the backlash, Boldt's landmark decision in *United States v. Washington* continues to protect Native American fishing rights to this day.

References

Brown, Shana. 2020. "Treaties in the Pacific Northwest Promises Made and Broken." Native Knowledge 360: The Fish Wars: What Kinds of Actions Can Lead to Justice? n.d.

Chrisman, Gabriel. 2007. "The Fish-in Protests at Franks Landing." The Seattle Civil Rights and Labor History Project. https://depts.washington.edu/civilr/fish-ins.html.

Johnstonbaugh, Laurie. 2006. "Indian Civil Rights Hearings: U.S. Commission on Civil Rights Comes to Seattle, 1977." The Seattle Civil Rights and Labor History Project. https://depts.washington.edu/civilr/CRcommission.htm.

Lac Courte Oreiles Band of Lake Superior Chippewa Indians v. State of Wisconsin (740 F. Supp. 1400 (W.D. Wis. 1990).

LeMay, Michael. 2009. *The Perennial Struggle*. 3rd ed. Upper Saddle River, NJ: Prentice-Hall.

Northwest Justice Project. 2018. "Indian Civil Rights Act." *Washington LawHelp,* March 20, 2018.

See article VI, United States Constitution.

David Zeh is a recent graduate of the University of Wisconsin-Oshkosh, majoring in history. In his research, Zeh specialized in Native American Indian history and the Oneida Tribe.

Introduction

This chapter presents profiles of important organizations and civil rights activists who advocated for the expansion of the civil rights and liberty protections guaranteed to American citizens by the Constitution of the United States. They did so by fighting in the halls of Congress to enact civil rights laws. They did so in the courts of the United States to redefine the meaning of the fundamental rights articulated in the Bill of Rights. They fought to expand our understanding of who ought to be included in "We the People," and thereby guaranteed those rights. They did so by engaging state governments to ratify new proposed amendments to state constitutions, or to end discriminatory treatment of minorities in law (de jure) or custom (de facto). They did so by transforming U.S. government and society. The chapter describes some key stakeholder organizations advocating or implementing civil rights policies. Table 5.11 lists forty such activist organizations across time and by type of organization and the focus of their activism. Space does not allow profiling all of them, but samples representing ten types are presented here.

After describing exemplary organizations struggling to achieve greater civil rights protections and more effective

---

A tipi with an "American Indian Movement" sign, on the grounds of the Washington Monument, Washington, D.C., during the "Longest Walk" on July 11, 1978. The walk was the largest demonstration of AIM. (Library of Congress)

limits on government intrusion of those rights, the chapter profiles twenty-seven individual actors in the political arena, including government officials of the federal government and leading activists from nongovernmental groups who impacted civil rights issues across a spectrum of problems and historical eras. Some lesser-known organizations are purposely profiled here, as some of the individual profiles feature persons from the better-known organizations. These organizations, and then the individual profiles, are presented in alphabetical order.

Organizations

Aids Coalition to Unleash Power (ACT UP)

The Aids Coalition to Unleash Power was an international grassroots political group advocating to end the AIDS pandemic. It began in New York City in 1987, founded by such activists as Larry Kramer, Didlier Lestrade, and Michael Petrelis. Act Up represents sexual-oriented organizations employing the new-style radicalism strategy and tactics. ACT UP emerged after using demonstrations on Wall Street in 1987 to push for greater access to experimental AIDS drugs, to radically reduce the costs of those drugs, and to speed up their approval and availability by the FDA. They used symbolically related demonstrations to change public perceptions of AIDS and of gays and lesbians more generally. In 1988, Act Up was featured in a *Cosmopolitan* article, after which the Act Up Women's Caucus was formed. The Women's Caucus advocated changing the way the Center for Disease Control (CDC) defined AIDS and described its symptoms. In October 1988, Act Up launched demonstrations in Washington, D.C., shutting down the FDA's offices there, much like AIM took over the Bureau of Indian Affairs offices in the early 1970s. Act Up also held a "die-in" demonstration at New York City's St. Patrick Cathedral to oppose the way in which the church characterized gays, lesbians, and AIDS. The "die-ins" simulated dead persons, some in "body bags," and essentially copied the Black civil rights movement's use of "sit-ins" in the early 1960s.

In the 1980s, Act Up organized itself into a number of committees to direct its activism: Action, Finance, Outreach, Treatment and Research, Media, Graphics, and Housing. Act Up was especially effective in using graphic art and in organizing "symbolic" protests to make their points about policy changes they wanted the appropriate government agencies to pursue or change. For example, in 1988 they picketed Boston's Health and Human Services office, and in 1990, they demonstrated at the National Institute of Health in Washington, D.C. In 1991, Act Up's Seattle chapter organized protests at Seattle schools in which they handed out "safe sex" packets to high school students. In 1991, they covered the house of Senator Jesse Helms, a noted antigay politician, in a giant condom.

Like many civil rights organizations, Act Up factionalized and spun off affiliated or associated groups: Act Up Women's Caucus, Act Up/LA, Act Up/RI, Bash Back, Fed Up Queers, Lesbian Avengers, and Queer Nation. By the 2000s, as the AIDS pandemic eased and a cocktail of drugs proved effective in treating AIDS, Act Up modified its strategy and tactics. As public opinion shifted regarding gays and lesbians, and as greater awareness of the nature of the spread of the virus (increasingly no longer being viewed as a "gay disease"), Act Up became more accommodationist, and diminished as an activist organization. They increasingly supported openly gay politicians who began to be elected to local, state, and even national-level offices (Faderman 2011; Fisher 1978).

American Association of People with Disabilities (AAPD)

AAPD is a national cross-disability organization advocating for the full civil rights of the more than 60 million Americans with disabilities. It promotes equal opportunity, economic power, independent living, and political participation. AAPD exemplifies organizations that use the political accommodation strategy and tactics. It was founded in 1947 by Justin Dart, Bob Dole, and a number of others coming from the various organizations involved in disability matters (typically organized around a specific type of disability). AAPD's current president and CEO is Maria Town. It is headquartered in Washington, D.C. People with disabilities sat in at federal buildings, obstructed the movement of inaccessible buses, and marched through the streets to protest injustice. AAPD used the courts and lobbied in the halls of Congress. A significant shift in disability-related public policy came with enactment of Section 504 of the Rehabilitation Act of September 26, 1973 (87 Stat. 355). The Rehabilitation Act prohibits discrimination based on disability in (1) programs of federal agencies, (2) programs receiving federal assistance, (3) federal employment, and (4) employment practices of federal contractors. It adds disability to the previous "protected" categories of race, ethnic origin, and sex discrimination. With its passage, for the first time, the exclusion and segregation of people with disabilities was viewed as discrimination rather than simply problems of unemployment and lack of education imposed by the physical or mental limitations of the disability itself. For the first time, persons with disabilities were viewed as a legal class—a protected minority group. AAPD mobilized a successful campaign in 1977 that eventually helped enact the Americans with Disabilities Act. In the 1980s, AAPD blocked the Reagan and Bush administrations' plan to deregulate Section 504 as part of its general "deregulation" of government efforts. AAPD joined a coalition of civil rights groups to enact the Civil Rights Restoration Act of 1988. The 1988 Act was aimed at overturning *Grove City College v. Bell* (465 U.S. 555, 1984). In *Grove City College* the Supreme Court had restricted laws that prohibited discrimination on the basis of race, ethnic origin, sex, or disability by recipients of federal funds. Also in 1988, the Fair Housing Act was passed, which included antidiscrimination legislation on the basis of disability.

In the 1980s, an affiliated group to the AADP worked in coalition with it. The Disability Rights Education and Defense Fund (DREDF), like MALDEF in the 1970s, filed amicus briefs on behalf of sixty-three national, state, and local organizations advocating for the civil rights of persons with disabilities. In *School Board of Nassau County v. Arline* (480 U.S. 273, 1987), the Supreme Court laid the foundation of coverage of people with AIDS. Like all landmark decisions, it influenced subsequent court cases and Congressional actions. In 1987, the National Council on Disability was established as an independent federal agency and its members were appointed by President Ronald Reagan. In 1988, Senator Lowell Wiecker (R-CT) and Representative Tony Coelho (D-CA) introduced the bill that ultimately became the Americans with Disabilities Act (ADA). Justin Dart, then Chair of the Congressional Task Force on the Rights and Empowerment of People with Disabilities, launched a nation-wide series of public hearings on the matter. In 1989, Senators Tom Harkin (D-Iowa) and David Durrenberger (R-MN) introduced a new ADA bill. ADA was signed into law on July 26, 1990 (42 U.S. 126). Since the passage of the American with Disabilities Act in 1990, the AAPD has worked to ensure that ADA is implemented at federal, state, and local levels as a codification of simple justice,

American Association of Retired Persons (AARP)

AARP (formerly the American Association of Retired Persons) is a nonprofit 501(c)(4) nonprofit organization with headquartered in Washington, D.C., and with branch offices in all fifty states, the District of Columbia, Puerto Rico, and the Virgin Islands. It was founded in 1958, by Dr. Ethel Percy Andrus, a California educator, and Leonard Davis, an insurance company executive. Today, its CEO is Jo Ann Jenkins. AARP well exemplifies an organization using the accommodation approach; it is a classic lobbying group, with 38 million members and a reputation for being one of the most influential lobbying organizations in Washington, D.C. AARP officially changed its name to the initials AARP in 1999, as it no longer requires members to be retired. AARP's stated mission is "empower people as they age." It has established several affiliated organizational platforms: AARP Foundation, AARP Financial Services, and AARP Insurance Plan.

It publishes *AARP: The Magazine*, which is sent to 37 million members. AARP advocates to protect and to improve the Medicare Prescription Drug Improvement and Modernization Act that created Medicare Part D in 2003. In 2012, AARP campaigned to strengthen Social Security and Medicare. AARP opposed the American Health Care Act of 2017, charging that it would increase premiums and provide smaller tax credits. AARP's former chief lobbyist, John Rother, has been criticized for opposing single-payer plans. In 2019, AARP was embroiled in controversy when a class-action suit was filed, alleging that AARP deceived its members regarding Medicare by inducing Medicare patients into paying an undisclosed commission when they enrolled in AARP-branded supplemental health insurance plans (Lynch 2011).

American-Arab Anti-Discrimination Committee (ADC)

The American-Arab Anti-Discrimination Committee is a civil rights organization whose mission is to defend the rights of people of Arab descent and to promote the cultural heritage of all Arab Americans. ADC was cofounded in 1980 by U.S. Senator James Abourezk (D-SD). It went on to become the largest American Arab grassroots organization in the United States. ADC supports the human and civil rights of all people and opposes racism, bigotry, and discrimination in any form. ADC is open to participation and support of people of all ethnic, racial, and religious backgrounds. Headquartered in Washington, D.C., ADC's objectives are to do the following: (1) defend and promote human rights, civil rights, and liberties of American Arabs and other persons of Arab heritage; (2) combat stereotyping and discrimination against the Arab American community; (3) serve as the public voice of the Arab American community with regard to both domestic and foreign policy matters and issues; (4) educate the American public in order to promote greater understanding of Arab history and culture; and (5) organize and mobilize the American-Arab community to further ADC's objectives (LeMay 2018a: 159–160).

ADC claims members in all fifty states, about three million Americans who trace their ancestry to an Arab country. It sponsors a number of programs to combat discrimination and bias against Arabs and Muslims. It is an organizational member of the Leadership Council on Civil Rights. One of its founders, James Abourezk, was the first Arab American to serve in the U.S. Senate. Another cofounder, New York attorney Samer Khalaf, became ADC's national president in 2013. Another ADC cofounder, James Zogby, also founded the Arab-American Institute in Washington, D.C. Among ADC's advisory board were Muhammad Ali, Queen Noor of Jordan, the late actor and voice actor Casey Kasem, United States Representatives John Conyers (D-MI), Darell Issa (R-CA), Nick Joe Rahall (D-WVA), and Paul Findley (R-IL). A prominent ADC board member is Philip Saliba, the Archbishop of New York and Metropolitan of All North America of the Antiochian Orthodox Christian Church.

ADC's legal department offers counsel in all cases of discrimination, defamation, and hate crimes. It participates in selected litigation in hundreds of cases against airlines and employers for discrimination on the basis of ethnicity and national origin and against the U.S. government for discriminatory detention without probable cause (that is, racial profiling) of Arabs and Muslims after the September 11, 2001, attacks. ADC's communications department challenges defamation, stereotyping, and ethnic bias in films, television programs, and news reporting. ADC spokespersons are considered an authoritative voice on Arab American affairs. ADC's government affairs department works with the U.S. Congress, the White House, and the U.S. Departments of State and of Justice to promote the interests of the Arab American community by lobbying. ADC contributes to the National Association of Arab-American Anti-Discrimination Committee (NAAAADC). Its political action committee supports political candidates for federal office of both major political parties. Its research institute, begun in 1981, sponsors research studies, seminars, conferences, and publications about discrimination faced by Arab Americans and promotes understanding of Arab cultural heritage. It provides lesson plans, background articles, fact sheets, bibliographies, and related resources to educators.

ADC's offices suffered a series of violent attacks in 1985, as did several mosques in southern California. In 1991, during the Gulf War, ADC was the target of anti-Arab telephone messages, and that year, ADC documented more than one hundred hate crimes against Arab Americans. The 1996 Antiterrorism and Effective Death Penalty Act and the Illegal Immigration Reform and Responsibility Act allowed for the deportation of immigrants for minor offenses. They allowed the government to use secret, classified evidence to deny bond for those under threat of deportation. In 1999, the Supreme Court ruled on the targeting of Arab Americans in *Reno v. American-Arab Anti-Discrimination Committee* (525 U.S. 471). In its 8–1 decision, delivered by Justice Antonin Scalia and joined by Chief Justice Rehnquist and Associate Justices O'Connor, Kennedy, and Thomas, with concurring opinions by Justices Breyer, Ginsburg, and Stevens, the Supreme Court denied the case on the basis of the federal courts being deprived of jurisdiction over the respondent's suit. Justice Souter wrote the sole dissenting opinion. The Court upheld the general rule that revised procedures for removing aliens do not apply to noncitizen aliens. Justice David Souter wrote a dissenting opinion in the case (LeMay 2018a: 161).

American Civil Liberties Union (ACLU)

The ACLU is a nonpartisan, nonprofit organization formed to defend and preserve individual rights and liberties of every person in America as guaranteed by the Constitution and the laws of the United States. ACLU was founded in 1920 in reaction to the Attorney General Mitchell Palmer's "Red Scare" raids. Those raids rounded up thousands of radicals and deported hundreds, arrested without warrants and without regard to constitutional protections against unlawful search and seizure. The raids literally constituted "guilt by association." Among the small group of founders of ACLU were Hellen Keller, Roger Nash Baldwin, Jane Addams, Walter Nelles, Elizabeth Gurley Flynn, Felix Frankfurter, Norman Thomas, and Crystal Eastman (www.aclu.org/about/aclu-history). As of 2020, ACLU is headquartered in New York City and is led by its CEO, Anthony Romero; its deputy CEO, Dorothy Ehrlich; and its National Legal Director, David Cole. Currently, ACLU claims a national membership of over 1.5 million. Its annual budget exceeds $234 million, and it has a staff of 300 attorneys as well as several thousand volunteer attorneys helping in offices throughout the United States. ACLU lobbies for a broad variety of policy positions: (1) opposition to the death penalty, which ACLU considers to be cruel and unusual punishment and unconstitutional on the basis of the Eighth Amendment; (2) support for same-sex marriage rights, other rights of LGBT people, and the ending of discrimination against them in employment, housing, adoption, and media stereotyping; (3) support for birth control and abortion rights and to protect against overturning *Roe v. Wade*; (4) elimination of discrimination against women in employment and compensation—equal pay for equal work; (5) support for the rights of prisoners and opposition to the use of torture; (6) opposition to government preference of religion over nonreligion, or for particular faiths over other faiths; and (7) support for the right to equal access to the ballot box (LeMay 2018a: 162–163).

ACLU comprises two separate but closely affiliated non-profits: the ACLU, a 501(c)(4) social welfare group; and the ACLU Foundation, a 501(c)(3) public charity. Both organizational platforms engage in civil rights litigation, advocacy, and education, but only the 501(c)(3) donations to the ACLU Foundation are tax deductible, and only the 501(c)(4) group can engage in unlimited political lobbying. The ACLU has supported countless suits by filing *amicus curiae* briefs. It has supported Native American suits to protect their rights to use controlled substances in religious ceremonies. It has supported the rights of Jehovah's Witnesses to canvass door-to-door, to resist the draft as conscientious objectors, and in their refusal to salute the flag. ACLU led battles over the separation of church and state in cases like *Everson v. Board of Education* (1947), and ACLU prevailed in *McCullum v. Board of Education* (1948) and in *Engel v. Vitale* (1962). It has lobbied to oppose the School Prayer constitutional amendment. ACLU has been largely unsuccessful but nonetheless a champion in efforts to end Sunday closing laws. Most recently, it has opposed President Donald Trump's Muslim travel ban.

Some of ACLU's more famous battles were partnering with Clarence Darrow to defend John Scopes in the Scopes Trial of 1925; the defense of Japanese American citizens incarcerated in the internment camps in 1942; support for ending the "separate-but-equal" doctrine in *Brown v. Board of Education*; privacy rights in *Roe v. Wade;* defense of Nazi protestors in *Skokie*; opposition to the USA Patriot Act in 2001; defending the rights of immigrants; supporting enactment of the Americans with Disabilities Act; protesting free speech in *Tinker v. Des Moines* (1969); fighting against the compulsory teaching of creationism in Arkansas in 1981; internet free speech in 1997 in *ACLU v. Reno*; protection of gays in 2003 in *Lawrence v. Texas;* keeping religion out of science classrooms in 2005 in *Kitzmiller v. Dover Area School District;* and, in 2009, protecting the constitutional rights of a thirteen-year-old girl from being strip-searched in *Safford Unified School District v. Redding* (Cole 2016).

American Indian Movement (AIM)

What became the best known radical protest pan-Indian group, the American Indian Movement (AIM), began in 1968 in Minneapolis, Minnesota. Its founders were Clyde Bellecourt, a Chippewa; Dennis Banks, an Anishinabe Ojibwa; and Russell Means, an Oglala Lakota Sioux. All of them were born on reservations but lived in urban areas at the time they began AIM. They started by stressing community service programs, monitoring police violence against Native Americans, offering alcohol rehabilitation programs, and advocating school reforms. Their militant protests began when they linked with a group calling itself Indians of All Tribes that had staged a takeover of Alcatraz Island in San Francisco (November 1969 to May 1971). AIM and Indians of All Tribes laid claim to the island asserting rights under an 1868 treaty that had promised to return to Indian control unused federal property. Their protest action drew worldwide attention to their cause.

AIM had a knack for symbolic gestures that maximized power through publicity. On Thanksgiving Day, 1970, they seized the *Mayflower* replica and painted Plymouth Rock red. On July 4, 1971, they organized a countercelebration at Mount Rushmore in the sacred Black Hills of South Dakota. In 1972, AIM and other Native American organizations began protests they called the "Trail of Broken Treaties," going from the West Coast to Washington, D.C., where 500 demonstrators seized the Bureau of Indian Affairs offices for six days and released files embarrassing to the BIA. AIM's most militant protest occurred in 1973, when they staged a takeover of Wounded Knee, South Dakota. The ten-week siege began when Dennis Banks and Russell Means organized demonstrations at the Pine Ridge and the Rosebud reservations to protest the failure of authorities to arrest the suspected murderers of Raymond Yellow Thunder.

He was a fifty-one-year-old Sioux who had been stripped of his pants and assaulted by a group of drunken whites at a local American Legion Hall. His frozen body was later found in the back of a pickup truck. The siege at Wounded Knee was at the site of the 1890 massacre of 250 Sioux old men, women, and children by white soldiers who had termed it the last battle of the Plains Indian Wars (Brown 2012). Banks and Means led a group of 300 AIM members who took over the tiny hamlet, occupying it for seventy days. During the occupation, two FBI members were killed. The FBI arrested the demonstrators, and the incident brought national focus on conditions of life on the reservations. AIM spurred "Red Pride" and the use of the term "Red Power." Red Power is attributed to Vine Deloria, an AIM member and Standing Rock Sioux who later served as director of the National Council of American Indians (Johnson 2007; LeMay 2009: 311–312; Wilkins 2002: 218). Russell Means and Dennis Banks were cleared of any crimes during the Wounded Knee takeover, but were later imprisoned for other crimes. AIM agitated from 1976 to 1994 to win release of one of their leaders, Leonard Peltier, who had been sentenced to two consecutive life terms for the murder of the two FBI agents on the Pine Ridge Reservation. In 1978, AIM staged the "Longest Walk," a 3,000 mile trek from the West Coast to Washington, D.C. In 1994, their civil rights demonstrations culminated in the "Walk for Justice," and in 2008, AIM held the "Longest Walk–2." AIM advocates for redress of discrimination against Native Americans exemplified by high unemployment, by slum housing, by the protest over treaty rights (for example, by staging a "fish-in"), and by protests for the reclamation of tribal lands. A "fish-in" was a type of protest used first in the Seattle, Washington, area in 1964, and then in Wisconsin in 1968. The Chippewa and Menominee Tribes of Wisconsin led a nine-year legal battle to ensure their treaty rights to fish and hunt. Their legal battle culminated in *Menominee Tribe v. United States* (391 U.S. 404, 1968) (Banks and Erdoes 2006; Deloria 1988; Johnson 2007; LeMay 2009; Stern 2002; Wilkins 2002).

Congress of Racial Equality (CORE)

CORE was a civil rights organization founded in Chicago, Illinois, in 1942 by James Farmer, George Houser, and Bernice Fisher, with help and inspiration from Bayard Rustin. It played a pivotal role in the Black Civil Rights movement. It originally was organized with twenty-eight men and twenty-twowomen, and stated its mission as: "To bring about equality for all people regardless of race, creed, sex, age, disability, sexual orientation, religion, or ethnic background" (Meier and Rudwick 1975: 3). CORE evolved out of the Fellowship of Reconciliation, a pacifist organization. CORE was greatly influenced by the philosophy and the nonviolent, civil disobedience tactics of Mahatma Gandhi. In the 1960s, CORE began its push against Jim Crow racial segregation in the South and against voting rights, employment, and housing discrimination in the North. CORE had fifty-three chapters in the United States, located mostly in urban centers in the Northeast, Midwest, Mid-Atlantic, and West Coast. In the South, it had chapters in Louisiana, Mississippi, Florida, South Carolina, and Kentucky. CORE's first president, James Farmer, dealt with tensions within CORE between factions of its original members with a faction advocating more radical tactics, Black nationalism, and Black Power. Farmer retired from CORE in 1966 and was replaced by Floyd McKissick, a "Black Power" advocate. In 1961, CORE developed the tactic of Freedom Rides, which echoed the 1947 Journey of Reconciliation. In 1961, however, the Freedom Riders were met with severe violence in the Deep South, particularly in Birmingham and Montgomery, Alabama. CORE pushed for desegregation of Chicago public schools in 1960–1963, when it staged "sit-ins" that copied the "sit-in" tactic used at segregated lunch counters in the South. In 1963, CORE worked with SCLC, SNCC, and other civil rights groups to help organize the March on Washington at which MLK gave his famous "I Have a Dream" speech. In the summer of 1964,

CORE, SNCC, SCLC, and even the NAACP (pushed to use more activist tactics by the other civil rights groups) helped organize the Mississippi Freedom Democratic Party (LeMay 2009: 291–296). By the mid-1960s, CORE turned increasingly toward community involvement. By 1968, it virtually collapsed and no longer held conferences, protests, or other activist activities (Farmer 1985; Frazier 2017; Meier and Rudwick 1975).

Japanese American Citizens League (JACL)

The Japanese American Citizens League is the oldest and largest Asian American civil rights organization in the United States. It began in California in 1929 and published the *Nikkei Shimin* newspaper. It held its first national convention in Seattle, Washington, in 1930. JACL monitors and reacts to issues that threaten the civil rights of all Americans, and advocates for effective, positive changes for the Asian Pacific American community. An accommodationist organization, in its strategy and tactics it parallels the NAACP. It promotes honoring the diversity of American society and respect for the values of fairness, equality, and social justice. JACL seeks to secure and maintain the rights of Japanese Americans and others victimized by injustice and bigotry. It works to promote cultural, educational, and social values that preserve the heritage and legacy of the Japanese-American community (www.jacl.org/about.)

In 1931, JACL lobbied Congress to amend the 1922 Cable Act (also known aa the Married Woman's Act) to restore U.S. citizenship to American women of Japanese ancestry who married Japanese nationals (Act of March 3, 1931, 46 Stat. 1511, LeMay and Barkan 1999: 169–170). In 1941, after Pearl Harbor was attacked and the United States entered World War II, President Franklin Roosevelt issued executive order 9066 on March 21, 1942. By FDR's order, some 50,000 Japanese immigrants (the Issei) and 70,000 Japanese American native-born citizens (the Nisei) were rounded up, relocated, and interned in ten American concentration camps (Armor and Wright 1988;

Hosokawa 1969; Kitano 1976; LeMay 2009: 85–87; LeMay and Barkan 1999: 192–194; Ng 2001). The JACL soon joined the ACLU and assorted church groups to work with the War Relocation Authority to resettle Americans of Japanese ancestry from the internment camps to Eastern and Midwestern states. In 1943, JACL opened a Midwest office in Chicago to help implement that resettlement. In 1944, JACL supported two members, Gordon Hirabayashi and Fred Korematsu, in filing suits to challenge the relocation and internment camp orders as unconstitutional. However, the Supreme Court ruled the orders constitutional in *Hirabayashi v. United States* (June 21, 1943, 320 U.S. 81) and *Korematsu v. United States* (December 18, 1944, 323 U.S. 214) (LeMay and Barkan 1999: 194–200). But the JACL won a case in *Ex Parte Mitsuye Endo* (323 U.S. 283–310,1944; Kitano 1997; LeMay and Barkan 1999: 201–203). In *Endo*, the Supreme Court ruled that a citizen who was loyal could not be presumed a spy or saboteur based solely on the person's ancestry, and that because the detention was to prevent against sabotage, "detention which has no relationship to that objective is unauthorized." Mitsuye Endo was ordered released from the camp. JACL secured the right of many internees to join the U.S. military, and the 442nd Regimental Combat Team was formed of Japanese American volunteers. It went on to become the most decorated combat unit in the European theatre. In 1946, President Truman honored them. That same year, the JACL opened its Anti-Discrimination Committee offices in Washington, D.C., which led the organization's lobbying efforts that secured, for example, amendment to the Soldier Brides Act to admit Japanese wives of U.S. soldiers to the United States.

Many western states had enacted Alien Land Acts after California's laws of 1913. The JACL fought a series of court cases in 1947 and 1948 that eventually succeeded in securing repeal of those land laws in several states. In *Oyama v. California* (332 U.S. 633, 1948), the Supreme Court ruled California's land laws were unconstitutional, and thus, so were all other state laws not yet repealed. JACL lobbied for enactment of the McCarran-Walter Act of June 27, 1952 (66 Stat. 163; LeMay and Barkan 1999: 220–225). It amended the quota system's immigration law by giving some quotas to Japanese immigrants and, more importantly from JACL's perspective, allowed for the naturalization of the Issei.

JACL joined with the NAACP in filing an amicus brief for the 1954 *Brown v. Board of Education* case. *Brown*, in effect, ruled as unconstitutional the public school segregation laws based on race (against both Asians and Blacks) in Kansas, Delaware, South Carolina, Virginia, and Washington, D.C. In 1959, JACL won repeal of Idaho's miscegenation law. JACL joined with the NAACP and SCLC in 1963 for the March on Washington. JACL successfully lobbied for enactment of the Civil Rights Acts of 1964, 1965, 1968, and especially enactment of the Immigration and Naturalization Act of October 3, 1965 (79 Stat. 911), which eliminated the quota system (LeMay and Barkan 1999: 257–261). In 1976, JACL succeeded in lobbying President Gerald Ford to rescind Executive Order 9066. President Ford also granted a pardon to Iva Toguri (aka Tokyo Rose) in 1977. In 1983, Congress established the Commission on Wartime Relocation and the Internment of Civilians, and JACL secured overturning the conviction of Fred Korematsu. After sustained lobbying by the JACL, Congress enacted the Civil Liberties Act of August 10, 1988 (102 Stat. 904). It authorized the payment of reparations and issued an official apology to an estimated 60,000 former internment camp internees. In 1989, President George H. W. Bush signed the appropriations bill that funded those redress payments.

Anti-Japanese sentiment still occasionally broke out, for example, in the firebombing of the Sacramento office of the JACL in 1993. But since the 1960s, anti-Japanese sentiment has declined markedly, and JACL has increasingly supported electoral politics by Japanese Americans, exemplified by the election of such national-level politicians as (1) U.S. Senators Daniel Inouye (1963–2012, D-Hawaii), a Medal of Honor recipient for his heroism in World War II; (2) S. I. Hayakawa (1977–1983, R-CA); (3) Spark Matsunaga (1977–1990, D-Hawaii); and (4) Mazie Hirano (2013–present, D-Hawaii). Members of the House of Representatives include (1) Doris Matsui (2005 to present, D-CA); (2) Mike Honda (2001–2017, D-CA); (3) Patsy Mink (1965–1977, D-Hawaii); (4) Norman Mineta (1975–1995, D-CA); (5) Bob Matsui (1979–2005, D-CA); (6) Pat Saiki (1987–1991, R-Hawaii); (7) Colleen Hanabusa (2011–2019, D-Hawaii); and (8) Mark Takano (2013–present, D-CA). As of 2019, there are three U.S. senators and thirteen representatives of Asian American descent.

League of Women Voters (LWV)

The League of Women Voters is a nonpartisan educational and advocacy organization that encourages informed and active participation in government and increased understanding of major public policy issues. LWV works to register voters and provide them with election information through voter guides, candidate and issue forums, and debates. An accommodationist organization, it does so through its education fund. LWV's stated mission is to empower voters and to defend democracy. It believes in the power of women to create a more perfect democracy. LWV is committed to diversity, equity, and inclusion. It was founded on February 14, 1920, by Emma Smith DeVoe and Carrie Chapman Catt. It grew out of the merger between the National American Women's Suffrage Association (1909) and the National Council of Women Voters (1911). LWV began in Chicago, Illinois, where it launched its "mighty political experiment" designed to help 20 million women carry out their new responsibilities as voters following the successful ratification of the Nineteenth Amendment on August 26, 1920. Suffrage leaders, like DeVoe and Catt, mobilized to press their political campaigns in the states (www.lwv.org /about-us/history; Lee, Young, and Young 1989; Laughlin and Castledine 2010).

In 1944–1945, the LWV pressed for establishment of the United Nations. It was one of the first organizations to be recognized by the UN as a non-governmental organization (NGO). LWV maintains that status to this day. In 1957, the League established its Education Fund to take on a more active advocacy rule for registration and information. In 1972, after Congress passed the Equal Rights Amendment (ERA), the LWV supported its goal to ensure "equal rights for all regardless of sex." It campaigned heavily for ratification before the ending date of 1982. Although the ERA failed to be ratified by then, the LWV continues to push for ERA ratification today and legislation (a joint resolution) has been introduced in the Congress that would extend its termination date to allow for ratification. To date, thirty-eight states have ratified the ERA. That is the number needed for the amendment to be ratified and become law, but the extension of the original time limit needs to be passed by the U.S. Congress, so the issue is still pending.

In the 1980s, the LWV sponsored the televised general election presidential debates in 1980 and 1984, as well as presidential primary "forums" in 1980, 1984, and 1988. These events focused on nonpartisan issues with the goal of informing voters. In 1988, the LWV withdrew its sponsorship of the debates and forums when the major parties and candidates demanded increasingly partisan conditions for them. The LWV began a grassroots campaign for national legislation to reform voter registration. It succeeded with enactment of the National Voter Registration Act (107 Stat. 77; the NVRA), also known as the "motor-voter" law. The NVRA's goal was to increase accessibility to the electoral process by enabling citizens to register to vote at motor vehicle agencies automatically, when getting or renewing their driver's license. It allowed for automatic voter registration, as well as by mail and at agencies that service the public, like Health and Human Services and Social Security. NVRA was signed into law by President William Clinton on May 20, 1993, and took effect January 1, 1995.

The 2000 presidential election exposed problems facing the electoral system, as exemplified by the need to finalize voter recounts in Florida. The recount battle necessitated the Supreme Court's decision of *Gore v. Bush* (531 U.S. 98, 2000). After the *Gore* ruling, the LWV began a campaign of electoral reform, working with a coalition of civil rights groups. It helped draft the Help America Vote Act (HAVA), passed in 2002. HAVA established the use of provisional balloting, requirements for updating voting systems, and establishment of the Election Assistance Commission (signed October 29, 2002, 116 Stat. 1666).

In 2006, LWV launched VOTE411.org. It is a website dedicated to voter information by a "one-stop shop" for all election-related information. VOTE411 provides both general and state-specific, nonpartisan resources to the voting public, including a nationwide polling place locator, a ballot look-up tool, and candidate positions on assorted issues. On June 27, 2019, the U.S. Supreme Court, by a 5–4 decision that followed party affiliation of the justices, ruled in *Rucho et al. v. Common Cause,* that partisan gerrymandering cannot be solved by federal courts. In response to *Rucho,* the LWV launched another initiative, the "People Powered Fair Maps Campaign." It is a coordinated effort across all fifty states and Washington, D.C., to create fair and transparent, people-powered redistricting processes designed to eliminate partisan and racial gerrymandering in the creation of electoral districts (www.lwv.org/about).

United Farm Workers (UFW)

The United Farm Workers was founded in 1962 by Cesar Chavez and Dolores Huerta. UFW's current president is Arturo Rodriquez, and it is headquartered in Keene, California. UFW works to promote nonviolence and educate its members, estimated between 10,000 and 11,000, on politics and social issues. It began as a social movement, emerging out of the Community Service Organization with which both Cesar Chavez and Dolores Huerta were affiliated. UFW used a radical protest strategy and tactics to pursue its goals. In 1960, Dolores Huerta was working in Stockton, California when she created the Agricultural Workers Association (AWA). In 1962, Huerta, Cesar Chavez, and Filipino labor leader Larry Itliong organized the Agricultural Workers Organizing Committee (AWOC) to lead a grape pickers' strike in Delano, California. UFW was formed from the AWOC. UFW quickly became a leading organization in the Hispanic civil rights movement, adopting the nonviolence strategy and tactics of Mahatma Gandhi and Martin Luther King Jr. Between 1965 and 1975, UFW held more than 1,000 farmworkers' strikes, boycotts, protests, marches, and hunger strikes (Araiza 2014; Flores 2016; Ganz 2009; Honor 2002; LeMay 2009: 3300–3303; Meier and Gutiérrez 2000; Shaw 2008). The UFW opposed the Bracero Program and helped secure its ending in 1964 (Calavita 1992; LeMay 2019).

In 1966, UFW went to Texas and supported a Texas melon workers' strike (1971–1972) independent of Cesar Chavez. The 1970s were a decade of growth and also growing pains for the UFW and its leaders. In 1977, UFW joined the Teamsters; then in 1980, it joined the AFL-CIO, which helped it launch its national "Wrath of Grapes" campaign. In the 1980s, the UFW opposed bills to enact employer sanctions, which nonetheless became law in 1986 (the Immigration Reform and Control Act of November 6, 1986, 100 Stat. 3360; LeMay and Barkan 1999: 282–288). Tomas Villanueva of the AFC-CIO helped the UFW organize rallies across the country. In 2005–2006, dissatisfied with its relationship with the AFL-CIO, UFW left them to join the labor federation "Change to Win," a labor federation of affiliated unions that promotes a more robust, somewhat more radical approach to unionism than does the AFL-CIO. In 2013, the UFW organized against the Peach Producers, after they had de-certified the UFW. In 2014, UFW supported a lawsuit against the Darigold milk producers by supporting the "Darigold Dozen" in their suit. Also In 2014, the bio-picture *Cesar Chavez* was released (https://doloreshuerta .ogr/dolores-huerta; ufw.org/research/history/ufw-history).

People—Government

There are literally hundreds of government officials for whom pro-files would be appropriate. Length constraints, however, limit this section to ten individuals to exemplify the group. It profiles a Con-gressman, a founding father who drafted the Bill of Rights, four U.S. presidents, and four justices of the U.S. Supreme Court, all of whom influenced civil rights by their careers in government ser-vice. They are presented here in alphabetical order.

Frank, Barney (1940–)

Former Representative Barney Frank (D-MA, 1981–2013) is an excellent example of a gay rights activist who used the political accommodation route to successfully advocate for civil rights (LeMay 2009: 162). Barney Frank was born in Bay-onne, New Jersey, in 1940, into a Jewish working class family. Frank earned a BA in political science at Harvard University in 1962. He taught undergraduate classes in government at Harvard while working toward a PhD degree. Before earning his doctorate, however, Frank left Harvard to work as the chief of staff to Boston Mayor Kevin White. Frank then served as assistant to U.S. Representative Michael Harrington (D-MA). In 1972, Frank was elected to a seat in the Massachusetts state legislature. He supported liberal causes and sponsored a bill to prohibit discrimination in housing and employment on the basis of sexual orientation, the first attempt to protect gay rights in Massachusetts.

While serving in the state legislature, Frank entered Har-vard Law School and earned his law degree in 1977. He served in the state legislature until 1980 and taught part-time at the University of Massachusetts, Boston, at the John F. Kennedy School of Government at Harvard, and at Boston University. Frank passed the Massachusetts bar in 1979. He ran for and won election to the U.S. House of Representa-tives in 1980. Frank quickly emerged as a leader of the liberal wing of the Democratic Party and as an outspoken critic on human rights issues. Frank earned a 100 percent rating from NARAL Pro-Choice America for his pro-choice voting record. He voted against the Partial Birth Abortion Ban bill. Frank chaired the House Judiciary Subcommittee on Administrative Law and Government Relations. He staunchly supported the redress and reparations to Japanese Americans interned in the camps. In 2001, Frank cosponsored an equal rights amendment based on gender. Frank had a 93 percent rating from the ACLU. In 1987, he came out of the closet and declared his homosexuality, the first member of House to do so. In 1998, Frank founded the National Stonewall Democrats, the National LGBT Democratic organization. In 2006, Frank "outed" closeted gay Republicans who had advocated or voted for antigay bills, an action that came to be called the "Frank Rule" (LeMay 2009: 162). In 2009, Frank signed a bill recognizing the fortieth anniversary of the Stonewall Riots and the hundredth anniversary of the NAACP.

Frank was easily reelected to the House in 1990. After the housing market collapse in 2007-2008, which happened while Frank was chair of the House Finance Committee (2007-2011), he and Senator Chris Dodd (D-CT) coauthored the Wall Street Reform and Consumer Protection Act of 2010, known as the Dodd-Frank Act (124 Stat. 1376–2223). Frank won reelection in 2010. In 2013, he wed his longtime partner to become the first sitting representative to enter a same-sex marriage. In 2006, the Human Rights Campaign rated him 100 percent, and in 2014, they named Frank "Humanist of the Year" (Weisberg 2009). Barney Frank retired from the U.S. House of Representatives in 2013, choosing not to run for reelection in the 2014 election. Frank wrote his autobiography, published in 2015 (Frank 2015).

Ginsburg, Ruth Bader (1933–2020)

Ruth Bader Ginsburg (known affectionately simply by RBG) was appointed an associate justice to the U.S. Supreme Court in August 1993 by President William Clinton. She filled the seat vacated by Justice Byron White. RBG was the unquestioned leader of the Supreme Court's liberal ideological bloc, regularly joined by Justices Stephen Breyer, Sonia Sotomayor, and Elena. Kagan. Given the ideological makeup of the current Supreme Court, they often cast dissenting opinions (Wainwright 2019). Since her appointment, Justice Ginsburg was involved in several dozens of important Supreme Court decisions on civil rights and liberty issues. Justice Ginsburg wrote the majority opinion in some; joined with the majority decision on some others; or voted with the liberal justices in dissenting opinions on many others (Carmon 2015; Kanefield 2016; Wainwright 2019). Throughout Justice Ginsburg's long and respected career, she was notably vocal about gender discrimination. Important for civil rights and liberties issues, RBG ruled on fourteen First Amendment cases; two Second Amendment decisions, eight Fourth Amendment cases; five Fifth Amendment cases; five Sixth Amendment cases, and four capital punishment cases.

Justice Ginsburg earned her bachelor's degree from Cornell University, attended Harvard Law, and received her law degree from Columbia Law School, where she graduated first in her class. She clerked for Edmund Palmieri, a judge of the U.S. District Court for the Southern District of New York, from 1959 to 1961. From 1961 to 1963, Ginsburg was a research associate of the Columbia Law School Project on International Procedure, living in Sweden, where she published a book on Swedish civil procedure. In 1963, Ginsburg became a professor at Rutgers University Law School. In 1972, she began teaching at Columbia Law, the first female to earn tenure there. She directed the Women's Rights Project for the ACLU, successfully arguing six landmark cases before the Supreme Court. In 1977–1978, Ginsburg was a fellow at the Center for Advanced Study in the Behavioral Sciences at Stanford University. In 1980, President Jimmy Carter appointed Ruth Bader Ginsburg to the U.S. Court of Appeals for the District of Columbia, a court that has often been a stepping stone to appointment to the U.S. Supreme Court. She served on the Court of Appeals until President Clinton appointed her to the U.S. Supreme Court in 1993.

LBG was born Ruth Bader in Brooklyn, New York. She married Martin Ginsburg in 1954. They had a son and daughter. Martin battled cancer off and on from 1956 until he passed away in 2010. Although she disagreed with Justice Antonin Scalia on most of the cases they heard, Ginsburg and Scalia were close friends in their personal lives, sharing a love for the opera. They voted together, however, on four religious freedom cases: *Church of the Lukumi Bahalu v. City of Hialeah* (1993), *Elk Grove v. Newdow* (2004), *Gonzales v. U.D.V.* (2006), and *Hosanna-Tabor v. E.E.O.C.* (2012).

Ginsburg wrote the majority opinions in *Chandler v. Miller* (1997), an 8–1 Fourth Amendment ruling, and in *Vermont v. Brillon* , a 7–2 ruling regarding the Sixth Amendment's right to a speedy trial. Justice Ginsburg dissented in two Second Amendment cases that were decided 5–4. She participated in several 9–0 rulings on civil rights matters, for example: on the Fourth Amendment challenge of a stop and frisk case (*Florida v. J. l.,* 2000); in *Berghuis v. Smith* (2010) and *Thaler v. Haynes* (2010). Justice Ginsburg voted with the majority in four landmark capital punishment cases: *Harris v. Alabama* (1995, 8–1), *Atkins v. Virginia* (2000, 6–3), *Roper v. Simons* (2005, 5–4), and *Hurst v. Florida* (8–1) (LeMay 2018a: 182–184). Having achieved nearly rock-star status (Carmon 2015), Ruth Bader Ginsburg's life was featured in the biodocumentary, feature-length film released in 2018, titled simply RBG. It was nominated for an academy award for best documentary film. She wrote her autobiography, *My Own Words*, published in 2018. RBG died of pancreatic cancer, after many years of battling cancer, on September 18, 2020. She was much respected by all her colleagues on the Court and on both sides of the aisle in the U.S. Congress.

Jefferson, Thomas (1743–1826)

Thomas Jefferson was one of the Founding Fathers and known as the principle author of the Declaration of Independence, and its expression of the "inalienable rights of life, liberty, and the pursuit of happiness." By that expression, Jefferson meant that those civil and human rights could not be taken away or nullified by government. He served as the first secretary of state (1789–1794), as the second vice president (1787–1801), and as the third president (1801–1809) (Jefferson 1914; Meacham 2012).

Thomas Jefferson was an early advocate of the total separation of church and state, and he drafted the Virginia Statute of Religious Liberty in 1777, which was finally ratified in 1786. That accomplishment was one of three lifetime achievements that Jefferson had ordered to be inscribed on his gravestone (Yarbough 2006). He was Virginia's representative to the Second Continental Congress in 1875. Jefferson was born in Virginia in 1743, and died there, at Monticello, on July 4, 1826. Jefferson attended William and Mary College. In drafting the Declaration of Independence, Jefferson became known as the "Apostle of Liberty." Along with fellow Founding Father, George Mason, Jefferson was instrumental in drafting the Bill of Rights. Jefferson interpreted the First Amendment as having built a "wall of separation between church and state," the idea of which was cited by the Supreme Court in several decisions involving challenges based on the establishment clause. Jefferson also notably supported the expansion of voting rights by dropping the property requirements for suffrage (Keyssar 2009; Yarbough 2006).

As president, Jefferson was responsible for negotiating the Louisiana Purchase from France in 1803. It essentially doubled the size of the United States, and added a significant population of Roman Catholic adherents (from the Spanish and French colonies) to the American population at a time when Catholics were still highly suspected as to their essential loyalty, and often discriminated against by the Protestant majority in the United States (LeMay 2018b; Zentner and LeMay 2020). Residents of the Louisiana Purchase territory became U.S. citizens by treaty right. Jefferson negotiated the purchase despite the fact that the Constitution made no provision for the acquisition of new land. The newly acquired Louisiana Purchase lands were allowed to enter the United States as slave states.

Jefferson owned a huge plantation, known as Monticello, with some 200 slaves. Over his lifetime, he may have owned as many as 600 slaves, who made possible the construction of Monticello and the running of his huge estate. In 1800, Jefferson became president when the U.S. House of Representatives selected him to break a tie with Aaron Burr in the Electoral College vote. He went on to win reelection in 1804 and is considered (along with James Madison) as the architect of the Democratic-Republican Party and establishment of the first American political party regime (Zentner and LeMay 2020: 25). Jefferson opposed and saw the ending of the infamous Alien and Sedition Acts (1 Stat. 570, June 25, 1798; LeMay and Barkan 1999: 15–16). Jefferson and the Jeffersonian Democratic-Republicans opposed the Federalist Party's position on naturalization, and Jefferson signed into law the Act of April 14, 1802 (54 Stat. 1172). It set the residency requirement for naturalization back from fourteen years under the Federalists to the current five-year residency requirement, thereby speeding up the process for immigrants to acquire citizenship status and the civil rights and liberties "privileges and immunities" that come with citizenship (Jefferson 1914; Meacham 2012; Keyssar 2009; Yarbough 2006).

Johnson, Lyndon (1908–1973)

Then–Vice President Lyndon B. Johnson became the thirty-sixth president on November 22, 1963, assuming the office upon the assassination of President John F. Kennedy. Lyndon Johnson arguably had the most extensive impact on civil rights legislation of any U.S. president, notably with his signing of the Civil Rights Acts of 1964, 1965, and 1968. He had earlier impacted the first amendment freedoms issue of tax exemption when, in 1954, as then United States Senator from Texas and Senate Majority Leader, Lyndon Johnson sponsored what came to be known as the "Johnson Amendment." It made significant changes to the IRS tax code by essentially prohibiting tax-exempt religious organizations from either endorsing or opposing candidates for elective political office. The amendment affected churches and other 501(c) tax-exempt organizations. The religious right launched a vigorous and concerted attempt to repeal the Johnson Amendment, to date without success. Critics of the amendment, however, note that the IRS has been extraordinarily lax in enforcement of the ban.

As president, Lyndon Johnson appointed Abe Fortas as associate justice of the Supreme Court. Fortas served from 1965 to 1969 and wrote the majority opinion in *Epperson v. Arkansas* (393 U.S. 97, 1968), a 7–2 ruling that banned teaching creationism from public school curricula.

Lyndon Johnson was born in 1908, in Texas, not far from Johnson City, which his family had founded. He worked his way through Southwest Texas State Teachers College and taught Mexican American students. In 1937, Johnson was elected to the U.S. House of Representatives. When the United States entered World War II, Johnson left Congress to serve in the U.S. Navy as a navy lieutenant commander in the South Pacific, and he earned a Silver Star. After the war, in the 1948 elections, Johnson won the U.S. Senate from Texas. In 1960, he was elected vice president. He ran for president and won by a landslide in 1964, defeating the Republican nominee, Senator Barry Goldwater (R-AZ), with 61 percent of the popular vote. As elected president who could claim a mandate, Johnson proposed a package of bills he called the "Great Society." LBJ strove to achieve an FDR-like First 100 Days. He urged passage of a baker's dozen bills considered part of the Great Society program: (1) the Higher Education Facilities Act of 1963 (77 Stat. 363), (2) the Equal Opportunity Act of 1964 (20 Stat. 1701), (3) the Housing Act of 1964 (82 Stat. 73), (4) the Civil Rights Act of 1964 (78 Stat. 241), (5) the Civil Rights Act of 1965 (79 Stat. 437), (6) a major tax cut, (7) enactment of the 1965 Medicare amendment to the Social Security Act of

1965 (79 Stat. 286), (8) the Freedom of Information Act of 1966 (80 Stat. 250), (9) the Age Discrimination in Employment Act of 1967 (81 Stat. 602), (10) the Bilingual Education Act of 1968 (81 Stat. 816), (12) the Gun Control Act of 1968 (82 Stat. 1213), and (13) the Fair Housing Act of 1968 (82 Stat. 73). That 1968 law dealt with racial discrimination in housing and ensured Native American civil rights (Caro 2012).

President Johnson worked notably and publicly with Reverend Martin Luther King Jr. President Johnson's success in getting the 1964, 1965, and 1968 Civil Rights Acts passed helped enormously in shifting African American electoral support to the Democratic Party (Zentner and LeMay 2020: 196–203). As the Vietnam War escalated, Johnson approved a massive increase in military forces engaged in the conflict (Woods 2006). Subsequent intense political controversy over the Vietnam War led Johnson to withdraw as a candidate for reelection to the presidency in 1968 (Gould 2010). He died suddenly of a heart attack at his Texas ranch on January 22, 1973.

Lewis, John (1940–2020)

John Lewis served as a member of the U.S. House of Representatives from the Fifth District of Georgia from 1987 until his death in 2020. He was hailed as the "conscience of the Congress." He was a giant in the civil rights movement. He exemplifies the direct-action "new-style radicalism" approach to civil rights advocacy, and he went on to become a leading voice in the U.S. House of Representative, thereby also exemplifying the political accommodation style (LeMay 2009).

John Lewis was the son a sharecroppers, born outside of Troy, Alabama. He was inspired to civil rights activism by the Montgomery Bus Boycott and the preaching of the Rev. Martin Luther King Jr. He remained at the vanguard of progressive social movements and the struggle for human rights ever since, most recently giving prominent support to the Black Lives Matter movement. Lewis was a spellbinding preacher and orator who moved the public and his fellow Congressmen with his eloquence and his moral leadership example. Lewis graduated from the American Baptist Theological Seminary in Nashville, Tennessee and was an ordained Baptist minister. He went on to study at Fisk University, earning a bachelor's degree in religion and philosophy. While in Nashville, Lewis organized the Nashville Student Movement that pioneered sit-ins at segregated lunch counters. In 1961, he was one of the original thirteen Freedom Riders sponsored by CORE, after the Supreme Court ruling against segregation laws regarding interstate busing, in the decision in *Boyton v. Virginia* (364 U.S. 454, 1960). Lewis and all the Riders suffered extreme violence committed against them. From 1963 to 1966, Lewis was chairman of the Student Nonviolent Coordinating Committee (SNCC), and at age twenty-three, he was recognized as one of the "Big Six" civil rights leaders (comprising the Rev. Martin Luther King Jr. of the Southern Christian Leadership Conference, James Farmer of CORE, John Lewis of SNCC, A. Philip Randolph, founder of the Brotherhood of Sleeping Car Porters; Roy Wilkins of the NAACP, and Whitney Young of the National Urban League). Lewis was one of the major organizers of the 1963 March on Washington and the youngest person to speak at the Lincoln Memorial event at which Martin Luther King Jr. delivered his famous "I Have a Dream" speech. In 1964 Lewis coordinated SNCC's "Mississippi Freedom Summer." On March 7, 1965, at age twenty-five, Lewis led 600 marchers across the Edmund Pettus Bridge in Selma, Alabama, in the event that came to be known as "Bloody Sunday," during which he was nearly beaten to death and suffered severe head injuries evident for the remainder of his life. He was arrested more than forty times, sustaining physical attacks and serious injuries, yet always remained an advocate of nonviolent protest and civil disobedience in an effort to overturn Jim Crow–era de jure segregation laws.

In 1977 Lewis served in the Carter administration as director of ACTION, running the VISTA program and directing more than 250,000 volunteers. Lewis went on to be elected to the Atlanta City Council in 1981, serving from 1982 to 1985. In 1986 he was elected to the U.S. House of Representatives. In the House he served on the powerful Committee on Ways and Means and on the Joint Committee on Taxation. He was a leading member of the Congressional Black Caucus and the Congressional Progressive Caucus. In 1991, Lewis was selected to the party leadership as Senior Chief Deputy Whip of the Democratic Caucus. In 1988, he first introduced a bill to establish a National Museum of African American History and Culture and campaigned for the bill annually for fifteen years before President George W. Bush signed the bill into law in 2003. The museum was constructed in the Smithsonian complex, adjacent to the Washington Memorial, and was opened on September 25, 2016. In 2008 Lewis backed then-senator Barack Obama in his presidential bid, serving as a superdelegate to the national convention. Lewis backed Hillary Clinton for president in 2016. Also notably in 2016, Lewis led his fellow House Democratic members in a "sit-in" on the House floor, when they were in the minority, to advocate for firearms safety. Lewis was a frequent and outspoken opponent of President Trump's policies.

John Lewis was the recipient of numerous awards and fifty honorary degrees from prestigious universities. In 2011, he was honored with the Medal of Freedom by President Barack Obama. He received the Capital Award from the National Council of La Raza, the Martin Luther King Jr. Non-Violent Peace Prize, the NAACP's Spingarn Medal, the National Education Association's Martin Luther King Jr. Memorial Award, and the John F. Kennedy Profile in Courage Award for Lifetime Achievement by the John F. Kennedy Library Foundation.

John Lewis authored several books: *Across That Bridge* (with Brenda Jones, 2012) and his 1998 autobiography, *Walking with the Wind: A Memoir of the Movement* (with Mike D'Orso). He coauthored a three-book series of graphic novels (with Andrew Aydin) that made the *New York Times* best-selling list and are used in schools across the nation to teach the Civil

Rights Movement to the next generation of young activists. He is the subject of two notable biographies: *John Lewis in the Lead: A Story of the Civil Rights Movement* (Haskins and Benson, 2006) and *John Lewis: From Freedom Rides to Congressman* (Hill, 2002).

John Lewis died from pancreatic cancer on July 17, 2020, much revered on both sides of the aisle and in both chambers of the U.S. Congress.

Lincoln, Abraham (1809–1865)

Abraham Lincoln was the sixteenth president of the United States, and historians have consistently rated him number one among presidents (Goodwin 2005). As president, Lincoln led the United States successfully through the Civil War, abolished slavery, strengthened the federal government, and modernized the U.S. economy. Abraham Lincoln was a self-made lawyer, a leader of the Whig Party (prior to 1854), and leader of the Republican Party (1854–1864) (Foner 1995; Gould 2003). He put his stamp on the Republican Party that emphasized personal liberty and equality (Zentner and LeMay 2020: 120–121).

Lincoln served in the Illinois House of Representatives as a Whig from 1834 to 1842. In the state house, Lincoln became noted for his antislavery views. Lincoln had previously served in the Illinois militia in 1832, during the Black Hawk War. In 1842 Lincoln married Mary Todd. In 1847–1849, Lincoln served in the U.S. House of Representatives, again as a Whig. While in the House, Lincoln notably opposed the Mexican-American War (1848). He emerged as a Republican Party leader in 1854, and in 1856 Lincoln opposed the Kansas-Nebraska Act. In 1858 Lincoln ran for the U.S. Senate, against Stephen Douglas. The Lincoln-Douglas debates gained him national prominence. Although he lost the Senate race to Douglas, he is considered to have "won" the debates, as they propelled him to the nomination of the party for president in 1860. In 1858, Lincoln delivered his famous "A House

Divided" speech, and in 1860, he gave the "Cooper-Union" speech, both of which were instrumental in his securing the nomination and election to the presidency. Lincoln won the office in the 1860 election with 38.8 percent of the vote in a four-person race. Lincoln received 180 electoral college votes to Southern Democrat John Breckenridge's 72, Constitutional Union Party's John Bell's 39, and Northern Democrat Stephen Douglas's 12. Lincoln took office in a deeply divided country that soon broke out into the Civil War.

Lincoln appointed thirty-two federal district judges during his presidency and, importantly, five justices to the U.S. Supreme Court: Noah Swayne in 1862, Samuel Miller in 1862, David Davis in 1862, Stephen Field in 1863, and Salmon Chase, as Chief Justice, in 1864.

Lincoln signed the Homestead Act of 1862, which granted land to homesteaders and greatly attracted immigrants and settlers to the western states. In1862, he also signed the Pacific Railway Act, which contributed federal funds to the construction of the transcontinental railroad. He strengthened the U.S. economy as well by signing the National Banking Act of 1862. In 1863, Lincoln declared Thanksgiving Day as a national holiday—a symbolic gesture that Lincoln took to help unify a divided nation. During Lincoln's presidency, two states were added to the Union: West Virginia in 1863, and Nevada in 1864. Lincoln became known as "the Great Emancipator" when he issued the Emancipation Proclamation on September 22, 1862, which took effect January 1, 1863. It affirmed the freedom of slaves in 10 Confederate states. Lincoln gave his famous "Gettysburg Address" on November 19, 1863. It is considered to be the most often-quoted speech in American history. Lincoln won reelection in 1864 and delivered his second inaugural address on March 4, 1865. In it, Lincoln supported a moderate approach to reconstruction. He pardoned a group of Native Americans from sentences to hanging and was chided that his decision cost him votes. He reportedly said, "I could not afford to hang men for votes." Although he died before he could see the law passed, Lincoln supported what became the Civil Rights Act of April 6, 1866 (14 Stat. 27–60). It passed by an override of President Andrew Johnson's veto. Lincoln supported the Thirteenth Amendment, abolishing slavery, which passed in the Senate on April 8, 1864, and in the House on April 14, 1865. Lincoln was assassinated on April 15, 1865. The Thirteenth Amendment was ratified and became law on December 6, 1865.

Madison, James (1751–1836)

James Madison was a founding father, and the fourth president (1809–1817). The Virginia-born Madison composed the first drafts of the Constitution and the Bill of Rights, earning him the nickname "Father of the Constitution." He was a principal advocate of their passage in the Congress and a strong spokesperson for their ratification. Along with Thomas Jefferson, he founded the Democratic-Republican Party, America's first opposition party (to the Federalists) (Zentner and LeMay 2020). James Madison served President Thomas Jefferson as secretary of state, negotiating the Louisiana Purchase from France in 1803. Having been a coauthor of the Virginia religious freedom law, Madison supported the citizenship of the many Roman Catholics—then an often discriminated-against religious minority—who resided in the Louisiana territory.

Madison was born in Virginia in 1761, the oldest of twelve children. He was raised on the family plantation, Montpelier. In 1769, Madison attended the College of New Jersey (today's Princeton University). In 1776, he represented Orange County at the Virginia Constitutional Convention and to organize a new government independent of Britain. While in the Virginia legislature, he and his lifelong friend, Thomas Jefferson, fought for a religious freedom statute. The Virginia Statute for Religious Freedom advocated both freedom of conscience and the principle of the separation of church and state. It was enacted into law by the Virginia General Assembly in 1786 and is widely viewed as the direct forerunner of the First

Amendment's religious freedom clauses (both the Establishment Clause and the Free Exercise Clause). In 1780, he became a Virginia delegate to the Continental Congress in Philadelphia, held to amend the Articles of Confederation. In 1787, at the Constitutional Convention, Madison presented the "Virginia Plan." It detailed a separation of powers and a system of checks and balances with three parts: legislative, executive, and judicial branches. Madison led the efforts to get the new Constitution ratified, writing a number of essays anonymously under the title "The Federalist Papers." In all, the Federalist Papers contained eighty-five essays written between 1787 and 1788. The other two authors were Alexander Hamilton and John Jay. When the Constitution was ratified in 1788, Madison was elected to the newly formed House of Representatives, where he served from 1789 to 1797. He drafted the Bill of Rights along with George Mason, as he had promised to do during the Constitutional Convention. The original proposal had twelve amendments, but only ten were ratified and became what is now known as the Bill or Rights. Madison and Jefferson founded the Democratic-Republican Party in 1792. Madison, Jefferson, and Monroe became Democratic-Republicans elected to the presidency. In 1794, Madison, at age forty-three, married twenty-six year old Dolly Todd, a Quaker, at the time, a widow with one son. During their forty-one years of marriage they were rarely apart. In 1803, Madison was party to the Supreme Court case *Marbury v. Madison* (5 U.S. 137, 1803), by which Chief Justice John Marshall declared the Supreme Court's power of judicial review. Then the secretary of state to President Thomas Jefferson, James Madison refused to deliver a justice of the peace commission to William Marbury. The case concerned Madison's denial of an appointment of Marbury, which Chief Justice Marshall and the U.S. Supreme Court held to be illegal and unconstitutional. When Jefferson became the third president, he appointed Madison as his secretary of state (1801–1809). In 1809, Madison defeated Federalist Charles Pinckney to win the presidential office. In 1811, Madison appointed two justices to the U.S. Supreme Court—Gabriel Duvall and Joseph Story—but neither altered the Federalist leanings of the Supreme Court. Madison also appointed eleven other federal appellate judges and nine federal district judges. Madison died at Montpelier at age eighty-five in June 1836 (Hagedorn and LeMay 2019: 202–204).

Marshall, Thurgood (1908–1993)

Thurgood Marshall was, arguably, one of the most significant contributors to civil rights law in United States history—as a lawyer advocate of the NAACP, as U.S. Solicitor General, and finally as an associate justice of the U.S. Supreme Court (Davis and Clark 1992; Rawn 2010; Marshall and Tushnet 2001; Tushnet 1994). Marshall was the grandson of a slave. He graduated from Lincoln University (a predominantly black institution) in 1930. He went on to Howard University Law School and earned his law degree in 1933. At Howard, Marshall was greatly influenced by its dean, Charles Hamilton Houston (Rawn 2010). After graduating from Howard, he became a special counsel for the Baltimore branch of the NAACP (Mack 2012). His first successful case was in 1935–1936, when Marshall won a Maryland Court of Appeals case against the University of Maryland for refusing to admit Donald Murray (*Murray v. Pearson,*169 Md 478, 1936). Marshall went on to win twenty-nine Supreme Court cases, among them, successfully arguing against the South's white primary in *Smith v. Allwright* (321 U.S. 649, 1944). In 1948, he won *Shelley v. Kraemer*, which struck down racially restrictive covenants. In 1950, Marshall won two cases, *Sweat v. Painter* (339 U.S. 629) and *McLaurin v. Oklahoma State Regents* (339 U.S. 637), which overturned segregated graduate schools. In 1954, Marshall successfully argued the landmark case of *Brown v. Board of Education of Topeka, Kansas* (347 U.S. 483). It overturned *Plessy v. Ferguson's* separate-but-equal doctrine and held all segregated public schools unconstitutional. In the view of many historians, *Brown* launched the modern Black civil rights movement (Davis and Clark 1992; Mack 2012; Rawn 2010; Tushnet 1994; Vile 2003).

In 1961, President John F. Kennedy appointed Marshall to the Second Court of Appeals. As Court of Appeals judge, Marshall made 112 rulings, all of which were upheld by the U.S. Supreme Court. In 1965, President Lyndon Johnson appointed Marshall as U.S. Solicitor General (1965–1967), during which time he won fourteen of the nineteen cases that he argued for the government. Over his career, Marshall won more cases before the Supreme Court than any other American (Vile 2003). In 1967, President Johnson named him to the U.S. Supreme Court, the first African American to so serve. Thurgood Marshall served on the highest court until 1991.

While on the Supreme Court, Marshall was its most consistent proponent of civil rights and one of its most influential liberal justices. He wrote the majority opinion in *United States v. Lovasco* (1977), the 8–1 decision on the Sixth Amendment. During the 1960s and 1970s, Marshall joined in a number of unanimous decisions, such as other Sixth Amendment cases like *Smith v. Hooey* (1969), *Dickey v. Florida* (1970), *Baker v. Wingo* (1972), and *Strunk v. United States* (1973). Thurgood Marshall joined the majority in the Fourth Amendment case of *Terry v. Ohio* (8–1, 1968), the Fifth Amendment case of *Roe v. Wade* (7–2, 1973), the Sixth Amendment case of *Braden v. 30th Circuit Court, Kentucky* (6–3, 1973), and *Regents of the University of California v. Bakke* (8–1, 1978), an affirmative action case (Davis and Clark 1992; Vile 2003).

In the 1980s, however, when the Court became more conservative under Chief Justice William Rehnquist, Justice Marshall increasingly joined the dissent side, for example, on such Second Amendment cases as *Lewis v. United States* (6–3, 1980) and *United States v. Verdugo-Urquirdez* (6–3, 1990), or the Fourth Amendment case *United States v. Ross* (6–3, 1982). Marshall dissented in Sixth Amendment cases like *United States v. McDonald* (6–3, 1982) and *United States v. Loud Hawk* (5–4, 1986) and in two capital punishment cases, *Spaziano v. Florida*

(6–3, 1984) and *Walton v. Arizona* (5–4, 1990). Indeed, Marshall has been described as a warrior at the bar and a rebel on the bench (Davis and Clark 1992; Marshall and Tushnet 2001; Tushnet 2008). Thurgood Marshall retired from the Supreme Court in 1991, in declining health, and passed away in 1993.

Mason, George (1725–1792)

George Mason has been called the "Forgotten Father" (Broadwater 2006). Mason was a delegate to the Constitutional Convention of 1787 from the state of Virginia. He was one of three delegates who refused to sign the document (the other two were Eldridge Gerry, from Massachusetts, and Edmund Randolph, also from Virginia). Mason refused to sign the Constitution because it lacked a Bill of Rights. George Mason was the primary author of the Virginia Declaration of Rights (other contributors were James Madison, Thomas Jefferson, Thomas Lee, and Robert Nichols). It became the basis for the U.S. Bill of Rights, of which Mason is also considered the primary author. He and fellow Virginia delegate James Madison also drafted the Virginia Plan. Whereas James Madison is one of the unnamed authors of the Federalist Papers, written to justify ratification of the new constitution, George Mason wrote *Objections to the Constitution* "a document circulated among many of the delegates and later published in the *Virginia Journal*," in October 1787, laying out his argument that it needed to have a Bill of Rights (Rutland 1980).

George Mason was born in Virginia, near present-day Fairfax, on December 11, 1725, and he died there at his manor, Gunston Hall, on October 7, 1792. He authored the constitution for the state of Virginia and served as a delegate from the state to the Constitutional Convention of 1788 during which he strenuously, but unsuccessfully, fought to include a Bill of Rights. His arguments, however, prepared the way for James Madison to include them during the first Congress in 1789.

In 1747, Mason was named a judge of Fairfax County. His experience as judge influenced his legal thinking and convinced him of the need for a listing of rights. He served as a colonel in the Fairfax militia. He married Ann Elbeck and thereby joined the Mason and Elbeck estates to form one of the largest land-holdings in the Virginia colony. In 1755, he built Gunston Hall, the estate's manor house. Mason was a friend of George Washington until their rift over the U.S. Constitution (Rutland 1980). From 1758 until 1775, Mason served in the Virginia House of Burgesses. It was during that time that Mason became increasingly dissatisfied with the English government's policies toward the colonies, and he gradually became a rebel. He opposed the Sugar Tax of 1764 and the Stamp Act of 1765. He helped pass the Virginia Resolves (probably written by Patrick Henry). His views on the Resolves were echoed in the Virginia Declaration of Rights, which Mason drafted in 1775, along with a plan for a Virginia government that became its constitution in 1776. It established the Commonwealth of Virginia. In the Virginia government plan, Mason stressed "toleration of religion," where James Madison insisted on full religious liberty. In it, Mason stressed the concept that all sovereign power stems from the people (Miller 1975). Mason served in the Virginia House of Delegates from 1776 to 1781.

Although George Mason owned slaves all his life, he supported the abolishment of trade in slavery. But Mason supported the provision in the Constitution that protected slavery as an institution. The view that retention of slavery was an economic necessity for the South became the "original sin" of the new Constitution, but this view was common to all of the delegates to the convention from the South. Some of Mason's biographers maintain that he personally opposed slavery. Supreme Court Justice Sandra Day O'Connor is noted as saying: "George Mason's greatest contribution to the present-day constitution was his influence on the Bill of Rights" (cited in Miller 1975: 153).

Rehnquist, William (1924–2005)

William Rehnquist was born in Milwaukee, Wisconsin, in 1924. He married Natalie Cornell in 1953. Rehnquist graduated from Harvard University (a BA and MA in political science) and earned his JD from Stanford Law School, graduating in the same law class as Sandra Day O'Connor. Rehnquist served in the U.S. Army Air Force during World War II (LeMay 2018a: 190–191).

With a total of thirty-three years on the Court, William Rehnquist was one of the longest serving U.S. Supreme Court justices. He was an associate justice from 1972 to 1986 and was Chief Justice from 1986 to 2005. As Chief Justice, Rehnquist led the Court toward what has been described as "judicial activism of the right," tilting the Court increasingly toward conservative rulings (Schwartz 2003). During Rehnquist's years as Chief Justice, the Supreme Court trended toward more split-decision rulings (e.g., more 5–4 or 6–3 decisions, as opposed to the 7–2, 8–1, or even unanimous rulings more common during the Warren Court) (LeMay 2009; Hudson 2006; Schwartz 2003; Tushnet 2005).

During his years as associate justice William Rehnquist often wrote dissenting opinions, sometimes even notable solo dissents (Tushnet 2008; Vile 2003). He dissented in the Fourth Amendment case *Florida v. Royer* (5–4, 1983) and the Fifth Amendment case of *Roe v. Wade* (7–2, 1973). He also dissented on the Sixth Amendment case of *Braden v. 30th Circuit Court* (6–3, 1973) and on the capital punishment cases of *Woodson v. North Carolina* (5–4, 1976) and *Godfrey v. Georgia* (6–3, 1980).

As Chief Justice, Rehnquist wrote several notable majority opinions: a Second Amendment case, *United States v. Verdugo-Urqirdez* (6–3, 1990) and a Fourth Amendment case, *Ohio v. Robinette* (8–1, 1996). He wrote the majority opinion in the Fifth Amendment case, a unanimous ruling in *United States v. Felix* (1992). Rehnquist influenced the Court by managing its docket. Notable cases in which Rehnquist dissented while Chief Justice include the Second Amendment case of *Planned Parenthood v. Casey* (5–4, 1992) and the Fourth Amendment case *Chandler v. Miller* (8–1, 1997, in which Rehnquist wrote the sole dissenting opinion). Rehnquist was among the dissenting votes in several Fifth Amendment cases: *Lawrence v. Texas* (6–3, 2003), *Rasul v. Bush* (6–3, 2004), *Kelo v. City of New London* (5–4, 2005), and in the capital punishment case of *Atkins v. Virginia* (6–3, 2002). His record on civil rights and liberties cases can be described as consistently conservative rather than expansive of such rights.

Justice Rehnquist wrote the majority opinion of four First Amendment freedom of religion cases, all decided by 5–4 votes: *Stone v. Graham* (1980), *Bowen v. Kendrick* (1988), *Zobrest v. Catalina Foothills School District* (1993), and *Zelman v. Simmons-Harris* (2002) (LeMay 2020).

As Chief Justice, and as per the constitutional provision, Justice Rehnquist presided over the U.S. Senate impeachment trial of President William Clinton. He also managed the Supreme Court in its highly controversial 5–4 decision in *Bush v. Gore* (2000) (Hudson 2006; Obermayer 2009). The *Bush v. Gore* ruling has been criticized as blatantly partisan, and the decision injected the Court into electoral politics in a way that historically has been more often eschewed by the Court. The *Bush v.* Gore decision undoubtedly contributed to his reputation as being a "judicial activist of the right" (Schwartz 2003). Rehnquist died of thyroid cancer, while on the bench, in September 2005.

Warren, Earl (1891–1974)

If William Rehnquist is characterized as a "judicial activist of the right," Earl Warren is widely viewed as the Supreme Court's primary judicial activist of the left (Belknap 2005; Newton 2006; Tushnet 1996). Earl Warren was Chief Justice of the U.S. Supreme Court from 1953 to 1969. He led the Court during its most activist period regarding civil rights and civil liberties. Warren guided the Court when it developed and most often used the judicial doctrine of incorporation to extend the protections of the Bill of Rights to state and local governments (Powe 2000; Urofsky 2001).

Earl Warren was born in Los Angeles in 1891. Warren attended the University of California, Berkeley, earning his BA in political science in 1913 and his LLB in 1914. During World War I, Warren served in the U.S. Army as a first lieutenant (1917–1918). He was chair of the Republican Party of California from 1932 to 1939 and was district attorney of Alameda County from 1925 to 1939. Earl Warren was elected attorney general of California in 1938, and it was while he was attorney general that Warren supported the Japanese relocation and internment programs in 1942, a decision he came to regret by 1944. He wrote in his memoirs: "Whenever I thought of the innocent little children who were torn from home, school, friends, and congenial surroundings, I was conscience stricken. . . . It was wrong to react so impulsively, without positive evidence of disloyalty" (Warren 1977; LeMay 2009: 83–85). At the time, however, it was unquestionably the popular stand to take, and Warren was elected to and served as Governor of California from 1943 to 1953. He was appointed as Chief Justice of the Supreme Court by President Dwight Eisenhower in 1953. President Eisenhower appointed him Chief Justice, believing that in doing so, he was getting a solid conservative. Eisenhower later indicated that his appointment of Warren was one of his biggest mistakes as president, and one that he regretted making (Hitchcock 2018; LeMay 2009: 284–285).

As Chief Justice, Warren wrote the majority opinion in a number of landmark civil rights–relevant cases: *Brown v. Board of Education* (1954, a unanimous ruling), *Klopfer v. North Carolina* (1967, an unanimous Sixth Amendment ruling), *Reynolds v. Sims* (1964, an 8–1 ruling), *Miranda v. Arizona* (1966, a 6–3 Fifth Amendment decision), and *Loving v. Virginia* (1967, a unanimous Tenth and Fourteenth Amendment ruling). In managing the Court, Warren worked hard at achieving unanimous or highly consensus decisions (that is, more than seven justices agreeing with the rulings).

Under Chief Justice Earl Warren, the Court issued "incorporation" rulings (saying that the Bill of Rights applies to state and local government, and not just federal) in such notable cases as *Mapp v. Ohio* (1961), *Engle v. Vitale* (1962), *Gideon v. Wainwright* (1963), *Escobedo v. Illinois* (1964), *New York Times v. Sullivan* (1964), *Reynolds v. Sims* (1964), *Wesberry v. Sanders* (1964), *United States v. Seeger* (1965), *Griswold v. Connecticut* (1965), *Miranda v. Arizona* (1966), *United States v. O'Brien* (1968), *Tinker v. Des Moines* (1969), and *Brandenburg v. Ohio* (1969). The Court also upheld the constitutionality of the 1964 Civil Rights Act under Chief Justice Earl Warren in *Heart of Atlanta Motel Inc. v. United States* (1964).

Chief Justice Warren concurred in the 1962 decision of *Fong Foo v. United States* (7–2, regarding the Fifth Amendment) and in *Katz v. United States* (1967, 7–1) and in two Sixth Amendment decisions, *United States v. Ewell* (1966, 7–2) and a unanimous decision in *Smith v. Hooey* (1969).

After President Kennedy's assassination, Earl Warren led the Warren Commission's investigation into the assassination. Earl Warren retired from the Court in 1969. He timed his retirement to enable President Johnson to replace him on the Court and to prevent President Nixon from having the opportunity to do so (Warren 1977). Earl Warren died in California in 1974.

People—Nongovernment

There are many dozens of civil rights activists who could appropriately be profiled here, but space constraints limit this section to fifteen. They are selected to exemplify the various strategies and tactics used (accommodation, economic or political; separatism, physical or psychological; or radicalism, old-style or new-style). They were selected to represent various groups for which discrimination was a problem (e.g., age, gender, national origin, race, religion, and sexual orientation). They span various times in the civil rights struggle (LeMay 2009).

Addams, Jane (1860–1936)

Jane Addams was an American settlement activist, social reformer, early sociologist, social worker, women's suffrage activist, and public administrator. She exemplifies economic accommodation. She cofounded the Hull House and the ACLU. When she died in 1936, she was arguably the best known female public figure in the United States and among its most prominent reformers.

Jane Addams's father was an active Republican who supported Abraham Lincoln. Jane attended the Rockford Female Seminary, graduating in 1881, and was a Phi Beta Kappa member. In 1888 she and Ellen Gates Starr cofounded the Hull House, in Chicago. It became a center for research, empirical analysis, study, and debate. It studied issues like housing, midwifery, tuberculosis, typhoid, addiction, and truancy—all problems facing the wide mixture of immigrant groups that populated the neighborhood served by Hull House. Addams and Starr also cofounded the Chicago Public School Art Society. In 1901, they cofounded the Juvenile Protective Association. Jane Addams became known as the "Mother of Social Work" and was a charter member of the American Sociological Society (1905). She was a lifelong lesbian, in long-term relationships with Starr and Mary Rozel Smith. In 1898, she joined the Peace Movement and the Anti-Imperialist League and, in 1915, the Women's Peace Party. In 1917, Addams joined the Fellowship of Reconciliation. In recognition of her work, she was the first woman to be awarded the Nobel Peace Prize in 1931. Addams was the first woman to be awarded an honorary degree by Yale University (Berson 2004; Knight 2010; Joselin 2004; Tyrkus, Bronski, and Gomez 1997).

Andrus, Ethel Percy (1884–1967)

Ethel Percy Andrus was a teacher, activist for the elderly, and founder of the AARP. She exemplifies the economic accommodation approach to coping with discrimination. She was born in San Francisco in 1884, but raised in Chicago. Ethel Andrus earned an undergraduate degree in philosophy from the University of Chicago in 1903 and began her lifetime career in education. She began teaching in Chicago and became active with the Hull House and the Chicago Commons social movements. In 1910, Andrus moved to California, where she taught German, English, and manual arts at the Santa Paula High School. At age thirty-two, Ethel Andrus was appointed principal of Abraham Lincoln High School, California's first-ever female high school principal. In 1927, Andrus organized the Foundation to Assist California Teachers. She became active with the California Retired Teachers Association. In 1947, she founded the National Retired Teachers Association, which became the AARP in 1958. In 1961, Andrus began "Freedom Home" in Washington, D.C., for the White House Conference on Aging. She was inducted into the National Women's Hall of Fame in 1993. Andrus vigorously promoted AARP and the civil rights of the elderly until her death in 1967 at age eighty-three. Coincidentally, that year AARP reached the milestone of one million members (www.aarp.org/politics-society/history /ethel-percy-andrus; Walker 2018).

Baker, Ella (1903–1986)

Ella Baker was an African American civil rights and human rights activist. She exemplifies the new-style radicalism approach (LeMay 2009: 45). Ella Baker was born in Norfolk, Virginia, in 1903. She attended Shaw University in Raleigh, North Carolina. In the 1930s, during the Great Depression, Ella worked as an editorial assistant at the *Negro National News* (www.ellabakercenter.org/about/who-was-ella-baker). Baker then worked for the Worker's Education Project in the Works Progress Administration, a program of FDR's New Deal. In 1938, Ella Baker became active with the NAACP, becoming one of their best recruiters in the South (Moye 2013). In 1944–1946, Baker directed the NAACP's Leadership Conferences in Chicago and Atlanta. Ella Baker worked with all the major civil rights leaders: W.E.B. Du Bois, Thurgood Marshall, A. Philip Randolph, and Martin Luther King Jr. She helped form the SCLC in 1957–1958 and worked on its voter registration campaign. Baker was hired as Associate Director of the

SCLC. In the early 1960s, she advocated for a more collectivist leadership in the SCLC and in the civil rights movement more generally. In 1960, she helped form the SNCC, resigning from SCLC in 1961 to do so. She worked with SNCC and CORE and mentored such activists as Diane Nash, Stokely Carmichael, Rosa Parks, and Bob Moses. Ella promoted grassroots organizing, radical democracy, and the ability of the oppressed to advocate for themselves (Ransby 2003). During the early to mid-1960s, Baker was the primary advisor and strategist of the SNCC. In 1961 she helped SNCC and CORE to organize the Freedom Rides (LeMay 2009: 286–291). She promoted radical democratic social change and influenced the Students for a Democratic Society. In 1964, Ella Baker helped organize the Mississippi Freedom Democratic Party and went with its delegation to the 1964 Democratic National Convention. In 1964–1965 SNCC moved toward "Black power." Largely due to her declining health, Baker began to back off from her heavy involvement with SNCC. From 1962 to 1967, she worked for the Southern Conference Education Fund. Baker returned to New York City in 1967 and allied with the Third World Women's Alliance and with the Women's International League for Peace and Freedom. She remained active with them and with the civil rights movement until, on her eighty-third birthday in 1986, she passed away (Ransby 2003).

Berger, Victor (1860–1928)

Victor Louis Berger was born in 1860 in Austria-Hungary. He attended the universities of Budapest and Vienna. Victor and his parents immigrated to the United States in 1878, to Bridgeport, Connecticut. Berger moved to Milwaukee in 1881 to work as a schoolteacher and newspaper editor. He published several papers in both English and German—the *Social Democratic Herald* (1901–1913) and the *Milwaukee Leader* (1911–1929). He was a labor leader with the Milwaukee Federated Trade council. It was through them that Berger joined the socialist movement. He was a delegate to the People's Party

Convention held in St. Louis in 1896 and helped organize (with Eugene Debs, Morris Hillquit, and others) the Social Democratic Party, in 1897, which later became known simply as the Socialist Party. The party split by factionalism: one faction followed Daniel DeLeon, and Victor Berger became the leader of the other—the more moderate and electorally successful wing (LeMay 2009: 252).

Milwaukee socialism, led by Berger, came to be known as the "Sewer Socialists" for their back-to-basics strategy and legacy that sought to reform the more dire conditions resulting from the industrial revolution. Berger was noted for pushing local government reforms, such as cleaning up neighborhoods and factories with a new sanitary system, promoting community parks, and improved public education. Berger, along with other German immigrants, started the first "kindergarten" system in Milwaukee. In economic policy, Berger proposed replacing the capitalist system with a planned economy and state-owned industries that would protect workers from the increasingly oppressive capitalist business class. Rather than advocating violent change, like the Western Syndicalist faction of the Socialist Party, Berger supported achieving their goals through public opinion education, at the ballot box, and with more efficient administration of government, especially at the local level. He became the very symbol of the Sewer Socialists of Milwaukee's socialism movement. Berger established what became a socialist-party machine. He was the first ever avowed socialist to run a major American city (Quint 1953; Beck 1982).

Berger ran for Congress in 1904 but lost that election. In 1910 he was elected to represent Wisconsin's fifth Congressional district, and Berger was the first socialist to serve in the U.S. Congress. He advocated voting rights for the District of Columbia, which at the time was considered a radical proposal. He advocated elimination of the presidential veto (which would require a constitutional amendment) and for the social takeover of major industries. He gained national attention by pushing for old-age pensions, proposing what eventually became the Social Security System. Berger lost reelection bids in 1912, 1914, and 1916 but remained active in Wisconsin politics and in national Socialist Party politics. When World War I broke out, he opposed U.S. entrance into the war, and enactment of the Espionage Act of 1917. Berger and many Socialist Party leaders were indicted under the act in 1918. Berger was convicted and sentenced to prison in 1919, but the conviction was appealed and overturned in 1921. Despite his indictment, Berger was again elected to Congress. When he arrived to claim his seat, Congress formed a special committee to determine whether a convicted felon and war opponent could serve. In 1919, Congress ruled that he could not and declared the seat vacant. A special election was held to fill the seat, and Milwaukee voters again elected Berger, and the House again refused to seat him. The office remained vacant until 1921, when a Republican, William Stafford, was elected to represent the district. Berger defeated Stafford in 1922 and was reelected in 1924 and 1926, after the wartime hysteria had passed. Berger served both his terms. He proposed old age pensions again, as well as unemployment insurance and public housing (both considered radical at the time). He advocated recognition of the Soviet Union and proposed revisions to the Versailles Treaty. He lost his reelection bid in 1928, again to Republican William Stafford, and returned to Milwaukee to continue his career as a newspaper editor. He died there in a streetcar accident in 1928 (LeMay 2009: 252; Beck 1982; Quint 1953).

Debs, Eugene (1855–1926)

Eugene Debs was born in Terre Haute, Indiana, in 1855. He was a labor organizer and five-time candidate for president of the United States on the Socialist Party ticket, in 1900, 1904, 1908, 1912, and 1920 (he refused the nomination in 1916). Debs left home at age fourteen to work on the railroad and became a fireman. Debs helped form the Brotherhood of

Locomotive Fireman in 1880. He served as the city clerk of Terre Haute from 1879 to 1883. He served in the Indiana legislature in 1884–1885. Debs helped establish and was president of the American Railway Union in 1893. He led their strike in 1894 against the Chicago Pullman Palace Car company and was jailed for that in 1895. Debs supported William Jennings Bryan for president in 1896. He became an avowed socialist and helped form the Socialist Party of America in 1897, and he ran for the presidency as its 1900 candidate. In 1995, Debs helped establish the Industrial Workers of the World.

A spellbinding speaker, Debs was well ahead of his times on civil rights and related Progressive Era reforms. He advocated abolishing child labor laws. He supported women's suffrage. He advocated for the graduated income tax, the direct election of U.S. senators, unemployment insurance, and employer liability laws. Debs advocated for establishment of a federal department of education and of health. He attacked Jim Crow laws, supported equal rights for Blacks, supported Black suffrage, and tried to recruit Black members to the Socialist Party, though never very successfully so. He advocated for prison reform (LeMay 2009: 149–150). His evangelistic style of socialism cost him influence with the Milwaukee Sewer Socialists to rival Victor Berger. Debs was tried, convicted, and sentenced to prison under the Espionage Act of 1917. He was stripped of citizenship in 1918 (and it was only restored posthumously in 1976). He has been correctly described as a "gentle rebel" in contrast to other more radical socialists, like the Wobblies with whom he was imprisoned (Constantine 1995; George and Wilcox 1992).

After being released from prison, Debs advocated for prison reform. He suffered declining health because of conditions during his imprisonment. He published a small tract, *Unionism and Socialism* (in 1904, reprinted in 2009), and wrote his memoirs, published posthumously as *Walls and*

Bars (1927, reprinted in 2000). Debs died in suburban Chicago in 1926.

Deer, Ada (1935–)

Ada Deer was born on the Menominee Indian Reservation in northwestern Wisconsin in 1935. Her mother was an Anglo-American from Philadelphia, a nurse for the Bureau of Indian Affairs (BIA). Her father, Joseph Deer, was a full-blooded Menominee Indian employed at the Menominee Indian Mills. Ada and her family lived in a log cabin near the Wolf River. It had no running water or electricity. Ada Deer graduated from the Shawano and Milwaukee public schools. She went on to the University of Wisconsin-Madison on a tribal scholarship and was the first Menominee Indian to graduate, with a BA in social work, in 1957. In 1961, Deer became the first Native American to earn a MSW from Columbia University. She worked for a time in New York City and then in the Milwaukee public school system. Deer joined the Peace Corps and served in Puerto Rico. Between 1964 and 1967, she worked with the BIA in Minnesota as a community service coordinator and then as coordinator of Indian Affairs in the University of Minnesota's Training Center for Community Programs. In 1969, Deer became a member of the national board of the Girl Scouts, where she served until 1975. She studied American Indian Law at the University of New Mexico and the University of Wisconsin's Law School. In 1954, Congress passed the Menominee Termination Act, imposing state jurisdiction and taxes that forced the tribe to sell ancestral lands. Deer left law school to head a campaign to regain tribal lands and reverse termination. In 1970, she helped form the Determination of Rights and Unity for Menominee Shareholders (DRUM) and organized a 220-mile protest march from Menominee to the state capital in Madison. From 1972 to 1973, Deer was vice president of a D.C. lobby firm, the National Committee to Save the Menominee People and Forest Inc. From 1974 to 1976, Ada Deer served as the first woman to chair the Menominee Tribe. Deer saw tribal rights restored in 1976. She became senior lecturer in the School of Social Work, and in the American Indian Studies Program at the University of Wisconsin-Madison, where she taught until 1993. She served as legislative liaison to the Native American Rights Fund. Dee ran for Wisconsin secretary of state, and as a delegate to the Democratic National Convention. Deer was vice-chair of the Mondale-Ferraro 1990 presidential campaign. In 1992, she ran, unsuccessfully, for the U.S. Congress. In May 1993, Ida Deer became the first woman to head the BIA, where she dealt with such issues as budget reductions, tribal conflicts over land management, water resources, mineral rights, tribal recognitions, education, and religious freedom. After leaving the BIA in 1999, she became director of the American Indian Studies Program at the University of Wisconsin-Madison (LeMay 2009: 192–193).

Du Bois, W.E.B. (1868–1963)

William Edward Burghardt Du Bois was one of the most distinguished and noted civil rights leaders. He was a leading activist, Pan-Africanist, sociologist, educator, historian, writer, editor, poet, and scholar. He was born in Massachusetts in 1868. He married Nina Gomer, and they had two children. W.E.B. Du Bois became a naturalized Ghana citizen in 1963, at the age of ninety-five, the year of his death (Appiah 2014).

Du Bois was one of the founders of the Niagara Movement, became its general secretary, and founded and edited the *Moon* (1906), and *Horizon* (1907–1910). In 1909, he cofounded the NAACP and directed its research and publicity from 1910 until 1934 (www.naacp.org/naacp-history/w-e-b-dubois.) Du Bois identified as a socialist and belonged to the Socialist Party from 1910 to 1912 (Johnson 2008; Marable 2005). He was the founder and editor of the NAACP's highly influential monthly magazine, *The Crisis*. In the years after World War I, the NAACP was the leading Black civil rights protest organization, and Du Bois was its leading figure, particularly of its anti-lynching campaign, along with Ida Wells (Dorien 2015). In 1934, Du Bois became more African American nationalist, and he resigned from the NAACP. He served as a consultant for founding the UN. He attended its convention and wrote "An Appeal to the World" in 1947 (Lewis 2009; Horne 2010).

Throughout his life, Du Bois was a gifted, prolific writer and scholar. He earned a BA from Fisk University in 1888, attended Harvard, and earned another BA. He studied history and economics at the University of Berlin from 1892 to 1894 and then taught Greek and Latin at Wilberforce University. In 1895, Du Bois became the first African American to receive a doctorate from Harvard (LeMay 2009: 157–158). He taught sociology at the University of Pennsylvania, doing pioneering research on an urban community, titled, "The Philadelphia Negro: A Social Study" (1899). Du Bois taught economics and history at Atlanta University, hosting several notable conferences and publishing several books, including *The Souls of Black Folks* (1903). He chaired Atlanta University's department of sociology from 1934 to 1944, and wrote on the role of African Americans in the Reconstruction. In 1948, Du Bois cochaired the Council on African Affairs and attended several international peace conferences. That year he ran for the U.S. Senate on the American Labor Party ticket. Du Bois was tried for but acquitted of being an agent of a foreign power (1950–1951). He traveled to Russia and China in 1958–1959. In 1961 he joined the Communist Party of the United States (Marable 2005). Du Bois moved to Ghana in 1961 at the request of President Kwame Nkrumah and died there on August 27, 1963, the eve of the civil rights march in Washington, D.C. He was given a state funeral in Ghana (Appiah 2014; Dorien 2015; Horne 2010; Johnson 2008; Lewis 2009; Marable 2005).

Farrakhan, Louis (1933–)

Louis Farrakhan was born Louis Walcott in the Bronx, New York, and raised in the West Indian community in Roxbury, Massachusetts. A gifted violinist, at age thirteen, Farrakhan played with the Boston College Orchestra and the Boston Civic Symphony. At age fourteen, he played on national television. He studied at Boston Latin School, and after graduating, attended Winston-Salem University's teaching college for two years. He became a professional musician, dancer, calypso singer, and recording artist. While performing in Chicago he attended the Nation of Islam's annual Savior's Day address by Elijah Muhammad. He joined the NOI in 1955, taking the name Louis X, and gave up his music career to become a leading preacher for NOI. Farrakhan became a minister of the Boston Mosque. In 1965, Farrakhan was appointed minister of the Harlem Mosque and served there until 1973.

Elijah Muhammad died in 1975, and Muhammad's son, Wallace Deen Muhammad, took over the NOI. Over several years' time, Wallace Deen Muhammad tried to transform NOI from its separatist orientation toward traditional Islam (Sunni). He became an imam of the American Society of Muslims, adopted traditional Islam theology, and accepted whites as fellow worshippers. Those moves alienated Minister Farrakhan.

Farrakhan led a small group in 1978 to rebuild the NOI and to espouse its founder's Black separatism and Black nationalism foundations. Minister Farrakhan established a NOI newspaper, *The Final Call*. In 1991, Farrakhan reintroduced the economic program first established by Elijah Muhammad, and in 1993, he wrote *Torchlight for America,* a compilation of guiding principles of the NOI (Gardell 1996). In 1993, Farrakhan led 2,000 members to Accra, Ghana, for the NOI's first-ever international Savior's Day convention. In 1995, Farrakhan publicly reconciled with Malcolm X's family and revived NOI mosques and study groups in 120 cities in the United States, Europe, the Caribbean, West Africa, and South Africa. In 1995, Farrakhan organized the largest march in American history, the so-called "Million Man March." By the late 1990s, NOI began to de-emphasize separatism. Farrakhan and NOI campaigned to register Black voters, supported Jesse Jackson's presidential campaign, and led a registration drive that resulted in an estimated new 1.7 million Black voters in the 1996 presidential elections. In 1997, NOI and the World Islamic People's Leadership hosted an International Islamic Conference in Chicago, with Muslim scholars attending from Europe, Asia, Africa, and the Middle East, and even some Christian and Native American spiritual leaders. In 2005, Farrakhan, the New Black Panther Party leader (Malik Shabazz), the Reverend Al Sharpton, then-senator Barack Obama (D-IL), and other prominent black leaders gathered to commemorate the tenth anniversary of the first Million Man March. Ideologically, Farrakhan moved from virulent anti-white and anti-Semitic rhetoric to a more centrist ideology. Farrakhan maintained that superiority and inferiority were determined by one's righteousness, not by their color (LeMay 2009: 225–226; Muhammad 2006; Gardell 1996).

Huerta, Dolores (1930–)

Dolores Fernandez Huerta was born in 1930 in Dawson, New Mexico. She is an excellent example of the new-style radicalism strategic approach to the struggle for civil rights (LeMay 2009: 301). Dolores was the daughter of a miner and a migrant agricultural worker. Her family moved to Stockton, California, where she grew up. In the 1950s, she met Cesar Chavez while helping organize the Community Service Organization (CSO) in Stockton. When Chavez left the CSO in 1962 to organize farm workers in Delano, Huerta left too. Since 1962, Dolores Huerta has dedicated her life to serving agricultural workers, mostly through the United Farm Workers (UFW), which she cofounded with Chavez. Dolores Huerta has worked as a union organizer, lobbyist, and direct-action protestor as a picket captain. She spent most of the 1960s organizing migrant workers in Stockton and Modesto, California. She worked at the UFW's central headquarters in Delano, becoming Cesar Chavez's most trusted and valuable associate. They frequently clashed about tactics and timing but never about the goals of the UFW. In 1963, Huerta was instrumental in securing welfare benefits for farm workers and their families in California.

She negotiated contracts to end the five-year-long Delano Grape Strike in 1970 and the ensuing off-and-on-again lettuce strike in the Salina, California. As an experienced union organizer, Huerta served as vice president of the UFW (from 1970 to 1973). She remains to this day the First Vice President Emeritus of the UFW. Huerta was critical in the UFW's joining the AFL-CIO and was the spokesperson for the union. She developed labor contracts and was the UFW's chief negotiator, boycott strategist, and effective lobbyist. She is credited with the UFW's policy of nonviolence, maintained even when violence was used against UFW's members. While an advocate of farm workers' rights, Dolores Huerta was arrested twenty-two times for nonviolent, peaceful union activities.

In 1984, the California Senate presented Huerta with the Outstanding Labor Leader Award. In 1993, she was inducted into the National Women's Hall of Fame. Huerta was given the ACLU's Roger Baldwin Medal of Liberty Award. Huerta also received the Eugene Debs Foundation Outstanding American Award and the Ellis Island Medal of Freedom Award. She was named *Ms. Magazine's* Woman of the Year, as well as one of *Ladies Home Journal's* "100 Most Important Women of the 20th Century." She has been awarded three honorary doctorate degrees. In 2012, President Barack Obama awarded Huerta with the Presidential Medal of Freedom Award, the nation's highest civilian award.

Huerta served for years as the secretary-treasurer of the UFW, and was vice-president of the Labor Union Women's Association, and vice-president of the California AFL-CIO. She is a board member and advocate for the Fund for the Feminist Majority, advocating for political and equal rights for women. She served on numerous commissions, such as the Minority Apprentice Program Commission (1965), the Advisory Commission on Immigration (1980), and the Commission on Agricultural Workers (1988–1993). She served on two California state commissions: Industrial Welfare Commission (1960) and Board of Directors of the California State Library

Service (1980–1982). In 2003, she was appointed to the Board of Trustees of the University of California (LeMay 2009: 301; Meier and Gutiérrez 2000: 106–107).

Kaepernick, Colin Rand (1987–)

Colin Kaepernick is a civil rights activist and former National Football League starting quarterback for the San Francisco Forty-Niners. He exemplifies the nonviolent, protest politics and new-style radicalism approach to civil rights advocacy, using his celebrity status as a sports figure to draw attention to the protest movement against police brutality and racial inequality in the United States. He began the symbolic protest of "kneeling during the national anthem" at the start of NFL games, which helped to give prominence to the Black Lives Matter movement.

Colin Kaepernick was born in 1987 in Milwaukee, Wisconsin, to Heidi Russo, who is white, and an African American birth father of Ghanaian, Nigerian, and Ivorian descent. Kaepernick was adopted by Rick and Teresa Kaepernick, a white couple. He lived in Fond du Lac, Wisconsin, and in California. He was an outstanding high school football quarterback, winning MVP honors, and he played basketball and baseball as well. He played college football for the University of Nevada Wolf Pack, twice winning the Western Athletic Conference Offensive Player of the Year award. He was selected by the 49ers in the 2011 NFL draft. In 2013, in his first full season as their starting quarterback, Kaepernick led them to the NFC Championship Game.

In 2016, Kaepernick sat during the national anthem prior to the fourth game of the season to protest racial injustice, police brutality, and systemic racism, and afterward for the remaining games of the season, he began kneeling during the anthem. Kaepernick received highly polarized reactions, and his symbolic protests led to wider protests against racism. Kaepernick pledge to donate $1 million to organizations working for civil rights in oppressed communities, and he donated $25,000 to

Mothers against Police Brutality. In 2018, he pledged another $100,000 in the form of $10,000 donations to charities that were matched by donations from other celebrities. His San Francisco teammates awarded him the team's Len Eshmont Award as the player who best epitomized inspirational and courageous play. He cofounded (with his wife) the "Know Your Rights Camp" that held free seminars to disadvantaged youth to teach them about self-empowerment, U.S. history, and legal rights. Also in 2018, Nike released an ad featuring Kaepernick with the text, "Believe in something, even if it means sacrificing everything," in recognition of Kaepernick's social justice campaign.

Kaepernick sacrificed significantly in his career. In September 2017, President Donald Trump called on NFL owners to fire players who protested during the national anthem, and Trump directed most of his ire at Kaepernick. Kaepernick became a free agent in the 2017 season, but no other team would hire him. He filed a grievance against the NFL and its owners, accusing them of colluding to keep him out of the league for political reasons. He reached a confidential settlement with the NFL in 2019. His protests received renewed attention and much greater acceptance in 2020, following the George Floyd homicide by Minneapolis police officers. That event sparked a renewed importance of the Black Lives Matter protest movement against police brutality and systemic racism. In April 2020, the Know Your Rights Camp launched a relief fund for COVID-19 pandemic survivors, and Kaepernick donated $100,000 to the fund (Yorkey 2013; Towler, Crawford, and Bennett 2020).

King, Martin Luther, Jr. (1929–1968)

No profiles of civil rights leaders would be complete without one for Martin Luther King Jr., the founder of the SCLC and arguably the most influential civil rights leader of the 1960s. He was born Michael Luther King Jr. but later followed his father's example and action by legally changing his first name to Martin, in honor of Martin Luther. Like his grandfather, he followed his family's long tenure as pastor of the Ebenezer Baptist Church in Atlanta, Georgia. He served as its copastor until his assassination in 1968.

King received a BA degree in 1948 from Morehouse College in Atlanta, of which both his father and grandfather were alumni. He studied theology at Crozer Theological Seminary in Pennsylvania, where he was elected class president of the predominantly white senior class. Martin earned a BD in 1951, and while on a scholarship at Crozer, he enrolled in graduate studies at Boston University, from which he took his doctorate, receiving the degree in 1955. In Boston, he met and married Coretta Scott, with whom he had two sons and two daughters.

In 1954, Martin became pastor of the Dexter Avenue Baptist Church in Montgomery, Alabama. He worked avidly for civil rights and was a member of the executive committee of the NAACP. In 1955, following protests begun by Rosa Parks, King became the leader of the Montgomery Improvement Association (MIA), leading the nonviolent demonstrations against Montgomery's segregated bus system. MIA launched a bus boycott that lasted 382 days. In December, 1956, the U.S. Supreme Court ruled laws requiring segregation on public buses as unconstitutional, and thereafter, Blacks and whites rode the buses as equals. During the boycott, King was arrested, his home was firebombed, and King was subjected to personal abuse and to a secret campaign by J. Edgar Hoover and the FBI designed to get King to cease his civil rights activism. In 1957, King and others formed the Southern Christian Leadership Council (SCLC). King was elected its president. SCLC quickly provided new leadership to the civil rights movement. The ideals of SCLC were based on Christianity, and the tactics and operational techniques were from Mahatma Gandhi. Between 1957 and 1968, King traveled more than six million miles and spoke more than 2,500 times. King appeared across the nation, whenever and wherever injustice and protest actions called on him. Over his lifetime, King wrote five books. He led civil rights protests in Birmingham, Alabama. He inspired the national conscience with his famous "Letter from a Birmingham Jail," which became a virtual manifesto of the Black civil rights movement. He planned voter registration drives and directed peaceful marches. In Washington, D.C., where the March on Washington attended by an estimated 250,000 people, King delivered his "I Have a Dream" speech. King conferred with President John F. Kennedy and campaigned for LBJ. King was arrested over twenty times, and seriously physically assaulted four times. He was awarded five honorary degrees and was selected as *Time Magazine*'s "Man of the Year" in 1963. In 1964, King was the youngest man to be awarded the Nobel Peace Prize. He worked with LBJ and Congress, advocating enactment of the 1964, 1965, and 1968 Civil Rights Acts. He was assassinated on April 4, 1968, while in Memphis, the day after delivering his "I Have Seen the Promised Land" speech. Martin Luther King is the only non-government official to be honored with a national holiday to commemorate his birthday. He is also the only civilian person to have a national monument in the nation's capital. He is considered by many to be the "Moses" of African Americans, and the "Second Emancipator" (after Abraham Lincoln) for freeing Black Americans from "de jure segregation." His books are *The Measure of a Man* (1959), *The Strength to Love* (1963), *Stride toward Freedom* (1958); *The Trumpet of Conscience* (1968), *Where Do We Go from Here? Chaos or Community* (1967), and *Why We Can't Wait* (1963). Some major biographies of Dr. Martin Luther King Jr. are Branch 1998, *Pillar of Fire: America in the King Years*; Frady 2002, *Martin Luther King, Jr.: A Life*; King and West 2015, *The Radical King*; King, Coretta Scott 1993, *My Life with Martin Luther King, Jr.*; Waldschmidt, Nelson and Britta 2012, *Dreams and Nightmares: Martin Luther King, Jr. Malcolm X, and the Struggle for Black Equality*.

Martin, Del (1921–2008)

Del Martin (Taliaferro) was a lesbian rights activist born in San Francisco in 1921. She, along with her lifelong partner and later wife, Phyllis Lyon, was at the forefront of the battles for gay and lesbian rights for more than fifty years. Del Martin exemplifies the political accommodation approach to civil rights activism. After a brief failed marriage, in 1955, Martin and Lyon cofounded the Daughters of Bilitis, the first advocacy group for lesbians. They founded it as an alternative to the lesbian bar scene in San Francisco. The organization grew to several chapters in a number of cities. It disbanded in 1970. Martin and Lyon coedited its newsletter, *The Ladder*. Del and Phyllis wrote two landmark books: *Lesbian Woman* (1972), and *Lesbian Love and Liberation* (1973). Martin later wrote *Battered Wives* (1976). She was an early member of the National Organization of Women (NOW) and was the first openly lesbian activist to serve on its board of directors. They formed the Council of Religion and the Homosexual to work with ministers to accept homosexuals into churches. They advocated to end the criminalization of homosexuality in the late 1960s and early 1970s. In 1972, Del Martin and Phyllis Lyon founded the Alice B. Toklas Democratic Club, the first gay political organization in the United States. Through the club, they influenced then–San Francisco Mayor Dianne Feinstein to sponsor a proposed city ordinance to outlaw employment discrimination against gays and lesbians. In 1989, Martin and Lyon joined Old Lesbians Organizing for Change. In 1995, with the Clinton administration, they served in the White House Council on Aging. In 2004, when San Francisco Mayor Gavin Newsom directed that marriage licenses be issued to same-sex couples, Martin and Lyon were the first couple to be married. The California Supreme Court nullified Newsom's directive. Martin and Lyon sued in a civil lawsuit. In May 2018, in the case *In re Marriage Cases*, the California Supreme Court ruled that the state's ban on same-sex marriage was unconstitutional. In June 2018, Martin and Lyon became the first couple in California to be legally wed. In 2019, Del Martin was among the inaugural fifty American "pioneers, trailblazers, and heroes" inducted into the Stonewall National Monument in New York

City (Gallo 2007). Del Martin died in August 2008 in San Francisco (Bullough 2002; Gallo 2007).

Parks, Rosa (1913–2005)

If any single person can be credited with launching the modern Black civil rights movement, it is arguably Rosa Parks. Born Rosa Louise McCauley in 1913, in Tuskegee, Alabama, Rose Parks came from a poor family and humble background, but she went on to become an icon of the civil rights movement and the first woman ever to lie in state in the capitol rotunda, an honor normally reserved for Presidents and United States Senators. The U.S. Congress recognized Rosa Parks as the "Mother of the Modern Day Civil Rights Movement." Her father was a carpenter, and her mother a grade school teacher. When her parents separated, Rosa and her mother moved to the Montgomery area, and Rosa grew up on a farm with her maternal grandparents. She was a lifelong member of the African Methodist Episcopal Church (AME). She was homeschooled by her mother and, as a teenager, at the Industrial School for Girls in Montgomery (a facility twice burned down by anti-Black arsonists). She did not graduate, as she had to drop out of school to care for her ailing mother and grandmother.

In the 1950s, Jim Crow laws segregated all aspects of life for Blacks, including public transportation. She grew up in highly segregated Montgomery and experienced KKK marches in front of her home. Blatant racism was impossible to ignore and purposively designed to strike terror in Blacks. In 1932, Rosa married Raymond Parks, a local barber and active member of the NAACP. Her husband helped raise funds to defend the Scottsboro Boys, a group of Black men falsely accused of raping two white women. Rosa Parks worked several jobs, including domestic work and as a hospital aide. She finished high school in 1933. Despite Jim Crow laws and intimidation, and after three tries to do so, Rosa Parks registered to vote.

Rosa joined the NAACP in 1943, and served as Montgomery chapter secretary. In 1944, she began to work at the Maxwell

Airforce base where the trolley was integrated, an experience that she noted "opened her eyes up." A Montgomery ordinance stipulated that the first four rows were reserved for whites, and all buses had a "colored" section at the back. At the time, 75 percent of public bus riders were Black. A local ordinance forbade Blacks from sitting across the aisle from whites. When white riders filled the first four rows, additional white passengers moved toward the middle section, and the bus driver or conductor ordered Black passengers to move to the back or to stand to vacate their seats for whites. On December 1, 1955, after a long day of work at the Montgomery Fair department store, Parks took a bus home, sitting in the first row of seats designated for Blacks. When whites filled their rows, and two white men were standing, the conductor ordered four Black people to vacate their seats and stand in the back of the bus. Three Black men complied, but Rosa Parks refused. A police officer was called, and he arrested Rosa for violating the law. She spent the night in jail before being bailed out by some NAACP staff. Parks was fined $10, plus $4 in court costs. The NAACP announced a bus boycott, and the local paper spread the word. Several Black church leaders formed the Montgomery Alabama Improvement Association (MIA), soon led by Martin Luther King Jr. About 40,000 Blacks carpooled or walked to work. For some that was as far as twenty miles. The boycott lasted from December 5, 1955, to December 20, 1956 382 days3and violence was directed at Blacks—bombing or burning churches and the homes of Dr. King and Reverend Ralph Abernathy. The boycott led to the founding of the SCLC. On November 13, 1956, the U.S. Supreme Court declared the state's segregated bus law and the Montgomery municipal ordinance as unconstitutional, applying the precedent set by *Brown v. Board of Education* (1954). With the boycott, the Black civil rights movement in the South was launched.

Rosa Parks continued to work as a seamstress until she joined the staff of Representative John Conyers (D-MI). She worked for Conyers until 1988, when she retired. In 1992, she wrote her autobiography, *Quiet Strength*. An icon of the civil rights movement, she was often honored later in her life, such as the NAACP's Spingarn Medal and, in 1980, the MLK Award. In 1992, Rosa Parks was awarded the Peace Abbey Courage Award, and in that year, she published her autobiography, *Rosa Parks: My Story*. In 1994, she received an honorary doctorate from Florida State University. In 1995, she authored her memoir, *Quiet Strength*. In 1996, President Clinton awarded her the Presidential Medal of Freedom. In 1999, Congress awarded her its highest honor, the Congressional Gold Medal. *Time* hailed her as one of the twenty most influential and iconic figures of the twentieth century. In 2000, Alabama inducted her into its Academy of Honor, and she was the first person awarded the governor's Medal of Honor for Extraordinary Courage. She died in 2005. President Bush ordered all flags to fly at half-mast in her honor and memory. On the fiftieth anniversary of her arrest, President Bush directed that a statue of Parks be placed in the United States Capitol's Statuary Hall (Brinkley 2005; LeMay 2009: 287–288; Parks and Haskins 1992; Theohans 2015).

Randolph, A. Philip (1889–1979)

Asa Philip Randolph was born in 1889 in Crescent City, Florida, the son of an AME minister. He moved to New York City's Harlem in 1911, intending to become an actor. While studying at City College of New York, he switched to political science and economics. While there, he met Chandler Owen, a sociology and political science student at Columbia University. They began to publish *The Messenger*, in 1919, espousing their socialist views. They were charged with breaking the Espionage Act of 1917 but were not convicted. They hailed the IWW as the only labor organization that drew no racial or color lines. Randolph ran as a socialist for several elective offices but was never elected. He organized Blacks working in the laundry, clothing, and cinema industries. In 1929, Randolph founded the Brotherhood of Sleeping Car Porters and undertook efforts to organize employees of the Pullman Company, finally winning bargaining rights in 1935. The union won their first contract in 1937. Randolph led the Brotherhood to join the AFL but moved the union to the CIO when the AFL failed to fight discrimination in its own ranks. He emerged as an effective and visible spokesman for African American rights. When the United States entered World War I, Randolph proposed a "March on Washington" to protest racial discrimination in the armed forces. Randolph canceled the march when President Franklin D. Roosevelt proposed the Fair Employment Act in 1941. In 1947, Randolph organized the Committee against Jim Crow in the Military Service, later called the League for Non-Violent Civil Disobedience. President Harry Truman reacted positively to the campaign and issued the executive order ending racial segregation in the armed forces. Randolph, Roy Wilkins of the NAACP, and Arnold Aronson of the National Jewish Community Relations Council formed the Leadership Conference on Civil Rights. It was soon involved in every civil rights law fight after 1957. In 1963, Randolph, MLK, and others organized the March on Washington (for Jobs and Freedom), drawing an estimated 400,000 people, Blacks and whites. At the march, MLK gave his "I Have a Dream" speech. Randolph came to the forefront of the civil rights movement in the 1960s, often addressing the nation on behalf of African Americans involved in the civil rights struggle for voting rights, to end segregation, and to end discrimination in public accommodations. Randolph worked closely with Bayard Rustin and the AFL-CIO. He died in New York City in 1979 (Kersten 2006; Kersten and Yang 2015; Taylor 2006).

Wells, Ida (1862–1931)

Ida B. Wells-Barnett was an African American journalist and rights activist who led the anti-lynching crusade in the United States in the 1890s. She exemplifies the political accommodation strategy and tactics (LeMay 2009: 122). Ida Wells was born a slave in Mississippi in July 1862. Her family was freed by the Emancipation Proclamation about six months after her birth. During Reconstruction, her father was involved with the Freedman's Aid Society and helped start and served on the board of Shaw University. It was at Shaw that Ida Wells received her schooling. When her parents died in a yellow fever outbreak, she began teaching. In 1882, she moved to Memphis and continued her education at nearby Fisk University. She became a writer and owner of the *Memphis Free Speech and Headlight*, later simply the *Free Speech*. In 1884 she was forced off a train for refusing to move from her first-class car to the car for African Americans. That experience began her civil rights activism as a journalist and publisher. She taught in the segregated public schools in Memphis. In 1892, a lynching of three Black men in Memphis prompted her to begin her anti-lynching campaign. She moved to New York City, narrowly escaping being killed herself. She wrote a series on lynching for the *New York Age* newspaper, and in 1893, she published *A Red Record*, an anti-lynching pamphlet. In 1898, Ida Wells brought her anti-lynching campaign to the White House, leading a protest and calling on President William McKinley to make reform.

In 1895, Ida married Ferdinand Barnett. In 1896, she formed the National Association of Colored Women, and she is considered a cofounder of the NAACP. Ida worked with the National Equal Rights League and created the first African American kindergarten. She fought for women's suffrage. She died in 1931, of kidney failure, in Chicago (Bay 2009; Effinger-Cricklow 2014; Giddings 2008; and Silkey 2015).

Wiesel, Elie (1928–2016)

Elie Wiesel was a Holocaust survivor, professor, writer, lecturer, Nobel laureate, and founder of the Elie Wiesel Foundation for Humanity. He exemplified the accommodation strategy and illustrated the power of the individual example and witness. He was born in Romania, and during World War II, he, his family, and the Jews from his village were deported to Nazi concentration and extermination camps. Wiesel was first sent to

Auschwitz, where his mother and younger sister died. He and his father were then sent to Buchenwald, where his father died. Elie and two older sisters survived. After liberation in 1945, Elie went to Paris, where he studied French and literature and graduated from the University of Paris. Wiesel taught Hebrew and wrote for newspapers, including the Yiddish-language paper, *Tsien in Kamf.*

In 1955, Wiesel moved to New York City, where he met and married his wife, Marion. He wrote some forty nonfiction books, including *Night* in 1960. It sold more than 10 million copies and has been translated into thirty languages. Wiesel became a naturalized U.S. citizen. He was a visiting scholar at Yale University, as well as a distinguished professor of Jewish studies at the City College of New York and a professor of humanities at Boston University. He lectured at countless other colleges and universities, and over his lifetime, received 90 honorary degrees. Wiesel chaired the U.S. Holocaust Memorial Council from 1980 to 1986. In 1986, Wiesel and Marion started the Elie Wiesel Foundation for Humanity. He was the recipient of numerous awards, including the Nobel Prize for Peace in 1986, for his speaking out against violence, repression, and racism. Wiesel received the Congressional Gold Medal in 1984. In 1992, President William Clinton awarded Wiesel the Presidential Medal of Freedom. Wiesel died in New York City in 2016 (www.nobelprize.org/prizes/peace/biographical; www .eliewieselfoundation.org/elie-wiesel; Downing 2008; Burger 2018).

References

Appiah, Kwame. 2014. *Lines of Descent: W.E.B. Du Bois and the Emergence of Identity.* Cambridge, MA: Harvard University Press.

Araiza, Lauren. 2014. *To March for Others: The Black Freedom Struggle and the United Farm Workers.* Philadelphia: University of Pennsylvania Press.

Armor, John, and Peter Wright. 1988. *Manzanar.* New York: Times Books.

Banks, Dennis, and Richard Erdoes. 2006. *Ojibwa Warrior: Dennis Banks and the Rise of the American Indian Movement.* Norman: University of Oklahoma Press.

Beck, Elmer. 1982. *The Sewer Socialists: A History of the Socialist Party of Wisconsin, 1895–1940.* Fenimore, WI: Westburg Associates Press.

Belknap, Michael. 2005. *The Supreme Court under Earl Warren, 1953–1969.* Columbia: University of South Carolina Press.

Berson, Robin. 2004. *Jane Addams: A Biography.* Westport, CT: Greenwood Press.

Branch, Taylor. 1998. *Pillar of Fire: America in the King Years, 1963–1965.* New York: Simon and Schuster.

Brinkley, Douglas. 2005. *Rosa Parks: A Life.* New York: Penguin Books.

Broadwater, Jeff. 2006. *George Mason: Forgotten Father.* Chapel Hill: University of North Carolina Press.

Brown, Dee. 2012. *Bury My Heart at Wounded Knee: An Indian History of the American West.* Maryville, TN: Open Roads Media.

Bullough, Vern L., ed. 2002. *Before Stonewall: Activists for Gay and Lesbian Rights in Historical Context.* New York: Harrington Park Press.

Burger, Ariel. 2018. *Witness: Lessons from Elie Wiesel's Classroom.* New York: Houghton Mifflin/Harcourt.

Calavita, Kitty. 1992. *Inside the State: The Bracero Program, Immigration and the INS.* New York: Routledge.

Carmon, Irwin. 2015. *Notorious RBG: The Life and Times of Ruth Bader Ginsburg.* New York: Dey Street Books/ HarperCollins.

Caro, Robert. 2012. *The Years of Lyndon Johnson: The Passage of Power.* New York: Knopf.

Cole, David. 2016. *Engines of Liberty: The Power of Citizen Activists to Make Constitutional Law.* New York: Basic Books.

Constantine, J. Robert, ed. 1995. *Gentle Rebel: Letters of Eugene Debs.* Urbana: University of Illinois Press.

Davis, Michael, and Hunter Clark. 1992. *Thurgood Marshall: Warrior at the Bar, Rebel on the Bench.* New York: Birch Lane Books.

Debs, Eugene. [1904] 2009. *Unionism and Socialism.* Whitefish, MT: Kessinger Publishing.

Debs, Eugene. [1927] 2000. *Walls and Bars.* Chicago, IL: Charles Kerr.

Deloria, Vine. 1988. *Custer Died for Your Sins: An Indian Manifesto.* Norman: University of Oklahoma Press.

Dorien, Gary. 2015. *The New Abolition: W.E.B. Du Bois and the Black Social Gospel.* New Haven, CT: Yale University Press.

Downing, Frederick. 2008. *Elie Wiesel: A Religious Biography.* Macon, GA: Mercer University Press.

Faderman, Lillian. 2011. *The Gay Revolution.* New York: Simon and Schuster.

Farmer, James. 1985. *Lay Bare the Heart: An Autobiography of the Civil Rights Movement.* Gettysburg, PA: Anchor House.

Farrakhan, Louis. 1993. *A Torchlight for America.* Chicago, IL: FCN Publishing.

Fisher, Peter. 1978. *The Gay Mystique: The Myth and Reality of Male Homosexuality.* New York: Stein and Day.

Flores, Lori. 2016. *A Grounds for Dreaming: Mexican Americans, Mexican Immigrants, and the California Farm Workers Union.* New Haven, CT: Yale University Press.

Foner, Eric. 1995. *Free Soil, Free Labor, Free Men: The Ideology of the Republican Party before the Civil War.* New York: Oxford University Press.

Frady, Marshall. 2002. *Martin Luther King, Jr.: A Life.* New York: Penguin.

Frank, Barney. 2015. *Frank: A Life in Politics from the Great Society to Same-Sex Marriage.* New York: Farrar, Strauss and Giroux.

Frazier, Nishani. 2017. *Harambee City: Congress of Racial Equality in Cleveland and the Rise of Black Power Populism.* Fayetteville: University of Arkansas Press.

Gallo, Marcia. 2007. *Different Daughters: A History of the Daughters of Bilitis and the Rise of the Lesbian Rights Movement.* Berkeley and New York: Seal Press.

Ganz, Marshall. 2009. *Why David Sometimes Wins: Leadership, Organization, and Strategy in the California Farmworkers Movement.* New York: Oxford University Press.

Gardell, Mattias. 1996. *In the Name of Elijah Mohammad: Louis Farrakhan and the Nation of Islam.* Durham, NC: Duke University Press.

George, John, and Laird Wilcox. 1992. *Nazis, Communists, Klansmen and Others on the Fringe: Political Extremism in America.* New York: Prometheus Books.

Ginsburg, Ruth Bader. 2018. *My Own Words.* New York: Simon and Schuster.

Goodwin, Doris Kearns. 2005. *Team of Rivals: The Political Genius of Abraham Lincoln.* New York: Simon and Schuster.

Gould, Lewis. 2003. *Grand Old Party: A History of the Republican Party.* New York: Random House.

Gould, Lewis. 2010. *1968: The Election that Changed America.* Chicago, IL: Ivan Dee.

Hagedorn, Sara, and Michael LeMay. 2019. *The American Congress: A Reference Handbook.* Santa Barbara: ABC-CLIO.

Haskins, Jim, and Kathleen Benson. 2006. *John Lewis in the Lead: A Story of the Civil Rights Movement.* New York: Lee and Low Books.

Hill, Christine. 2002. *John Lewis: From Freedom Rider to Congressman.* New York: Enslow Publishers.

Hitchcock, William. 2018. *The Age of Eisenhower: America and the World in the 1950s.* New York: Simon and Schuster.

Honor, Louise, ed. 2002. *Hispanic America: A Statistical Sourcebook.* Palo Alto, CA: Information Publications.

Horne, Gerald. 2010. *W.E.B. Du Bois: A Biography.* Westport, CT: Greenwood Press.

Hosokawa, William. 1969. *Nisei: The Quiet Americans.* New York: William Morrow.

Hudson, David. 2006. *The Rehnquist Court: Understanding Its Impact and Legacy.* New York: Praeger Press.

Jefferson, Thomas. 1914. *Autobiography of Thomas Jefferson, 1743–1790.* New York: Putnam's Sons.

Johnson, Brian. 2008. *W.E.B. Du Bois: Toward Agnosticism, 1868–1934.* Lanham, MD: Rowman and Littlefield.

Johnson, Troy. 2007. *Red Power: The Native American Civil Rights Movement.* New York: Chelsea House.

Joselin, Katherine. 2004. *Jane Addams: A Writers Life.* Champaign: University of Illinois Press.

Kanefield, Teri. 2016. *Free to Be Ruth Bader Ginsburg: The Story of Women and Law.* New York: Amazon Publishing.

Kersten, Andrew. 2006. *A. Philip Randolph: A Life in the Vanguard.* Lanham, MD: Rowman and Littlefield.

Kersten, Andrew, and Clarence Young, eds. 2015. *Reframing Randolph: Labor, Black Freedom, and the Legacies of A. Philip Randolph.* New York: New York University Press.

Keyssar, Alexander. 2009. *The Right to Vote: The Contested History of Democracy in the United States.* New York: Basic Books.

King, Coretta Scott. 1993. *My Life with Martin Luther King, Jr.* New York: Henry Holt.

King, Martin Luther, Jr., and Cornel West, eds. *The Radical King.* New York: Beacon Press.

Kitano, Harry. 1976. *Japanese Americans: The Evolution of a Subculture.* Englewood Cliffs, NJ: Prentice Hall.

Kitano, Harry. 1997. *Race Relations,* 5th ed. Upper Saddle River, NJ: Prentice Hall.

Knight, Louise. 2010. *Jane Addams: Spirit in Action.* New York: W. W. Norton.

Laughlin, Kathleen, and Jacqueline Castledine, eds. 2010. *Breaking the Wave: Women, Their Organizations, and Feminism, 1945–1985.* Abington, UK: Routledge.

Lee, Percy, Louise Young, and Ralph Young. 1989. *In the Public Interest: The League of Women Voters, 1920–1970.* Westport, CT: Greenwood Press.

LeMay, Michael. 2009. *The Perennial Struggle.* Upper Saddle River, NJ: Prentice Hall.

LeMay, Michael. 2018a. *Religious Freedom in America: A Reference Handbook.* Santa Barbara, CA: ABC-CLIO.

LeMay, Michael. 2018b. *U.S. Immigration Policy, Ethnicity, and Religion in American History.* Santa Barbara, CA: Praeger Press.

LeMay, Michael. 2019. *Immigration Reform: A Reference Handbook.* Santa Barbara, CA: ABC-CLIO.

LeMay, Michael. 2020. *First Amendment Freedoms: A Reference Handbook.* Santa Barbara: ABC-CLIO.

LeMay, Michael, and Elliott Barkan, eds. 1999. *U.S. Immigration and Naturalization Laws and Issues: A Documentary History.* Westport, CT: Greenwood Press.

Lewis, David. 2009. *W.E.B. Du Bois: A Biography.* New York: Henry Holt and Company.

Lewis, John. "Biography." https://johnlewis.house.gov /john-lewis/biography. Accessed July 28, 2020.

Lewis, John, with Mike D'Orso. 1998. *Walking with the Wind: A Memoir of the Movement.* New York: Simon and Schuster.

Lewis, John, with Brenda Jones. 2012. *Across That Bridge.* Westport, CT: Hyperion.

Lynch, Frederick. 2011. *One Nation under AARP: The Fight over Medicare, Social Security, and America's Future.* Berkeley: University of California Press.

Mack, Kenneth. 2012. *Representing the Race: The Creation of the Civil Rights Lawyer.* Cambridge, MA: Harvard University Press.

Marable, Manning. 2005. *W.E.B. Du Bois: Black Radical Democrat.* Boulder, CO: Paradigm.

Marshall, Thurgood, and Mark Tushnet, eds. 2001. *Thurgood Marshall: His Speeches, Writings, Arguments, Opinions, and Reminiscences.* Chicago, IL: Lawrence Hill Books.

Martin, Del. 1976. *Battered Wives.* Volcano, CA: Volcano Press.

Martin, Del, and Phyllis Lyon. 1972. *Lesbian Woman.* San Francisco, CA: Glide Publications.

Martin, Del, and Phyllis Lyon. 1973. *Lesbian Love and Liberation.* Irvine, CA: Multimedia Resources Center.

Meacham, Jon. 2012. *Thomas Jefferson: The Art of Power.* New York: Random House.

Meier, August, and Elliott Rudwick. 1975. *CORE: A Study in the Civil Rights Movement, 1942–1968.* Champaign: University of Illinois Press.

Meier, Matt, and Margo Gutiérrez. 2000. *Encyclopedia of Mexican American Civil Rights Movement.* Westport, CT: Greenwood Press.

Miller, Helen Hill. 1975. *George Mason: Gentleman Revolutionary.* Chapel Hill: University of North Carolina Press.

Moye, J. Todd. 2013. *Ella Baker: Community Organizer of the Civil Rights Movement.* Lanham, MD: Rowman and Littlefield.

Muhammad, Jabril. 2006. *Closing the Gap: Inner Views of the Heart, Mind, and Soul of the Honorable Minister Louis Farrakhan.* Chicago, IL: FCN Publishing.

Newton, Jim. 2006. *Justice for All: Earl Warren and the Nation He Led.* New York: Riverhead Books.

Ng, Wendy. 2001. *Japanese American Internment during World War II.* Westport, CT: Greenwood Press.

Obermayer, Herman. 2009. *Rehnquist: A Personal Portrait of the Distinguished Chief Justice of the United States.* New York: Oxford University Press.

Powe, Lucas. 2000. *The Warren Court and American Politics.* Cambridge, MA: Belknap Press/Harvard University Press.

Parks, Rosa, with James Haskins. 1992. *My Story.* Boston, MA: Beacon Press.

Quint, Howard. 1953. *The Forging of American Socialism: Origins of the Modern Movement.* Columbia: University of South Carolina Press.

Ransby, Barbara. 2003. *Ella Baker and the Black Freedom Movement: A Radical Democratic Vision.* Chapel Hill: University of North Carolina Press.

Rawn, James. 2010. *Root and Branch: Charles Hamilton Houston, Thurgood Marshall, and the Struggle to End Segregation.* New York: Bloomsbury Press.

Rutland, Robert. 1980. *George Mason: Reluctant Statesman.* Baton Rouge: Louisiana State University Press.

Schwartz, Herman. 2003. *The Rehnquist Court: Judicial Activism of the Right.* New York: Hill and Wang.

Shaw, Randy. 2008. *Beyond the Fields: Cesar Chavez, the UFW, and the Struggle for Justice in the 21st Century.* Berkeley: University of California Press.

Stern, Kenneth. 2002. *Loud Hawk: The United States versus the American Indian Movement.* Norman: University of Oklahoma Press.

Taylor, Cynthia. 2006. *Philip Randolph: The Religious Journey of an African American Labor Leader.* New York: New York University Press.

Theohans, Jeannie. 2015. *The Rebellious Life of Rosa Parks.* Boston, MA: Beacon Press.

Towler, Christopher, Nyron Crawford, and Robert Bennett. 2020. "Shut Up and Play: Black Athletes, Protest Politics, and Black Political Action." *Perspectives on Politics* 18(1): 111–127.

Tushnet, Mark. 1994. *Making Civil Rights Law: Thurgood Marshall and the Supreme Court, 1936–1961.* London: Oxford University Press.

Tushnet, Mark. 1996. *The Warren Court in Historical and Political Perspective.* Charlottesville: University of Virginia Press.

Tushnet, Mark. 2005. *A Court Divided: The Rehnquist Court and the Future of Constitutional Law.* New York: W. W. Norton.

Tushnet, Mark. 2008. *Dissent: Great Opposing Opinions in Landmark Supreme Court Cases.* Boston, MA: Beacon Press.

Tyrkus, Michael, Michael Bronski, and Jewelle Gomez. 1997. *Gay and Lesbian Biography.* Detroit, MI: St. James Press.

Urofsky, Melvin. 2001. *The Warren Court: Justices, Rulings, and Legacy.* Santa Barbara, CA: ABC-CLIO.

Vile, John, ed. 2003. *Great American Judges: An Encyclopedia.* Santa Barbara, CA: ABC-CLIO.

Wainwright, Susan. 2019. *In Defense of Justice: The Greatest Dissents of Ruth Bader Ginsburg.* Fairhope, AL: Mockingbird Press.

Waldschmidt-Nelson, and Britta. 2012. *Dreams and Nightmares: Martin Luther King, Jr., Malcolm X, and the Struggle for Black Equality.* Gainesville: University Press of Florida.

Walker, Craig. 2018. *Ethel Percy Andrus: One Woman Who Changed America.* Washington, D.C.: AARP Press.

Warren, Earl. 1977. *The Memoirs of Earl Warren.* Garden City, NY: Doubleday.

Weisberg, Stuart. 2009. *Barney Frank: The Story of America's Only Left-Handed, Gay, Jewish Congressman.* Amherst: University of Massachusetts Press.

Wilkins, David. 2002. *American Indian Politics and the American Political System.* Lanham, MD: Rowman and Littlefield.

Woods, Randall. 2006. *LBJ: Architect of American Ambition.* New York: Free Press.

Yarbough, Jean. 2006. *The Essential Jefferson.* Indianapolis, IN: Hackett Publishing.

Yorkey, Mike. 2013. *Playing with Purpose: Football: Inside the Lives and Faith of the NFL's Most Intriguing Personalities.* Uhrichsville, OH: Barbour Publishing.

Zentner, Scot, and Michael LeMay. 2020. *Party and Nation: Immigration and Regime Politics in American History.* Lanham, MD: Lexington Books.

Introduction

This chapter presents data and documents on civil rights and liberties over an extensive period of United States history. The data section presents important United States Supreme Court cases that rendered decisions on each of the Amendments to the Constitution that guarantee an important civil right or liberty. It offers tables of leading civil rights laws enacted by the United States Congress. It also presents tables of the key organizations and civil rights activists for critical minority groups seeking protection under the Constitution.

The documents section presents a number of documents that span 1776 to 2016. They are selected to be representative of acts of Congress, states, treaties, executive orders, and U.S. Supreme Court decisions excerpted to most relevant sections with regard to civil rights, or statements of principles of civil rights organizations. Collectively, they are indicative of various time periods. They are presented in chronological order.

"The Fearless Girl" statue in Lower Manhattan, erected to honor International Women's Day. (Cpenler/Dreamstime.com)

Data

Table 5.1. Articles of the United Nations' Universal Declaration of Human Rights

Table 5.1 lists the 30 articles adopted by the United Nations as its Declaration of Rights.

Number	Topic of Article
1	RIGHT TO EQUALITY
2	FREEDOM FROM DISCRIMINATION
3	RIGHT TO LIFE, LIBERTY, AND PERSONAL SECURITY
4	FREEDOM FROM SLAVERY
5	FREEDOM FROM TORTURE AND DEGRADING TREATMENT
6	RIGHT TO RECOGNITION AS A PERSON BEFORE THE LAW
7	RIGHT TO EQUALITY BEFORE THE LAW
8	RIGHT TO REMEDY BY COMPETENT TRIBUNAL
9	FREEDOM FROM ARBITRARY ARREST AND EXILE
10	RIGHT TO A FAIR PUBLIC HEARING
11	RIGHT TO BE CONSIDERED INNOCENT UNTIL PROVEN GUILTY
12	FREEDOM FROM INTERFERENCE WITH PRIVACY, FAMILY, HOME, AND CORRESPONDENCE
13	RIGHT TO FREE MOVEMENT IN AND OUT OF A COUNTRY
14	RIGHT TO ASYLUM IN OTHER COUNTRIES FROM PERSECUTION
15	RIGHT TO A NATIONALITY AND FREEDOM TO CHANGE IT
16	RIGHT TO MARRIAGE AND A FAMILY
17	RIGHT TO OWN PROPERTY
18	FREEDOM OF BELIEF AND RELIGION
19	FREEDOM OF OPINION AND INFORMATION
20	RIGHT OF PEACEFUL ASSEMBLY AND ASSOCIATION
21	RIGHT TO PARTICIPATE IN GOVERNMENT AND FREE ELECTIONS
22	RIGHT TO SOCIAL SECURITY
23	RIGHT TO DESIRABLE WORK AND TO JOIN TRADE UNIONS
24	RIGHT TO REST AND LEISURE
25	RIGHT TO ADEQUATE LIVING STANDARDS
26	RIGHT TO EDUCATION
27	RIGHT TO PARTICIPATE IN THE CULTURAL LIFE OF A COMMUNITY
28	RIGHT TO A SOCIAL ORDER THAT ADVOCATES THIS DOCUMENT

Table 5.1 (*continued*)

Number	Topic of Article
29	COMMUNITY DUTIES ESSENTIAL TO FREE AND FULL DEVELOPMENT
30	FREEDOM FROM STATE AND PERSONAL INTERFERENCE IN THE ABOVE RIGHTS

Source: United Nations. https://www.un.org/en/universal-declaration-human-rights/

Table 5.2. Second Amendment Decisions and Congressional Gun Control Measures

Table 5.2 lists United States Supreme Court cases regarding the Second Amendment and United States Congressional enactments regarding gun control measures.

SUPREME COURT DECISIONS REGARDING THE SECOND AMENDMENT RIGHT TO BEAR ARMS

United States v. Cruikshank (92 U.S. 542, 1876)
Presser v. Illinois (116 U.S. 252, 1886)
Miller v. Texas (153 U.S. 535, 1894)
Robertson v. Baldwin (165 U.S. 275, 1897)
United States v. Verdugo-Urquirdez (494 U.S. 259, 1990)
Lewis v. United States (445 U.S. 55, 1990)
Casey v. Planned Parenthood (503 U.S. 833, 1992)
District of Columbia v. Heller (554 U.S. 570, 2008)
McDonald v. City of Chicago (561 U.S. 242, 2010)

CONGRESSIONAL ENACTMENTS REGARDING GUN CONTROL MEASURES

National Firearms Act (48 Stat. 1236, 1934)
Federal Firearms Act (52 Stat. 1250, 1938)
Omnibus Crime Control and Safe Streets Act (42 Stat. 3789, 1968)
Firearm Owners Protection Act (100 Stat. 449, 1986)
Brady Handgun Violence Protection Act (107 Stat. 1536, 1993)
Violent Crime Control and Law Enforcement Act (108 Stat. 1796, 1994)
Protection of Lawful Commerce in Arms Act (119 Stat. 2095, 2005)

Table 5.3. Supreme Court Decisions Regarding the Fourth Amendment

Table 5.3 lists United States Supreme Court decisions regarding the Fourth Amendment rights.

Case	Citation	Regarding
Luther v. Borden	48 U.S 1, 1849	Recovery of damages to property during a search
Weeks v. United States	232 U.S. 383, 1914	Warrantless seizure unconstitutional
Schenck v. United States	249 U.S. 47, 1919	Draft evidence seized from socialists
Hester v. United States	265 U.S. 57, 1924	Established "open field" doctrine
Olmstead v. United States	277 U.S. 438, 1928	Evidence seized via a wiretap
Brinegar v. United States	338 U.S. 160, 1949	Reasonableness test, probable cause
Mapp v. Ohio	367U.S. 643, 1961	Exclusionary rule re: unreasonable search and seizure
Katz v. United States	389 U.S. 357, 1967	Katz test for expectation of privacy
Terry v. Ohio	392 U.S. 1, 1968	Stop and frisk is legal if there is a reasonable suspicion that a person is armed and dangerous
Coolidge v. New Hampshire	403 U.S. 443, 1971	Automobile exception to Fourth Amendment
United States v. Matlock	415 U.S. 164, 1974	Police consent from third party
Smith v. Maryland	442 U.S. 735, 1979	Use of pen register not a search
United States v. Ross	456 U.S. 798, 1982	Closed container in car searchable
Florida v. Royer	460 U.S. 491, 1983	Seizure of person and probable cause
California v. Greenwood	486 U.S. 35, 1986	Warrantless search of garage
Illinois v. Rodriquez	497 U.S. 177, 1990	Warrantless search and third-party consent
Ohio v. Robinette	519 U.S. 33, 1996	Police search of car at traffic stop
Chandler v. Miller	520 U.S. 305, 1997	Georgia law on drug test to run for elective office

(continued)

Table 5.3   *(continued)*

Case	Citation	Regarding
Florida v. J.L.	529 U.S. 266, 2000	Stop and frisk on anonymous tip
United States v. Drayton	546 U.S. 194, 2002	Consent and search on public bus
Ontario v. Quon	560 U.S. 746, 2010	Privacy and electronic communication in government workplace
United States v. Jones	132 U.S. 945, 2012	GPS tracking device equals a search
Maryland v. King	569 U.S. 435, 2013	Use of cheek swab like fingerprinting
Carpenter v. U.S.	585 U.S----, 2018	Cell-site location information without warrant issued on probable cause

Table 5.4. Supreme Court Decisions Regarding the Fifth Amendment

Table 5.4 lists Fifth Amendment United States Supreme Court decisions from 1803 to the most recent in 2005.

Case	Citation	Topic
Marbury v. Madison	5 U.S. 137, 1803	Gave power of judicial review to Supreme Court
Dred Scott v. Sanford	60 U.S. 393, 1857	Protected slave owners as slaves were property
Blockburger v. United States	284 U.S. 299, 1932	Standards re: double jeopardy
Chambers v. Florida	309 U.S. 227, 1940	Compelled confession inadmissible
Ashcraft v. Tennessee	322 U.S. 143, 1944	Extorted confessions
Johnson v. Eisentager	339 U.S. 763, 1950	Court jurisdiction regarding German war criminals
Burns v. Wilson	346 U.S. 137, 1953	Military courts questioning without being informed of rights
Fong Foo v. United States	369 U.S. 141, 1962	Double jeopardy clause of Fifth Amendment.
Miranda v. Arizona	384 U.S. 436, 1966	Miranda warnings, being informed of one's rights

(continued)

Table 5.4 *(continued)*

Case	Citation	Topic
Roe v. Wade	410 U.S. 113, 1973	Woman's right to privacy and abortion, Fifth and Fourteenth Amendment rights
Bowers v. Hardwick	478 U.S. 186, 1986	Right to privacy, homosexual acts
United States v. Felix	503 U.S. 378, 1992	Offense and conspiracy to commit offense not double jeopardy
Lawrence v. Texas	539 U.S. 558, 2003	Laws prohibiting homosexual acts by consenting adults in private not constitutional
Hiibel v. 6th D. Ct., Nevada	542 U.S. 177, 2004	A "Terry stop" allows police to briefly detain a person on reasonable suspicion of involvement in criminal activity, based on *Terry v. Ohio* (1968), Court rules an ID requirement not a violation of Fifth Amendment
Rasul v. Bush	542 U.S. 466, 2004	Foreign nationals at Guantanamo Bay no right to habeas corpus review
Hamadi v. Rumsfeld	542 U.S. 507, 2004	Enemy combatant detention and U.S. citizen due process rights to challenge enemy combatant status
Kelo v. City of New London	545 U.S. 469, 2005	Court rules approval of a taking clause and eminent domain seizure even when it involves private to private owners, rather than for public use.

Table 5.5. Supreme Court Decisions Regarding the Fair Trial Clause of the Sixth Amendment

Table 5.5 lists Sixth Amendment challenges regarding the fair trial clause.

Date	Case	Citation	Topic
1905	*Beaver v. Haubert*	198 U.S. 77	Speedy trial for potential defendant
1955	*United States v. Provoo*	352 U.S. 857	Speedy trial for prisoner of war

(continued)

Table 5.5 (*continued*)

Date	Case	Citation	Topic
1957	*Pollard v. United States*	352 U.S. 354	Speedy trial requirements
1966	*United States v. Ewell*	383 U.S. 116	19 months of time before trial in a drug case is too long
1967	*Klopfer v. North Carolina*	386 U.S. 214	2 years after a mistrial is too long
1969	*Smith v. Hooey*	393 U.S. 374	6-year delay from federal court to state court too long
1970	*Dickey v. Florida*	398 U.S. 374	7 years' delay too long
1971	*United States v. Marion*	404 U.S. 307	3 years before indictment OK, only time after accused counts
1972	*Baker v. Wingo*	407 U.S. 514	Right to speedy trial can be implicitly waived
1973	*Braden v. 30th Circuit Court*	410 U.S. 484	District court must have custody over prisoner
1973	*Strunk v. United States*	412 U.S. 434	Propriety of remedy of Court of Appeals and speedy trial
1977	*United States v. Lovasco*	431 U.S. 783	Reasons for delay must be considered; 18 months too long
1982	*United States v. McDonald*	456 U.S. 1	Speedy trial clause does not apply until indicted
1986	*United States v. Loud Hawk*	474 U.S. 302	Time between dismissal and new trial should not be excluded from length of delay
1992	*Doggett v. United States*	505 U.S. 647	8½-year delay between indictment and arrest violates right to speedy trial
2003	*Sell v. United States*	539 U.S. 166	Can defendant be involuntarily medicated to competency to stand trial?
2009	*Vermont v. Brillon*	129 U.S. 1382	If appointed counsel is responsible for delay, delay is attributable to defendant
2010	*Berhuis v. Smith*	130 U.S. 1382	Fair cross-section of a community required for a jury trial to be fair
2010	*Thaier v. Haynes*	130 U.S. 1171	Fifth Amendment self-incrimination clause and registration of firearms
2012	*Smith v. Cain*	132 U.S. 627	State must reveal exculpatory material

Table 5.6. Supreme Court Decisions on Capital Punishment

Table 5.6 specifies twelve exemplary capital punishment U.S. Supreme Court rulings.

Name of Case	Citation	Vote	Ruling
Rooney v. North Dakota	196 U.S. 196, 1905	9–0	Private vs. public execution
Francis v. Resweber	329 U.S. 459, 1947	5–4	Execution after failed attempt not cruel and unusual punishment
Woodson v. North Carolina	428 U.S. 280, 1976	5–4	Mandatory capital punishment laws are unconstitutional
Godfrey v. Georgia	466 U.S. 420, 1980	6–3	Murder must involve narrow and precise aggravating factors to be punishable by death
Spaziano v. Florida	468 U.S. 477, 1984	6–3	Judge v. jury on aggravating factors
Sumner v. Shuman	483 U.S. 66, 1987	6–3	No mandatory death penalty for prisoner service life sentence without parole
Walton v. Arizona	497 U.S. 639, 1990	5–4	Judge finding aggravating factors is constitutional (overruled in 2002)
Harris v. Alabama	513 U.S. 504, 1995	8–1	Law allowing judge to impose death penalty making jury recommendations nonbinding, even if it calls for life imprisonment, is constitutional
Atkins v. Virginia	536 U.S. 304, 2002	6–3	Execution of mentally impaired offender unconstitutional
Roper v. Simmons	543 U.S. 551, 2005	5–4	Death penalty for under 18 years of age unconstitutional
Kennedy v. Louisiana	554 U.S. 407, 2008	5–4	Death penalty for child rape, nonhomicidal, unconstitutional
Hurst v. Florida	577 U.S.--, 2016	8–1	Law giving judges power to decide facts related to Sixth Amendment requiring a jury to determine aggravating factors making a crime punishable by death, rather than by a judge.

Table 5.7. State Status Regarding Capital Punishment

Table 5.7 presents a list of states and their status regarding capital punishment.

STATES WITH CAPITAL PUNISHMENT

ALABAMA	NEBRASKA
ARIZONA	NEVADA
ARKANSAS	NORTH CAROLINA
CALIFORNIA	OHIO
FLORIDA	OKLAHOMA
GEORGIA	OREGON
IDAHO	PENNSYLVANIA
INDIANA	SOUTH CAROLINA
KANSAS	SOUTH DAKOTA
KENTUCKY	TENNESSEE
LOUISIANA	TEXAS
MISSISSIPPI	UTAH
MISSOURI	VIRGINIA
MONTANA	WYOMING

STATES WITH GUBERNATORIAL MORATORIUM	YEAR OF MORATORIUM
CALIFORNIA	2019
OREGON	2011
PENNSYLVANIA	2015

STATES WITH NO DEATH PENALTY, YEAR ABOLISHED

ALASKA (1957)	MINNESOTA (1911)
COLORADO (2020)	NEW HAMPSHIRE (2019)
CONNECTICUT (2012)	NEW JERSEY (2007)
DELAWARE (2016)	NEW MEXICO (2009)
HAWAII (1957)	NEW YORK (2007)
ILLINOIS (2011)	NORTH DAKOTA (1973)
IOWA (1965)	RHODE ISLAND (1984)
MAINE (1887)	VERMONT (1972)
MARYLAND (2013)	WASHINGTON (2018)
MASSACHUSETTS (1984)	WEST VIRGINIA (1965)
MICHIGAN (1847)	WISCONSIN (1853)

Table 5.8. Supreme Court Decisions Regarding the Tenth, Fourteenth, Nineteenth, Twenty-Fourth, and Twenty-Sixth Amendments

Table 5.8 lists cases dealing with the Tenth, Fourteenth, Nineteenth, Twenty-Fourth, and Twenty-Sixth Amendments

Case	Citation	Vote	Ruling
Slaughter House Cases	83 U.S. 36, 1873	5–4	Citizens' privileges and immunities vs. Louisiana state law
Plessy v. Ferguson	163 U.S. 537, 1896	7–1	Louisiana "separate" car act upheld, "separate-but-equal" doctrine
Lochner v. New York	198 U.S. 45, 1905	5–4	New York labor law violated Fourteenth Amendment "freedom of contract."
Gitlow v. New York	268 U.S. 652, 1925	7–2	Upheld criminal anarchy law, set "clear and present danger" test
Brown v. Board of Education	347 U.S. 483, 1954	9–0	Segregation laws inherently unequal, unconstitutional
Mapp v. Ohio	367 U.S. 643, 1961	6–3	Held exclusionary rule v. evidence obtained vs. Fourteenth Amendment applies to states, "selective incorporation" principle
Gideon v. Wainwright	372 U.S. 335, 1963	9–0	State must provide counsel to indigent
Griswold v. Connecticut	381 U.S. 479, 1965	7–2	Connecticut's "Comstock" law unconstitutional by Tenth and Fourteenth Amendments
Loving v. Virginia	388 U.S. 1, 1967	9–0	Virginia's interracial marriage ban unconstitutional; set precedent for same-sex marriage case
Regents UCA v. Bakke	438 U.S. 265, 1978	5–4	Racial quotas unconstitutional, affirmative action constitutional
Bond v. United States	564 U.S. 211, 2011	9–0	Individuals have standing to raise 10th Amendment challenge to federal laws
Leser v. Garnett	258 U.S. 130, 1922	9–0	Upheld Nineteenth Amendment as constitutional on voting rights for women
Harper v. Virginia Board of Elections	383 U.S. 663, 1966	6–3	Upheld Twenty-Fourth Amendment on the poll tax
Oregon v. Mitchell	400 U.S. 112, 1970	5–4	Upheld Twenty-Sixth Amendment on voting age for federal elections

Table 5.9. Major Civil Rights Acts Passed by the United States Congress

Table 5.9 presents the major civil rights enactments of the United States Congress, 1866–1991.

Year/Title	Citation	Also Known As
Act of April 6, 1886	14 Stat. 27	Civil Rights Act of 1866
Act of March 3, 1875	18 Stat. 335	The Enforcement Act
Act of August 9, 1957	71 Stat. 634	Eisenhower Civil Rights Act
Act of May 6, 1960	74 Stat. 89	Voter Registration/Poll Tax
Act of July 2, 1964	78 Stat. 241	Equal Employment Opportunity Act
Act of August 6, 1965	79 Stat. 437	Voting Rights Act
Act of April 11, 1968	82 Stat. 73	Fair Housing Act/Indian Civil Rights Act
Act of November 21, 1991	105 Stat. 1071	Equal Opportunity Act
Act of May 20, 1993	107 Stat. 77	National Voter Registration Act

Table 5.10. Exemplary Civil Rights Advocacy Groups, by Type

Table 5.10 presents a list of 40 exemplary civil rights advocacy groups, by type of group.

Type of Organization	Name of Organization, Date, Strategy Used
AGE	American Association of Retired People, AARP, 1958—**A**
	Students for a Democratic Society, SDS, 1960—**R**
AMERICAN ARAB/MUSLIM	American Arab Anti-Discrimination Committee, ADC, 1980—**A**
	Arab American Political Action Committee, AAPAC, 1980—**A**
	Council of American Islamic Relations, CAIR, 1994—**A**
	Nation of Islam, NOI, 1934—**S**
ASIAN AMERICAN	Asian American Legal Defense and Education Fund, AALDEF, 1974—**A**
	Japanese American Citizens League, JACL, 1929—**A**

(continued)

Table 5.10   *(continued)*

Type of Organization	Name of Organization, Date, Strategy Used
BLACK AMERICAN	Black Panther Party, BPP, 1966—**R**
	Congress of Racial Equality, CORE, 1942—**A**
	National Association for the Advancement of Colored People, NAACP, 1909—**A**
	Southern Christian Leadership Conference, SCLC, 1957—**R**
	Student Nonviolent Coordinating Committee, SNCC, 1960—**R**
	Universal Negro Improvement Association, UNIA, 1914—**S**
	Urban League, UL, 1910—**A**
DISABLED AMERICANS	American Association of People with Disabilities, AAPD, 1995—**A**
GENDER	League of Women Voters, LWV, 1920—**A**
	National Women Political Caucus, NWPC, 1971—**A**
	National Women's Suffrage Association, NWSA, 1869—**A**
GENERAL	American Civil Liberties Union, ACLU, 1920—**A**
	Human Rights Watch, HRW, 1978—**A**
	National Center for Civil and Human Rights, NCCHR, 2014—**A**
	National Rifle Association, NRA, 1871—**A**
	Southern Poverty Law Center, SPLC, 1971—**A**
HISPANIC	Association Federal dee Mercedes, AFM, 1963—**R**
	Community Service Organization, CSO, 1947—**A**
	Crusade for Justice, CJ, 1966—**R**
	League of United Latin American Citizens, LULAC, 1929—**A**
	Mexican American Legal Defense and Education Fund, MALDEF, 1968—**A**
	Mexican American Youth Organization, MAYO, 1967—**R**
	National Council of La Raza, 1968—**R**
	United Farm Workers, UFW, 1962—**R**
NATIVE AMERICAN	American Indian Movement, AIM, 1968—**R**
	National Council of American Indians, NCAI, 1944—**A**
	National Indian Youth Council, NIYC, 1961—**R**
SEXUAL ORIENTATION	ACT UP, 1987—**R**
	Daughters of Bilitis, DB, 1955—**A**
	Mattachine Society, 1950—**A**
	Transgender Education Association, 2003—**A**

A = Accommodation
S = Separatist
R = Radical

Table 5.11. Activists and Organizations Concerning Sexual Orientation Rights

Table 5.11 lists activists and activist organizations that advocated regarding sexual orientation rights.

Activist	Rights Fought for/Organization
Barbara Cameron (1954–2002)	Native American/Lesbian/Women's Rights
Barbara Gittings (1932–2007	Lesbian Rights
Steven Goldstein (1962–)	Gay Rights Advocate
Harry Hay (1912–2002)	Founder, Mattachine Society, LGBT Advocate
Marsha T. Johnson (1945–1992)	Gay Liberation, AIDs Activist with ACT UP
Frank Kamery (1925–2011)	Gay Rights Activist
Larry Kramer (1935–)	ACT UP Founder
Phyllis Lyon (1924–2020)	Cofounder, Daughters of Bilitis
Del Martin (1921–2008)	Cofounder, Daughters of Bilitis
Harvey Milk (1930–1978)	Gay Rights, LGBT Movement Activist, Assassinated
Christopher Scuderi (1972)	Transgender Education Advocates of Utah
Judy Shepard (1952–)	Gay Rights Activist/Speaker
Rebecca Wilde (1973)	Transgender Education Advocates of Utah

Table 5.12. Presidential Medals of Freedom Awarded for Civil Rights Activism

Table 5.12 presents the awardees of the prestigious Presidential Medal of Freedom for civil rights activism. They are presented by date the award was given, the recipient, and the president giving the award.

Year Awarded	Recipient of Award	President Awarding Medal
1964	Hellen Keller	Lyndon B. Johnson
1964	Philip Randolph	Lyndon B. Johnson
1967	Roy Wilkins	Lyndon B. Johnson
1969	Mary Lasker	Richard Nixon
1977 –P	Martin Luther King Jr.	Jimmy Carter
1980	Clarence Mitchell	Jimmy Carter
1981	Esther Peterson	Jimmy Carter

(continued)

Table 5.12   *(continued)*

Year Awarded	Recipient of Award	President Awarding Medal
1981	Andrew Young	Jimmy Carter
1981	Roger Nash Baldwin	Jimmy Carter
1984	Hector Garcia	Ronald Reagan
1989	Lech Welesa	George H. W. Bush
1994	Dorothy Height	Bill Clinton
1994—P	Cesar Chavez	Bill Clinton
1995—P	William C. Velasquez Jr.	Bill Clinton
1996	Ginetta Sagan	Bill Clinton
1998	Rosa Parks	Bill Clinton
1998	Mario G. Obiedo	Bill Clinton
1998	Fred Korematsu	Bill Clinton
1998	Justin Dart	Bill Clinton
1998	James Farmer Jr.	Bill Clinton
1998	Arnold Aronson	Bill Clinton
1998	Evelyn Dubrow	Bill Clinton
2000	George G. Higgins	Bill Clinton
2000	Millie Jeffrey	Bill Clinton
2000	Marian Wright Edelman	Bill Clinton
2006	Natan Sharansky	George W. Bush
2007	Benjamin Hooks	George W. Bush
2007	Oscar Elias Biscet	George W. Bush
2008	Rev. Joseph Lowery	Barack Obama
2009—P	Harvey Milk	Barack Obama
2011	Sylvia Mendez	Barack Obama
2011	John Lewis	Barack Obama
2012—P	Gordon Hirabayashi	Barack Obama
2012	Dolores Huerta	Barack Obama
2013	Gloria Steinem	Barack Obama
2013—P	Bayard Rustin	Barack Obama
2013	Cordy Tindell Vivian	Barack Obama
2014—P	Andrew Goodman	Barack Obama
2014—P	James Chaney	Barack Obama
2014	Suzan Shown Harjo	Barack Obama
2014	Ethel Kennedy	Barack Obama
2014—P	Michael Schwerner	Barack Obama
2015—P	Minoru Yasui	Barack Obama
2015—P	Bill Frank Jr.	Barack Obama
2015—P	Elouise Cobell	Barack Obama

P = Awarded Posthumously

Documents

Declaration of Independence (1776)

The Declaration of Independence, signed on July 4, 1776, justifying why the colonies sought independence at the risk of a revolutionary war, contains a list of particulars of offenses—they deemed them usurpations—by the Crown that give insight into what they considered their fundamental rights. The spelling and punctuation of the original are retained.

When in the Course of human events, it becomes necessary for one people to dissolve the political bands which have connected them with another, and to assume among the powers of the earth, the separate and equal station to which the Laws of Nature and of Nature's God entitle them, a decent respect to the operations of mankind requires that they should declare the causes which impel them to the separation.

We hold these truths to be self-evident, that all men are created equal, that they are endowed by the Creator with certain unalienable Rights, that among these are Life, Liberty and the pursuit of Happiness. That to secure these rights, Governments are instituted among Men, deriving their power from the consent of the governed. That whenever any Form of Government becomes destructive of those ends, it is the Right of the People to alter or to abolish it, and to institute a new Government, laying its foundation on such principles and organizing its powers in such form, as to them shall seem most likely to effect their Safety and Happiness. Prudence, indeed, will dictate that Governments, long established should not be changed for light and transient causes; and accordingly all experience that shewn, that mankind are more disposed to suffer, while evils are sufferable, than to right themselves by abolishing the forms to which they are accustomed. But when a long train of abuses and usurpations, pursuing invariably the same Object evinces a design to reduce them under absolute Despotism, it is their right, it is their duty, to throw off such

Government, and to provide new Guards for their future security. Such has been the patient sufferance of these Colonies; and such is now the necessity which constrains them to alter their former Systems of Government. The history of the present King of Great Britain is a history of repeated injuries and usurpations, all having in direct object the establishment of an absolute Tyranny over these States. To prove this, let Facts be submitted to a candid world.

He has refused his Assent to Laws, the most wholesome and necessary for the public good.

He has forbidden his Governors to pass Laws of immediate and pressing importance, unless suspended in their operation till his Assent should be obtained; and when so suspended, he has utterly neglected to attend to them.

He has refused to pass other Laws for the accommodation of large districts of people, unless those people would relinquish the right of Representation in the Legislature, a right inestimable to them and formidable to tyrants only.

He has called together legislative bodies at places unusual, uncomfortable, and distant from the depository of their public Records, for the sole purpose of fatiguing them into compliance with his measures.

He has dissolved Representative Houses repeatedly, for opposing with manly firmness his invasions on the rights of the people.

He has refused for a long time, after such dissolutions, to cause others to be elected; whereby the Legislative powers, incapable of Annihilation, have returned to the People at large for their exercise; the State remaining in the mean time exposed to all the dangers of invasion from without, and convulsions from within.

He has endeavored to prevent the population of these States; for that purpose obstructing the Laws of Naturalization of Foreigners; refusing to pass others to encourage their migrations hither, and raising the conditions of new Appropriations of Lands.

He has obstructed the Administration of Justice, by refusing his Assent to Laws for establishing Judiciary powers.

He has made Judges dependent on his Will along, for the tenure of their offices, and the amount and payment of their salaries.

He has erected a multitude of New Offices, and sent hither swarms of Officers to harass our people, and eat out their substance.

He has kept among us, in times of peace, Standing Armies without the Consent of our legislatures.

He has affected to render the Military independent of and superior to the Civil power.

He has combined with others to subject us to a jurisdiction foreign to our constitution, and unacknowledged by out laws; giving his Assent to their Acts of pretended Legislation:

For Quartering large bodies of armed troops among us;

For protecting them, by a mock Trial, from punishment for any Murders which they should commit on the inhabitants of these States:

For cutting off our Trade with all parts of the world:

For imposing Taxes on us without our Consent:

For depriving us in many cases, of the benefits of Trial by Jury:

For transporting us beyond Seas to be tried for pretended offences:

For abolishing the free System of English Laws in a neighboring Province, establishing therein an Arbitrary government, and enlarging its Boundaries so as to render it at once an example and fit instrument for introducing the same absolute rule into these Colonies:

For taking away our Charters, abolishing our most valuable Laws, and altering fundamentally the Forms of our Government:

For suspending our own Legislatures, and declaring themselves invested with power to legislate for us in all cases whatsoever:

He has abdicated Government here, by declaring us out of his Protection and waging War against us.

He has plundered our seas, ravaged our Coasts, burnt our towns, and destroyed the lives of our people.

He is at this time transporting large Armies of foreign Mercenaries to compleat the works of death, desolation and tyranny, already begun with circumstances of Cruelty and perfidy scarcely paralleled in the most barbarous ages, and totally unworthy the Head of a civilized nation.

He has constrained our fellow Citizens taken Captive on the high Seas to bear Arms against their Country, to become the executioners of their friends and Brethren, or to fall themselves by their Hands.

He has excited domestic insurrections amongst us, and has endeavored to bring on the inhabitants of our frontiers, the merciless Indian Savages, whose known rule of warfare, is an undistinguished destruction of all ages, sexes and conditions.

In every state of these Oppressions We have Petitioned for Redress in the most humble terms: Our repeated Petitions have been answered only by repeated injury. A Prince whose character is thus marked by every act which may define a Tyrant, is unfit to be the ruler of a free people.

Nor have We been wanting in attentions to our British brethren. We have warned them from time to time of attempts by their legislature to extend an unwarrantable jurisdiction over us. We have reminded them of the circumstances of our emigration and settlement here. We have appealed to their native justice and magnanimity, and we have conjured them by the ties of our common kindred to disavow these usurpations, which would inevitably interrupt our connections and correspondence. They too have been deaf to the voice of justice and of consanguinity. We must, therefore, acquiesce in the necessity, which denounces our Separation, and hold them, as we hold the rest of mankind, Enemies in War, in Peace Friends.

We, therefore, the Representatives of the United States of America, in General Congress Assembled, appealing to the

Supreme Judge of the world for the rectitude of our intentions, do, in the Name, and by Authority of the good People of these Colonies, solemnly publish and declare, That these United Colonies are, and of Right ought to be Free and Independent States; that they are Absolved from all Allegiance to the British Crown, and that all political connection between them and the State of Great Britain, is and ought to be totally dissolved; and that as Free and Independent States, they have full Power to levy War, conclude Peace, contract Alliances, establish Commerce, and to do all other Acts and Things which Independent States may of right do, And for the support of this Declaration, with a firm reliance on the protection of divine Providence, we mutually pledge to each other our lives, our Fortunes and our sacred Honor.

Source: U.S. National Archives. https://www.archives.gov /founding-docs/declaration-transcript.

Resolutions of the Seneca Falls Convention (1848)

In 1848, a group of suffragettes gathered in convention in Seneca Falls, New York. They drafted a Declaration of Sentiments and Resolutions calling for women's rights. In many ways, it reflected the Declaration of Independence of the United States.

Whereas, the great precept of nature is conceded to be, "that man shall pursue his own true and substantial happiness," Blackstone, in his Commentaries, remarks, that this law of Nature being coeval with mankind, and dictated by God himself, is of course superior in obligation to any other. It is binding over all the globe, in all countries, and at all times; no human laws are of any validity if contrary to this, and such of them as are valid, derive all their force, and all their validity, and all their authority, mediately and immediately, from this original; Therefore,

Resolved, That such laws as conflict, in any way, with the true and substantial happiness of woman, are contrary to the great precept of nature, and of no validity; for this is "superior in obligation to any other."

Resolved, That all laws which prevent woman from occupying such a station in society as her conscience shall dictate, or which place her in a position inferior to that of man, are contrary to the great precept of nature, and therefore of no force or authority.

Resolved, That woman is man's equal—was intended to be so by the Creator, and the highest good of the race demands that she should be recognized as such.

Resolved, That the women of this country ought to be enlightened in regard to the laws under which they live, that they may no longer publish their degradation, by declaring themselves satisfied with their present position, nor their ignorance, by asserting that they have all the rights they want.

Resolved, That inasmuch as man, while claiming for himself intellectual superiority, does accord to woman moral superiority, it is preeminently his duty to encourage her to speak, and teach, as she has an opportunity, in all religious assemblies.

Resolved, That the same amount of virtue, delicacy, and refinement of behavior, that is required of woman in the social state, should also be required of man, and the same transgressions should be visited with equal severity on both man and woman.

Resolved, that the objection of indelicacy and impropriety, which is so often brought against woman when she addresses a public audience, comes with a very ill grade from those who encourage, by their attendance, her appearance on the stage, in the concert, or in the feats of the circus.

Resolved, That woman has too long rested satisfied in the circumscribed limits which corrupt customs and a perverted application of the Scriptures have marked out for her, and that it is time she should move in the enlarged sphere which her great Creator has assigned her.

Resolved, That it is the duty of the women of this country to secure to themselves their sacred right to the elective franchise.

Resolved, That the equality of human rights results necessarily from the fact of the identity of the race in capabilities and responsibilities.

Resolved, therefore, That, being invested by the Creator with the same capabilities, and the same consciousness of responsibility for their exercise, it is demonstrably the right and duty of woman, equally with man, to promote every righteous cause, by every righteous means, and especially in regard to the great subjects of morals and religion, it is self-evidently their right to participate with her brother in teaching them, both in private and in public, by writing and by speaking, by any instrumentalities, proper to be used, and in any assemblies proper to be held; and this being a self-evident truth, growing out of the divinity implanted principles of human nature, any custom or authority adverse to it, whether modern or wearing the hoary sanction of antiquity, is to be regarded as self-evident falsehood, and at war with the interests of mankind

Source: Stanton, Elizabeth Cady. *Address Of Mrs. Elizabeth Cady Stanton, Delivered at Seneca Falls & Rochester, NY, July 19th & August 2d, 1848.* New York: R. J. Johnston, 1870.

Article VIII of the Treaty of Guadalupe Hidalgo (1848)

In 1848, the United States ended its war with Mexico by signing the Treaty of Guadalupe Hidalgo. Mexico ceded most of its northern territory to the United States, comprising all or parts of the following states: California, New Mexico, Arizona, Nevada, Utah, and Colorado. Importantly for civil rights, it contained Article VIII regarding the admission to U.S. citizenship—and thus to the privileges and immunities thereof, those Mexicans remaining in those territories ceded to the United States and not declaring their wish to remain citizens of Mexico. It is significant that at the time they were generally considered to be "nonwhite," yet prior to the Civil War and adoption of the Thirteenth Amendment, citizenship was reserved to "white" persons only. It confers citizenship by treaty right to that of native birth or naturalization.

Mexicans now established in territories previously belong to Mexico, and which remain for the future within the limits of the United States as defined by the present treaty, shall be free to continue where they now reside, or to remove at any time to the Mexican republic, retaining the property which they possess in the said territories, or disposing thereof, and removing the proceeds wherever they please, without their being subjected on this account, to any contribution, tax, or charge whatever.

Those who shall prefer to remain in the said territories, may either retain the title and rights of Mexican citizens, or acquire those of citizens of the United States. But they shall be under the obligation to make their election within one year from the date of the exchange of ratification of this treaty, and those who shall remain in the said territories after the expiration of that year, without having declared their intention to retain the character of Mexicans, shall be considered to have elected to become citizens of the United States.

Source: *Treaty of Peace, Friendship, Limits, and Settlement with the Republic of Mexico.* February 2, 1848. United States Treaties and Other International Agreements, vol. 9. Washington, D.C.: Government Printing Office, 1950, 922.

Mississippi Black Codes (1865)

The Mississippi Black Codes were enacted right after the Civil War ended. They were intended to formalize a racial hierarchy in which whites could restrict the freedoms of black laborers. They exemplify "de jure" segregation and discrimination.

1. Civil Rights of Freedmen in Mississippi.

All freedmen, free negroes and mulattoes may sue and be sued . . . may acquire personal property . . . and may dispose of the same in the same manner and to the same extent that white persons may: [but no] freedman, free negro or mulatto . . . [shall] rent or lease any lands or tenements except in incorporated cities or towns, in which places the corporate authorities shall control the same. . . .

All freedmen, free negroes or mulattoes who do now and have herebefore lived and cohabitated together as husband and wife shall be taken and held in law as legally married, and the issue shall be taken and held as legitimate for all purposes; and it shall not be lawful for any freedman, free negro or mulatto to intermarry with any white person; nor for any person to intermarry with any freedman, free negro or mulatto; and any person who shall so intermarry shall be deemed guilty of felony, and on conviction thereof shall be confined in the State penitentiary for life; and those shall be deemed freedmen, free negroes and mulattoes who are of pure negro blood, and those descended from a negro to the third generation, inclusive, though one ancestor in each generation may have been a white person. . . .

Freedman, free negroes, and mulattoes are now by law competent witnesses . . . in civil cases [and in criminal cases where they are the victims]. . . .

All contracts for labor made with freedmen, free negroes and mulattoes for a longer period than one month shall be in writing, and a duplicate, attested to and read to said freedman, free negroe or mulatto by a beat, city, or county officer, or two disinterested white persons of the county in which the labor is to be performed, of which each party shall have one: and said contract shall be taken and held as entire contracts, and if the laborer shall quit the service of the employer before the expiration of his term of service, without good cause, he shall forfeit his wages for that year up to the time of quitting.

Every civil officer shall, and every person may, arrest and carry back to his or her legal employer any freedman, free negro, or mulatto who shall have quit the service of his or her employer before the expiration of his or her term of service without good cause; and said officer and person shall be entitled to receive for arresting and carrying back every disserting employee aforesaid the sum of five dollars. . . .

If any person shall persuade or attempt to persuade, entice, or cause any freedman, free negro or mulatto to desert from the legal employment of any person before the expiration of his or her term of service, or shall knowingly employ any such disserting freedman, free negro or mulatto, or shall knowingly give or sell to any such disserting freedman, free negro or mulatto, any food, raiment, or other thing, he or she shall be guilty of a misdemeanor. . . .

2. Mississippi Apprentice Law

It shall be the duty of all sheriffs, justices of the peace, and other civil officers of the several counties in this State, to report to the probate courts of their respective counties semiannually, at the January and July terms of said courts, all freedmen, free negroes, and mulattoes, under the age of eighteen, in their respective counties, beats, or districts, who are orphans, or whose parent or parents have not the means or who refuse to provide for and support said minors; and thereupon it shall be the duty of said probate court to order the clear of said court to apprentice said minors to some competent and suitable person on such terms as the court may direct, having a particular care to the interest of said minor: *Provided,* that the former owner of said minors shall have the preference when, in the opinion of the court, he or she shall be a suitable person for that purpose.

In the management and control of said apprentice, said master or mistress shall have the power to inflict such moderate corporal chastisement as a father or guardian is allowed to inflict on his or her child or ward at common law; *Provided,* that in no case shall cruel or inhuman punishment be inflicted. . . .

3. Mississippi Vagrant Law

That all rogues and vagabonds, idle and dissipated persons, beggars, jugglers, or persons practicing unlawful games or plays, runaways, common drunkards, common night-walkers, pilferers, lewd, wanton, or lascivious persons, in speech or behavior, common railers and brawlers, persons who neglect their calling or employment, misspend what they earn, or do not provide for the support of themselves or their families, or dependents, and all other idle and disorderly persons, including all who neglect all lawful business, habitually misspend their time by frequenting houses of ill-fame, gaming-houses, or tippling shops, shall be deemed and considered vagrants, under the provisions of this act, and upon conviction thereof shall be fined not exceeding one hundred dollars . . . and be imprisoned, at the discretion of the court, not exceeding ten days.

All freedmen, free negroes and mulattoes in this State, over the age of eighteen years, found on the second Monday in January, 1866, or thereafter, with no lawful employment or business, or found unlawful assembling themselves together, either in the day or night time, and all white persons assembling themselves with freedmen, free negroes or mulattoes, or usually associating with freedmen, free negroes or mulattoes, on terms of equality, or living in adultery or fornication with a freed woman, freed negro or mulatto, shall be deemed vagrants, and on conviction thereof shall be fined in a sum not exceeding, in the case of a freedman, free negro or mulatto, fifty dollars, and a white man two hundred dollars, and imprisonment at the discretion of the court, the free negro not exceeding ten days, and the white man not exceeding six months. . . .

4. Penal Laws of Mississippi
That no freedman, free negro or mulatto, not in the military service of the United States government, and not licensed so to do by the board of police of his or her country, shall keep or carry fire-arms of any kind, or any ammunition, dirk or bowie knife...

Any freedman, free negro, or mulatto committing riots, routs, affrays, trespasses, malicious mischief, cruel treatment to animals, seditious speeches, insulting gestures, language, or acts, or assaults on any person, disturbance of the peace, exercising the function of a minister of the Gospel without license from some regularly organized church, vending spirituous or intoxicating liquors, or committing any other misdemeanor, the punishment of which is not specifically provided by law, shall, upon conviction thereof in the county court, be fined not less than ten dollars, and not more than one hundred dollars, and may be imprisoned at the discretion of the court, not exceeding thirty days. . . .

If any freedman, free negro, or mulatto, convicted of any of the misdemeanors provided against in this act, shall fail or refuse for the space of five days, after conviction, to pay the fine and costs imposed, such person shall be hired out by the sheriff or other officer, at public outcry, to any white person who will pay said fine and costs, and take said convict for the shortest time.

Source: *An Act to Confer Civil Rights on Freedmen, and for Other Purposes. Laws of Mississippi.* 1865. https://www.houseofrussell .com/legalhistory/alh/docs/lawsofmiss.html.

Civil Rights Act (April 9, 1866)

This document excerpts three sections of the Civil Rights Act of 1866 (14 Stat. 27). Enacted immediately after the Civil War, it exemplifies the attempts made during Reconstruction to protect the civil rights and liberties of the former slaves. Subsequent Supreme Court decisions rendered it very limited in its effectiveness and necessitated the civil rights laws of the 1960s.

Be it enacted by the Senate and the House of Representatives of the United States of America in Congress assembled, That all persons born in the United States and not subject to any foreign power, excluding Indians not taxed, are hereby declared to be citizens of the United States; and such citizens, of every race and color, without regard to any previous condition of slavery or involuntary servitude, except as a punishment for crime whereof the party shall have been duly convicted, shall have the same right in every State and Territory in the United States, to make and enforce contracts, to sue, be parties, and give evidence, to inherit, purchase, lease, sell, hold, and convey real and personal property, and to full and equal benefit of all laws and proceedings for the security of person and property, as is enjoyed by white citizens, and shall be subject to like punishment, pains, and penalties, and to none other, any law, statute, ordinance, regulation, or custom, to the contrary notwithstanding.

Sec. 2. *And be it further enacted,* That any person who, under color of any law, statute, ordinance, regulation, or custom, shall subject, or cause to be subjected, any inhabitant of any State or Territory to the deprivation of any right secured or protected by this act, or to different punishment, pains, or penalties on account of such person having at any time been held in a condition of slavery or involuntary servitude, except as punishment for crime whereof the party shall have been duly convicted, or by reason of his color or race, than is prescribed for the punishment of white persons, shall be deemed guilty of a misdemeanor, and, on conviction, shall be punished by fine not exceeding one thousand dollars, or imprisonment not exceeding one year, or both, in the discretion of the court.

Sec. 3. *And it is further enacted,* That the district courts of the United States, within their respective districts, shall have, exclusively of the courts of the several States, cognizance of all crimes and offenses committed against the provisions of this act, and also, concurrently with the circuit courts of the United States, of all causes, civil and criminal, affecting persons who are denied or cannot enforce in the courts or judicial tribunals of the State or locality where they may be any of the rights secured to them by the first section of this act; and if any suit or prosecution, civil or criminal, has been or shall be commenced in any State court, against any such person, for any causes whatsoever, or against any officer, civil or military, or other person, for any arrest or imprisonment, trespasses, or wrongs done or committed by virtue or under color of authority derived from this act or the act establishing a Bureau for the relief of Freedmen and Refugees, and all acts amendatory thereof, or for refusing to do any act upon the ground that it would be inconsistent with this act, such defendant shall have the right to remove such cause for trial to the proper district or circuit court in the manner prescribe by the "Act relating to habeas corpus and regulating judicial proceedings in certain cases," approved March three, eighteen hundred and sixty three, and all acts amendatory thereof.

Source: "An Act to Protect All Persons in the United States in their Civil Rights, and Furnish the Means of their Vindication," Chap. 31, *U.S. Statutes at Large* 14 (1866): 27–29.

The Espionage Act (June 15, 1917)

The Espionage Act of 1917 was used very directly and successfully to prosecute members, including native-born citizens, of the Socialist Party of America, the Communist Party of America, and of the International Workers of the World (IWW). The sweeping nature of the language in the law, particularly its conspiracy provision (Sec. 4) and harboring provision (Sec. 5) were used so as essentially to constitute guilt by association. Many U.S. citizens, naturalized citizens, and noncitizen resident aliens were imprisoned upon conviction under the Espionage Act, and several hundred immigrants not yet naturalized were summarily expelled under this law. Under the judicial concept of "wartime necessity," the law was upheld as constitutional by the United States Supreme Court in Schenck v. United States (249 U.S. 47, 1919).

Section 1. That: (a) whoever, for the purpose of obtaining information respecting the national defense with intent or reason to believe that the information to be obtained is to be used to the injury of the United States, or to the advantage of any foreign nation, goes upon, enters, flies over, or otherwise obtains information, concerning any vessel, aircraft, work of defence, navy yard, naval station, submarine base, coaling station, fort, battery, torpedo station, dockyard, canal, railroad, arsenal, camp, factory, mine, telegraph, telephone, wireless, or signal station, building, office, or other place connected with the national defence, owned or constructed, or in progress of construction by the United States, or under the control of the United States, or of any of its officers or agents, or within the exclusive jurisdiction of the United States, or any place in which any vessel, aircraft, arms, munitions, or other materials or instruments for use in time of war are being made, prepared, repaired, or stored, under any contract or agreement with the United States, or with any person on behalf of the United States, or otherwise on behalf of the United States, or any prohibited place with the meaning of section six of this title; or (b) whoever for the purpose aforesaid, and with like intent or reason to believe, copies, takes, makes, or obtains, or attempts, or induces or aids another to copy, take, make, or obtain, any sketch, photograph, photographic negative, blue print, plan, map, model, instrument, appliance, document, writing or not of anything connected with the national defence; or (c) whoever, for the purpose aforesaid, receives or obtains or agrees or attempts or induces or aids another to receive or obtain from any other person, or from any source whatever, any document, writing, code book, signal book, sketch, photograph, photographic negative, blue print, plan, map, model, instrument, appliance, or not, of anything connected with the national defence, knowing or having reason to believe, at the time he receives or obtains, or agrees or attempts or induces or aids another to receive or obtain it, that it has been or will be obtained, taken, made or disposed of by any persons contrary to the provisions of this title; or (d) whoever, lawfully or unlawfully having possession of, access to, control over, or being entrusted with any document, writing, code book, signal book, sketch, photograph, photographic negative, blue print, plan, map, model, instrument, appliance, or note relating to the national defence, willfully communicates or transmits or attempts to communicate or transmit the same and fails to deliver it on demand to the officer or employee of the United States entitled to receive it; or (c) whoever, being entrusted with or having lawful possession or control of any document, writing, code book, signal book, sketch, photograph, photographic negative, blue print, plan, map, model, note, or information relating to the national defence, through gross negligence permits the same to be removed from its proper place of custody or delivered to anyone in violation of his trust, or to be list, stolen, abstracted, or destroyed, shall be punished by a fine of not more than $10,000, or by imprisonment for not more than two years, or both.

Section 2. Whoever, with intent or reason to believe that it is to be used to the injury of the United States, or to the advantage of a foreign nation, communicated, delivers, or transmits, or attempt to, or aids, or induces another to, communicate, deliver or transmit, to any foreign government, or to any faction or party or military or naval force within a foreign country, whether recognized or unrecognized by the United States, or to any representative, officer, agent, employee, subject, or citizen thereof, either directly or indirectly any document, writing, code book, signal book, sketch, photograph, photographic negative, blue print, plan, map, model, not, instrument, appliance, or information relating to the national defence, shall be punished by imprisonment for not more than twenty years: Provided, That whoever shall violate the provisions of subsection (a) of this section in a time of war shall be punished by death or imprisonment for not more than thirty years, and (b) whoever, in time of war, with intent that the same shall be communicated to the enemy, shall collect, record, publish or communicate, or attempt to elicit any information with respect to the movement, numbers, description, condition, or disposition of any of the armed forces, ships, aircraft, or war materials of the United States, or with respect to the plans or conduct, or supposed plans for conduct of any naval or military operations, or with respect to any works or measures undertaken for or connected with, or intended for the fortification of any place, or any other information relating to the public defence, which might be useful to the enemy, shall be punished by death or by imprisonment for not more than thirty years.

Section 3. Whoever, when the United States is at war, shall willfully make or convey false reports or false information with intent to interfere with the operation or success of the military or naval forces of the United States or to promote the success of its enemies and whoever when the United States is at war, shall willfully cause or attempt to cause insubordination, disloyalty, mutiny, refusal of duty, in the military or naval forces of the United States, or shall willfully obstruct the recruiting or enlistment service of the United States, to the injury of the service or of the United States, shall be punished by a fine of not more than $10,000 or imprisonment for not more than twenty years, or both.

Section 4. If two or more persons conspire to violate the provisions of section two or three of this title, and one or more of such persons does nay act to effect the object of the conspiracy, each of the parties to such conspiracy shall be punished as in said sections provided in the case of the doing of the act the accomplishment of which is the object of such conspiracy. Except as above provided conspiracies to commit offences under this title shall be punished as provided in section thirty-seven of the Act to codify, revise, and amend the penal laws of the United States, approved March fourth, nineteen hundred and nine.

Section 5. Whoever harbours or conceals any person who he knows, or has reasonable grounds to believe or suspect, has committed, or is about to commit, any offence under this title shall be punished by a fine of not more than $10,000 or by imprisonment for not more than two years, or both.

Source: *Espionage Act. U.S. Statutes at Large 40* (1917): 217. https://law.jrank.org/pages/6568/Espionage-Act-1917.html.

Leser v. Garnett (1922)

The Nineteenth Amendment was passed in 1920, and was challenged in the United States Supreme Court in Leser v. Garnett *(258 U.S. 130, 1922). This document provides a synopsis of the majority opinion of the Court, written by Justice Louis Brandeis, upholding the constitutionality of the Nineteenth Amendment. Justice Brandeis was appointed to the Supreme Court by President Woodrow Wilson in 1916.*

On October 12, 1920, Cecilia Street Waters and Mary D. Randolph, citizens of Maryland, applied for and were granted registration as qualified voters in Baltimore City. To have their names stricken from the list, Oscar Leser and others brought this suit in the court of common pleas. The only disqualification alleged was that the applicants for registration were women, whereas the Constitution of Maryland limits the suffrage to men. Ratification of the amendment . . . known as the Nineteenth, 41 Stat. 362, has been proclaimed on August 26, 1920. The Legislature of Maryland had refused to ratify it. The petitioners contended, on several grounds, that the amendment had not become part of the federal Constitution. The trial court overruled the contention and dismissed the petition. Its judgment was affirmed by the Court of Appeals of the state (Maryland), and the case comes here on writ of error. That writ must be dismissed; but the petition for a writ of certiorari, also duly filed, is granted. The laws of Maryland authorize such a suit by a qualified voter against the board of registry. Whether the Nineteenth Amendment has become part of the federal Constitution is the question presented for decision.

The first contention is that the power of amendment conferred by the federal Constitution and sought to be exercised does not extend to this amendment because of its character. The argument is that so great an addition to the electorate, if made without the state's consent, destroys its autonomy as a political body. This amendment is in character and phraseology precisely similar to the Fifteenth. For each the same method of adoption was pursued. One cannot be valid and the other invalid. That the Fifteenth is valid, although rejected by six states, including Maryland, has been recognized for half a century. . . . The suggestion that the Fifteenth was not incorporated into the Constitution is not in accordance with law, but practically as a war measure which has been validated by acquiescence, cannot be entertained.

The second contention is that the Constitution of several of the 36 states named in the proclamation of the Secretary of State there are provisions which render inoperative the alleged ratification by their Legislatures. The argument is that by reason of these specific provisions the Legislature were without power to ratify. But the function of a state Legislature in ratifying a proposed amendment to the federal Constitution, like the function of Congress in proposing the amendment, is a federal function derived from the federal Constitution, and it transcends any limitations sought to be imposed by the people of a state...

The remaining contention is that the ratifying resolutions of Tennessee and of West Virginia are inoperative, because adopted in violation of the rules of legislative procedure prevailing in the respective states. The question raised may have been rendered immaterial by the fact that since the proclamation the Legislatures of two other states—Connecticut and Vermont—have adopted resolutions of ratification. But a broader answer should be given to the contention. The proclamation by the Secretary certified that from official documents on file in the Department of State it appeared that the proposed amendment was ratified by the Legislatures of 36 states, and that it "has become valid in all intents and purposes as a part of the Constitution of the United States." As the Legislatures of Tennessee and of West Virginia had power to adopt the resolution of ratification, official notice to the Secretary, duly authenticated, that they had done so, was conclusive upon him, and being certified to by his proclamation, is conclusive upon the courts. . . . Affirmed.

Source: *Leser v. Garnett*, 258 U.S. 130, 1922.

Executive Order 9066 (February 19, 1942)

In 1942, after Pearl Harbor, President Franklin Roosevelt issued an executive order that led to the evacuation and internment of 120,000 Japanese and Japanese Americans. Some 70,000 were native-born citizens of Japanese ancestry (the Nisei).

Now, therefore, by virtue of the authority vested in me as President of the United States, and Commander-in-Chief of the

Army and Navy, I hereby authorize and direct the Secretary of War, and the Military commanders whom he may from time to time designate, whenever he or any designated Commander deems such action necessary or desirable, to prescribe military areas in such places and of such extent as he or the appropriate Military Commander may determine, from which any and all persons to enter, remain in, or leave shall be subject to whatever restrictions the Secretary of War or the appropriate Military Commander may impose in his discretion. The Secretary of War is hereby authorized to provide for residents of any such area who are excluded therefrom, such transportation, food, shelter, and other accommodations as may be necessary, in the judgment of the Secretary of War, of the said Military Commander, and until other arrangements are made, to accomplish the express purpose of this order. The designation of military areas in any region or locality shall supersede designations of prohibited or restricted areas by the Attorney General under the proclamation of December 7 and 8, 1941, and shall supersede the responsibility and authority of the Attorney General under the said Proclamation in respect of such prohibited and restricted areas.

I hereby further authorize and direct the Secretary of War and the said Military Commanders to take such steps as he or the appropriate Military Commanders may deem advisable to enforce compliance with the restriction applicable to each Military area hereinabove authorized to be designated, including the use of Federal troops and other Federal Agencies, with authority to accept assistance of state and local agencies.

I hereby further authorize and direct all Executive commanders in carrying out this Executive Order, including the furnishing of medical aid, hospitalization, food, clothing, transportation, use of land, shelter, and other supplies, equipment and services.

This order shall not be construed as modifying or limiting in any way the authority granted under Executive Order 8972, dated December 12, 1941, nor shall it be construed as limiting or modifying the duty and responsibility of the Attorney General and the Department of Justice under the proclamations of December 7 and 8, 1941, prescribing regulations for the conduct and control of alien enemies, except as such duty and responsibility is superseded by the designation of military orders hereunder.

Source: Executive Order 9066, February 19, 1942; General Records of the Unites States Government; Record Group 11; National Archives.

Findings and Purposes of the National Voter Registration Act (1993)

In order to enhance voter participation in national elections, the Congress enacted the Act of May 20, 1993 (107 Stat. 77), known as the National Voter Registration Act and as the Motor Voter Act.

Section 1973gg Findings and purposes:

(a) Findings

The Congress finds that (1) the right of citizens of the United States to vote is a fundamental right, (2) it is the duty of Federal, State, and local governments to promote the exercise of that right, and (3) discriminatory and unfair registration laws and procedures can have a direct and damaging effect on voter participation in elections for Federal office and disproportionately harm voter participation by various groups, including racial minorities.

(b) Purposes

The purposes of this subchapter are (1) to establish procedures that will increase the number of eligible citizens who register to vote in elections for federal office; (2) to make it possible for Federal, State, and local governments to implement this subchapter in a manner that enhances the participation of eligible citizens as voters in elections for Federal office; (3) to protect the integrity of the electoral process; and (4) to ensure that accurate and current voter registration rolls are maintained.

Source: Pub. L. 103-31, Sec. 2, May 20, 1993, 107 Stat. 77.

Hurst v. Florida (2016)

Florida's death sentencing scheme violated the Sixth Amendment in light of the Supreme Court's decision in Ring v. Arizona. In Hurst v. Florida, 136 S.Ct. 616, 016, by an 8–1 decision, the Court ruled on the Florida sentencing scheme. The majority opinion was written by Justice Sonia Sotomayor, and a dissenting opinion was written by Justice Samuel Alito.

Majority

A Florida jury convicted Timothy Lee Hurst of murdering his co-worker, Cynthia Harrison. A penalty-phase jury recommended that Hurst's judge impose a death sentence. Notwithstanding this recommendation, Florida law required the judge to hold a separate hearing and determine whether sufficient aggravating circumstances existed to justify imposing the death penalty. The judge so found and sentenced Hurst to death.

We hold this sentencing scheme unconstitutional. The Sixth Amendment requires a jury, not a judge, to find each fact necessary to impose a sentence of death. A jury's mere recommendation is not enough.

[. . .]

The State fails to appreciate the central and singular role the judge plays under Florida law. As described above and by the Florida Supreme Court, the Florida sentencing statute does not make a defendant eligible for death until "findings *by the court* that such person shall be punished by death." Fla. Stat. §775.082(1) (emphasis added). The trial court *alone* must find "the facts . . . [t]hat sufficient aggravating circumstances exist" and "[t]hat there are insufficient mitigating circumstances to outweigh the aggravating circumstances." §921.141(3); see *Steele*, 921 So. 2d, at 546. "[T]he jury's function under the

Florida death penalty statute is advisory only." *Spaziano* v. *State*, 433 So. 2d 508, 512 (Fla. 1983). The State cannot now treat the advisory recommendation by the jury as the necessary factual finding that *Ring* [*v. Arizona*, 56 U.S. 584, 608, n. 6 (2002)] requires.

[. . .]

The Sixth Amendment protects a defendant's right to an impartial jury. This right required Florida to base Timothy Hurst's death sentence on a jury's verdict, not a judge's fact-finding. Florida's sentencing scheme, which required the judge alone to find the existence of an aggravating circumstance, is therefore unconstitutional.

Dissent

[. . .]

Although the Court suggests that today's holding follows ineluctably from *Ring*, the Arizona sentencing scheme at issue in that case was much different from the Florida procedure now before us. In *Ring*, the jury found the defendant guilty of felony murder and did no more. It did not make the findings required by the Eighth Amendment before the death penalty may be imposed in a felony murder case. See *id.*, at 591–592, 594; *Enmund* v. *Florida*, 458 U. S. 782 (1982) ; *Tison* v. *Arizona*, 481 U. S. 137 (1987) . Nor did the jury find the presence of any aggravating factor, as required for death eligibility under Arizona law. *Ring, supra,* at 592–593. Nor did it consider mitigating factors. And it did not determine whether a capital or noncapital sentence was appropriate. Under that system, the jury played *no* role in the capital sentencing process.

The Florida system is quite different. In Florida, the jury sits as the initial and primary adjudicator of the factors bearing on the death penalty. After unanimously determining guilt at trial, a Florida jury hears evidence of aggravating and mitigating circumstances. See Fla. Stat. §921.141(1) (2010). At the conclusion of this separate sentencing hearing, the jury may recommend a death sentence only if it finds that the State has proved one or more aggravating factors beyond a reasonable doubt and only after weighing the aggravating and mitigating factors. §921.141(2).

Once the jury has made this decision, the trial court performs what amounts, in practical terms, to a reviewing function. The judge duplicates the steps previously performed by the jury and, while the court can impose a sentence different from that recommended by the jury, the judge must accord the jury's recommendation "great weight." See *Lambrix* v. *Singletary*, 520 U. S. 518 –526 (1997) (recounting Florida law and procedure). Indeed, if the jury recommends a life sentence, the judge may override that decision only if "the facts suggesting a sentence of death were so clear and convincing that virtually no reasonable person could differ." *Tedder* v. *State*, 322 So. 2d 908, 910 (Fla. 1975) (*per curiam*). No Florida trial court has overruled a jury's recommendation of a life sentence for more than 15 years.

Under the Florida system, the jury plays a critically important role. Our decision in *Ring* did not decide whether this procedure violates the Sixth Amendment, and I would not extend *Ring* to cover the Florida system.

[. . .]

Source: *Hurst v. Florida*, 136 S.Ct. 616 (2016)

Introduction

This chapter lists and briefly annotates the major sources of information that the reader is encouraged to consult for further research and study on the topic. It begins with print resources, first discussing 185 scholarly books that are cited and annotated. Then twenty-one major scholarly journals that publish original research articles and book reviews on the subject are covered and described. Finally, the chapter discusses as nonprint resources eleven feature-length films available for viewing. They dramatically depict the issues and people involved, putting real faces to the numbers and statistics.

Books

Aberbach, Joel D. 2001. *Keeping a Watchful Eye: The Politics of Congressional Oversight.* Washington, D.C.: Brookings Institution Press.

> Aberbach examines the reasons for the growth of congressional oversight using original data. He demonstrates the increase in oversight activity and links it to the political environment, exploring the purposes and techniques of oversight to uncover activities of the federal bureaucracy.

Journalists at a press conference. Freedom of the press is a key clause of the first amendment and often considered among its most important. President Trump attacked the press relentlessly. (Viorel Dudau/Dreamstime.com)

Abrams, Paula. 2009. *Cross Purposes*. Ann Arbor: University of Michigan Press.

> The book is a definitive study of the *Pierce v. Sisters* case. It is a captivating examination of the clash between cultural pluralism and the ongoing struggle to control education of children and the formation of citizens.

Ackerman, Bruce, ed. 2002. *Bush v. Gore: The Question of Legitimacy*. New Haven, CT: Yale University Press.

> Ackerman's book brings together a collection of prominent legal scholars to examine the larger questions raided by *Bush v. Gore* and the Court's actions. It asks if the Court violated the rule of law. It asks whether the decision inaugurates an era of hyperpoliticized jurisprudence.

Alden, Edward. 2008. *The Closing of the American Border: Terrorism, Immigration, and Security Since 9/11*. New York: Harper Perennial.

> Reacting to the attacks of 9/11/2001, the government began to close its borders to fight terrorism. Alden uses extensive interviews to examine the effects of that attempt at closing the borders. The book is a compelling assessment of the dangers faced when the nation cuts itself off from the rest of the world.

Alexander, Michelle. 2010. *The New Jim Crow: Mass Incarceration in the Age of Colorblindness*. New York: New Press.

> Alexander, a civil rights litigator and legal scholar, discusses race-related issues and how they impact Black males and mass incarceration. She notes discrimination is prevalent among other minorities and socioeconomically disadvantaged populations.

Alley, Robert. 1999. *The Constitution and Religion: Leading Supreme Court Cases and Religion: Leading Supreme Court Cases in Church and State*. Amherst, NY: Prometheus Press.

A superb collection of essays that chronicle the most important church-state related cases over the past three decades. In concerns prayer in state legislatures, the pledge of allegiance, displays of the commandments in public buildings, religious displays on public property, school prayers, use of vouchers for religious schools, and religion in science classes.

Amar, Akhil Reed. 1998. *The Bill of Rights.* New Haven, CT: Yale University Press.

This award-winning history by Amar, Yale Law professor and a leading constitutional law scholar, provides insight into the impact, flexibility, and timeliness of the Bill of Rights that guarantees personal rights and shields society against authoritarianism. Amar emphasizes the counter-majoritarianism of the Bill of Rights and its impact over time, especially on state and local governments as the courts have incorporated the Bill of Rights by the Fourteenth Amendment.

Anderson, Jack. 1996. *Inside the NRA: Armed and Dangerous.* Beverly Hills, CA: Dove.

Anderson offers an intensely researched and powerful examination of one of the most influential lobbying groups in America. He scrutinizes the organization and how it evolved over time. He focuses on three leaders of the NRA and reveals a shocking dossier of their backgrounds.

Appiah, Kwame. 2014. *Lines of Dissent: W.E.B. Du Bois and the Emergence of Identity.* Cambridge, MA: Harvard University Press.

Appiah traces the twin lineages of Du Bois's American experience and his German apprenticeship in Berlin. He shows how those two shaped Du Bois's ideas of race and social identity. He argues Du Bois's challenge was to take the best of German intellectual life without its parochialism.

Araiza, Lauren. 2014. *To March for Others: The Black Freedom Struggle and the United Farm Workers*. Philadelphia: University of Pennsylvania Press.
Araiza's book adds to the body of scholarship on black-brown organizational relationships. She demonstrates convincingly that the UFW created alliances of varying length and strength with five leading black civil rights organizations.

Austin, Algernon. 2015. *America Is Not Post-Racial: Xenophobia, Islamophobia, Racism, and the 44th President*. Santa Barbara, CA: Praeger Press.
Austin's book is an in-depth examination of the 25 million Americans with the most intense hatred of President Barack Obama, and what the mindset of "Obama-Haters" teaches about race and ethnicity in America today. He shows how they are xenophobic, Islamophobic, and racists, rather than political conservatives motivated by just conservatism.

Baker, Jean. 2004. *Women and the United States Constitution, 1776–1920*. Washington, D.C.: American Historical Association.
Women played a peripheral role in constitutional history until 1920. Baker looks at their role as it developed throughout the nineteenth century, culminating with the passage of the women's suffrage amendment in 1920.

Ball, Howard. 2000. *The Bakke Case: Race, Education, and Affirmative Action*. Lawrence: University Press of Kansas.
Ball reviews the many issues raised by the Bakke case that placed affirmative action plans on trial. He examines the law and politics surrounding the case with evenhandedness. He discusses the key arguments put forth by both sides. He examines the impact of the Bakke case and its use as precedent.

Ball, Howard. 2017. *The Right to Die: A Reference Handbook.* Santa Barbara, CA: ABC-CLIO.

This reference book provides a comprehensive and contemporary examination of the right-to-die issue in light of the vast improvement in public health and medicine. He shows that people live longer, but often taking much longer to die, and often doing so in great pain and suffering.

Banks, Dennis, and Richard Erdoes. 2005. *Ojibwa Warrior: Dennis Banks and the Rise of the American Indian Movement.* Norman: University of Oklahoma Press.

Dennis Banks tells his own story to writer and photographer Richard Erdoes. He details the founding of the American Indian Movement, tracing its rise. The book offers an insider's understanding of AIM and its many protest events.

Barnes, Kenneth. 2016. *Anti-Catholicism in Arkansas: How Politicians, the Press, the Klan, and Religious Leaders Imagined an Enemy.* Fayetteville, AR: University of Arkansas Press.

Barnes's book illustrates how the dominant Protestant majority portrayed Catholics as a feared and disliked "other," a phenomenon that was particularly strong in Arkansas. He examines in detail the period of 1910–1960.

Bay, Mia. 2004. *To Tell the Truth Freely: The Life of Ida B. Wells.* New York: Hillaway.

Mia Bay presents a detailed profile of the civil rights pioneer from her early life in Mississippi and Tennessee to her famous campaign for justice, and her journalist's fight against lynching and racial injustice. It offers a comprehensive biography of Ida Wells.

Bedell, Kenneth B. 2017. *Realizing the Civil Rights Dream: Diagnosing and Treating American Racism.* Santa Barbara, CA: Praeger.

Bedell proposes a civil rights dream that grows out of American history yet speaks to the twenty-first-century reality. He makes the case that by adopting a larger perspective about the role of racism in preserving social, cultural, economic, and political institutions and practices, Americans can better understand why it has been so difficult to fulfill the promises of the 1960s civil rights movement. He uses sociological theories to explain why racism is still so prevalent in the United States. He concludes with identifying steps necessary to overcome racism.

Belknap, Michael. 2005. *The Supreme Court Under Earl Warren, 1954–1969.* Columbia: University of South Carolina Press.
Belknap recounts the eventful history of the Warren Court and its controversial decisions that are still hotly debated. He draws on internal memoranda as well as published opinions of the justices to reveal the philosophical debates and the personality conflicts behind the Court's major decisions. He places them in their political and social context.

Berman, Art. 2015. *Give Us the Ballot: The Modern Struggle for Voting Rights in America.* New York: Farrar, Strauss, and Giroux.
Berman's book is compelling history but also a cry for help in the recurring struggle to gain what is supposed to be an inalienable right. Berman is a political correspondent for *Nation* and a fellow at the Nation Institute.

Berson, Robin K. 2004. *Jane Addams: A Biography.* Westport, CT: Greenwood Press.
Berson chronicles Jane Addams's privileged childhood, her thirst for education, and her search for purpose and self-fulfillment. The book describes her help in cofounding the NAACP and her championing of women's suffrage. Berson's biography highlights the greatness of this lesser-known civil rights leader to a new generation.

Bharara, Preet. 2019. *Doing Justice: A Prosecutor's Thoughts on Crime, Punishment, and the Rule of Law.* New York: Knopf.

Bharara presents an important overview of the way the justice system in the United States actually works. He uses case histories as well as his own compelling personal experiences to describe what is needed to achieve justice within American society.

Boyd, Nan Alamilla. 2003. *Wide Open Town: A History of Queer in San Francisco.* Berkeley: University of California Press. Boyd traces the history of gay men and lesbians in San Francisco from 1900 to 1965. Her book describes the 1965 raid on gay bars that spurred the gay rights movement. She uses police and court records, oral histories, and manuscripts in archives to explain the growth of San Francisco as a "wide-open town."

Brest, Paul, Sanford Levinson, Jack Baldwin, Akeel Amar, and Reval Siegal. 2018. *Processes of Constitutional Decisionmaking,* 7th ed. New York: Wolter Kluwer. This casebook text traces the historical, political, and social development of constitutional law. It delivers strong chapters on the constitutional treatment of sex equality, race, civil rights, separation of powers, and federalism.

Brinkley, Douglas. 2005. *Rosa Parks: A Life.* New York: Penguin. Historian Brinkley brings to life midcentury America in this compelling examination of the life of an iconic heroine of the civil rights movement. It shows how her quiet dignity, hope, courage, and humor made her a living legend.

Broadwater, Jeff. 2006. *George Mason: Forgotten Founder.* Chapel Hill: University of North Carolina Press. Broadwater provides a comprehensive account of the birth of the governments of Virginia and the United States and the contributions made to both by George Mason. It shows his impact on the founding period of American history. His in-depth portrait of Mason and his times is a rich resource for the period.

Brown, Dee. 2012. *Bury My Heart at Wounded Knee: An Indian History of the American West.* Maryville, TN: Open Roads Media.

> A unique and disturbing narrative, Dee Brown's book is a meticulously documented account of the systematic destruction of the Native Americans during the second half of the nineteenth century. Importantly, the book uses the words of the great chiefs and warriors of the Dakotas, Utes, Sioux, and Cheyenne to tell the story of their battles, the massacres, and the trail of broken treaties.

Brown, Donathan L., and Michael L. Clemons. 2015. *Voting Rights under Fire: The Continuing Struggle for People of Color.* Santa Barbara, CA: Praeger.

> Brown and Clemons show how the struggle by people of color for their voting rights continues to this day. This interdisciplinary book connects past and present issues in the political debates, historical development, and court decisions on race and voting rights in the United States.

Brown, Nikki L., and Barry M. Stentiford, eds. 2014. *Jim Crow: A Historical Encyclopedia of the American Mosaic.* Santa Barbara, CA: Greenwood Press.

> This reference volume examines, in an encyclopedia format, a broad range of topics related to the establishment, maintenance and eventual dismantling of the discriminatory system known as Jim Crow. The book documents the methods used to create the system, and how courts and laws finally dismantled it.

Bruns, Roger. 2018. *Documents of the Chicano Movement.* Santa Barbara, CA: ABC-CLIO.

> This book provides original source documents regarding the Chicano movement from the 1960s through the 1970s. It covers key events, individuals, and political developments of *La Causa* and how Chicanos united to free themselves from exploitation.

Budiansky, Stephen. 2008. *The Bloody Shirt: Terror after the Civil War.* New York: Penguin Press.

This book documents the use of terrorist violence during the Reconstruction era when more than three thousand Blacks and their white allies were killed. Budiansky uses original letters, diaries, as well as published racist diatribes in this vivid narrative. He sheds new light on the violence, division, and heroism of the Reconstruction era.

Bullock, Charles, Ron Gaddle, and Justin Wert, eds. 2016. *The Rise and Fall of the Voting Rights Act.* Norman: University of Oklahoma Press.

The authors trace the development of the Voting Rights Act from its inception by exploring the political and legal aspects of the Jim Crow electoral regime. They detail the subsequent struggle to enact laws to end Jim Crowism. They present events since 2006 that made the ideological makeup of the Supreme Court ripe for the legal challenge to the Act.

Bullough, Vern L., ed. 2002. *Before Stonewall: Activists for Gay and Lesbian Rights in Historical Context.* New York: Harrington Park Press.

This book illuminates the lives of fifty individuals involved in the early struggles for gay and lesbian rights. It explores the early history of the movement through concise biographies of the pre-1969 barrier breakers.

Burger, Ariel. 2018. *Witness: Lessons from Elie Wiesel's Classroom.* New York: Houghton Mifflin/Harcourt.

Elie Wiesel's teaching assistant presents a primer on educating against indifference, on the urgency of memory and individual responsibility, and on the role of literature, music, and art in making the world a better place. His book shows Wiesel not only as an extraordinary human being but also as a master teacher.

Cameron, Christopher. 2014. *The Abolitionist Movement: Documents Decoded.* Santa Barbara, CA: ABC-CLIO.

This history text provides an engaging overview of the abolitionist movement. It uses primary source documents along with expert commentary to show readers how to critically evaluate key documents that chronicle a major American social movement. It shows the critical points in the history of slavery and abolition.

Campbell, Nadia. 2003. *More Justice, More Peace: The Black Person's Guide to the American Legal System.* Chicago, IL: Chicago Review Press.

This book provides legal information for activists to demand those in power to respect and honor their rights, no matter how difficult the situation. It shows how the legal system was created by white men for white men and how it fails to reflect the values and interests of Black men and women. Yet it shows how they can use this imperfect system to their advantage to exercise their rights.

Cannistraro, Philip, and Gerald Meyers, eds. 2003. *The Lost World of Italian American Radicalism: Politics, Labor, and Culture.* Westport, CT: Praeger Press.

This book is a collection of essays that explore the history of Italian American radicalism from the early 1900s to the present. It surveys the major events, trends, and individuals within the Italian American community. It provides essays on the socialist and anarchist movements and their appeal to Italian immigrants. It illustrates the radicalist approach to the effort of a minority to secure its civil rights and liberties.

Carmon, Irin, and Shana Knishnik. 2015. *Notorious RBG: The Life and Times of Ruth Bader Ginsburg.* New York: Dey Street Books/HarperCollins.

The authors draw an intimate look at RBG through interviews, reported narrative, annotated dissents, and archival documents to bring to life the story of a transformative woman who transcends generational divides over the struggle for gender equality and civil rights.

Caro, Robert. 2012. *The Years of Lyndon Johnson: The Passage of Power*. New York: Knopf.

This book is the fourth in the award-winning series in the life of Lyndon Johnson. It is a definitive history of his presidency, detailing his impact on American society and particularly on civil rights policy and law during the tumultuous years of the 1960s.

Carpenter, Dale. 2012. *Flagrant Conduct: The Story of Lawrence v. Texas*. New York: W. W. Norton.

Carpenter's book is a riveting account of the fight to overturn laws that made intimate and private homosexual relationships a crime. It provides background on all the participants in the landmark case of *Lawrence v. Texas* and shows how it reshaped American law.

Carter, Greg Lee. 2017. *Gun Control in the United States: A Reference Handbook*, 2nd ed. Santa Barbara, CA: ABC-CLIO.

Carter offers a concise, understandable and comprehensive coverage of gun rights, gun violence, gun control, government regulations, gun organizations, and court decisions on the topic. The topics covered are placed in historical and cross-cultural perspectives.

Cathcart, Kevin, and Leslie Gabel-Brett, eds. 2016. *Love Unites Us: Winning the Freedom to Marry in America*. New York: New Press.

This book relates the story of the landmark 2015 case of *Obergefell v. Hodges* that legalized same-sex marriage. It captures the story of the fight for marriage equality in states, in legislatures, and in courts across the country. It shows how gay and lesbian couples won the right to marry.

Chemerinsky, Erwin. 2014. *The Case against the Supreme Court.* New York: Penguin.

> An eminent constitutional scholar presents a hard-hitting analysis of the Supreme Court over its more than 200-year history. He argues that the Supreme Court has often failed at its most important tasks at its most important moments.

Chemerinsky, Erwin. 2017. *Constitutional Law: Principles and Policies*, 6th ed. New York: Wolters Kluwer.

> A treatise on constitutional law, the book identifies the underlying policy issues in each area of constitutional law. It provides thorough coverage of such critical topics as standing, congressional power, presidential power, school desegregation, abortion, voting rights, and freedom of speech and religion.

Cornell, Saul. 2008. *A Well-Regulated Militia: The Founding Fathers and the Origins of Gun Control in America.* Oxford and New York: Oxford University Press.

> Cornell, a leading constitutional historian, details how the founding fathers understood the right to bear arms as neither an individual right nor a collective right, but as a *civic* right as an obligation owed to the state to arm themselves so they could participate in a well-regulated militia. The book restores the lost meaning of the original Second Amendment but also provides an historical account of how we arrived at our current impasse.

Cox, Daniel, and Robert Jones, eds. 2019. *America's Changing Religious Identity.* Washington, D.C.: Public Religion Research Institute.

> This volume is a landmark report on America's religious landscape. It provides a detailed demographic analysis of all fifty states. It is the largest denominational identity study ever conducted, based on a sample of more

than 101,000 Americans with detailed information on their denominational ties, political affiliations, and other important demographic attributes.

Curran, Robert. 2014. *Papist Devils: Catholics in British America, 1574–1783*. Washington, D.C.: Catholic University Press of America.

Curran's book provides a readable history of the Catholic experience in British America and how their experience shaped the development of the colonies and the republic during the seventeenth and eighteenth centuries. It explains the Catholic exodus from England, Ireland, and Scotland. It demonstrates the deeply rooted view of Catholics as enemies of the political and religious traditions of the British.

Cushman, Clare. 2001. *Supreme Court Decisions and Women's Rights*. Washington, D.C.: Congressional Quarterly Press.

Cushman's book examines a range of hot-button women's issues before the Supreme Court from the nineteenth century to *Roe v. Wade*. It features more than one hundred cases and updated biographies. It is a complete study of all the important issues and movements involving the Supreme Court and the role the Court plays in shaping women's rights.

Dailey, Jane, Glenda Gilmore, and Bryant Simon, eds. 2000. *Jumpin' Jim Crow: Southern Politics from the Civil War to Civil Rights*. Princeton, NJ: Princeton University Press.

This book presents a clear picture of Jim Crowism and white supremacy, and how some Blacks and white women launched the strongest attacks on the Jim Crow system. It portrays change over time, showing how Strom Thurmond is not the reincarnation of Ben Tillman, nor is Rosa Parks the first black woman to say no to Jim Crow.

Dashefsky, Arnold, and Ira Sheskin, eds. 2019. *American Jewish Yearbook.* Basel, Switzerland: Springer Nature.

An annual record of North American Jewish communities, it has been published since 1899. It is an authoritative source of data on Jewish community life, including number and affiliations of synagogues.

Davis, Hugh. 2011. *We Will Be Satisfied with Nothing Less: The African American Struggle for Equal Rights in the North During Reconstruction.* Ithaca, NY: Cornell University Press.

Historian Hugh Davis examines two issues that African Americans in the North considered the most essential: Black male suffrage and equal access to public schools. His book connects the local and the national. It focuses on specific campaigns in cities like Cincinnati, Detroit, and San Francisco. It details the work of the National Equal Rights League and the National Executive Committee of Colored Persons. It examines the equal rights movement from 1864 to the end of Reconstruction.

Dierenfield, Bruce J. 2008. *The Civil Rights Movement.* Oxfordshire, UK: Routledge/Taylor Francis.

Dierenfield recounts the extraordinary and all-too-often bloody story of how thousands of ordinary African Americans overcame long odds to end segregation, to exercise the right to vote, and to improve their economic standing. He shows how their struggle required great courage and persistent agitation during which many activists sacrificed their homes, jobs, and even their lives in their struggle to achieve their basic civil rights.

Dorrien, Gary. 2015. *The New Abolition: W.E.B. Du Bois and the Black Social Gospel.* New Haven, CT: Yale University Press.

Dorrien describes the early history of the black social gospel from its nineteenth-century roots to its close association in the twentieth century with W.E.B. Du Bois. His book offers a new perspective on modern Christianity and the civil rights era. It delineates the traditions of social justice theology and activism that led to Martin Luther King Jr.

Douglas, Todd. 2017. *The Police in a Free Society: Safeguarding Rights While Enforcing the Law.* Santa Barbara, CA: Praeger Press.

Douglas offers a detailed look at the evolution of American police and their intended role of peacekeepers and guardians of citizen rights to calling themselves and acting primarily as "law enforcement officers." The book reveals realities and myths about police in American society and what can—and cannot—be done to improve relations and public confidence in police. Its sober assessment is all the more relevant in this post–George Floyd's killing and rising influence of the Black Lives Matter movement.

Downing, Frederick. 2008. *Elie Wiesel: A Religious Biography.* Macon, GA: Mercer University Press.

Downing's book shows Elie Wiesel's religious faith as the driving force behind his status as a moral authority. Wiesel is portrayed as a generative religious personality, a poet-prophet whose Jewish vision becomes a link with humanity. It shows how his existential struggle for meaningful identity joined with the quest of all oppressed people after the holocaust.

Dray, Philip. 2008. *Capitol Men: The Epic Story of Reconstruction through the Lives of the First Black Congressmen.* New York: Houghton Mifflin.

In his deep look at the first African American congressmen during the Reconstruction, Dray offers a look at the different issues in post–Civil War America. He shows how the congressmen attempted to fulfill the notion of post–Civil War democracy and equality, and how they came to be denied representation for eighty years thereafter as Jim Crowism triumphed.

Dudziak, Mary L. 2000. *Cold War, Civil Rights, Race and the Image of American Democracy.* Princeton, NJ: Princeton University Press.

This book offers an insightful analysis of how international relations affected domestic security. Dudziak interprets postwar civil rights as a Cold War feature. She argues that the Cold War helped facilitate social reforms, but notes how the focus on image limited the nature and extent of the progress.

Effinger-Crichlow, Marta. 2014. *Staging Migration Toward an American West: From Ida B. Wells to Rhodessa Jones.* Boulder: University Press of Colorado.

This book examines how black women's migration toward the American West exposed the complexities of their struggle for sociopolitical emancipation. She presents four case studies: Ida Wells, Sissieretta Jones, World War II female defense workers, and Rhodessa Jones. The book expands the understanding of the African American struggle for free movement and full citizenship in the United States.

Epps, Garrett. 2006. *Democracy Reborn: The Fourteenth Amendment and the Fight for Civil Rights in Post–Civil War America.* New York: Holt.

This narrative of the adoption of the Fourteenth Amendment shows how it revolutionized the Constitution and shaped the United States from the ashes of the Civil War. Over time, Epps argues, it provided African Americans with full citizenship by prohibiting the states from denying any citizen due process and equal protection under the law. The book tells the struggle from the halls of Congress to the bloody streets of Memphis and New Orleans.

Epstein, Richard. 2014. *The Classical Liberal Constitution.* Cambridge, MA: Harvard University Press.

Epstein's book steers clear of the well-worn debates between defenders of originalism and proponents of a living Constitution. He employs close textual reading, historical analysis, and political and economic theory to urge a return to the classical liberal theory of governance that animated the framers' constitutional design.

Eskridge, William. 2008. *Sodomy Laws in America, 1861–2003.* New York: Penguin Press.

Few issues are more controversial than gay rights. Eskridge demonstrates there is nothing new about this political and legal obsession. He shows how the American colonies and early states prohibited sodomy as a crime against nature but rarely punished it if it took place behind closed doors. The McCarthy era, however, targeted "degeneration." It was not until *Lawrence v. Texas* that private sex between consenting adults was decriminalized. Eskridge shows how American sodomy laws affected the lives of both homosexual and heterosexual Americans.

Farrelly, Maura Jane. 2017. *Anti-Catholicism in America: 1620–1860.* Cambridge, UK: Cambridge University Press.

Farrelly's book reveals the ironic role anti-Catholicism played in defining and sustaining some of the core values of American identity. Those values, she shows, animate our religious and political discussions today. Her book provides a framework for understanding what is at stake in the debate over the place of Muslims and other non-Christian groups in U.S. society.

Feldman, Paul, ed. 2013. *Routledge Revivals: Encyclopedia of American Civil Liberties.* Oxfordshire, UK: Routledge Press.

This comprehensive, three-volume set covers a broad range of topics on the subject of civil liberties in America.

It includes such topics as free speech, press, religion, assembly and petition, the Bill of Rights, slavery, censorship, crime, and war. It uses a multidisciplinary approach and an encyclopedia alphabetically arranged order.

Feldman, Richard. 2011. *Ricochet: Confessions of a Gun Lobbyist.* New York: Wiley and Sons.

Feldman's book casts an eye-opening spotlight on the shadowy world of behind-the-scenes gun politics. His memoir vividly describes the firearms debate in extraordinary detail.

Finley, Keith. 2008. *Delaying the Dream: Southern Senators and the Fight against Civil Rights, 1936–1965.* Baton Rouge: Louisiana State University Press.

Finley explores the gradation in opposition to equal rights by examining how senators addressed the civil rights question and developed a concerted plan to thwart legislation by using a strategy of delay. His book goes beyond traditional images of the quest for racial equality and adds a fresh perspective to the canon of the civil rights era in modern American history.

Fireside, Harvey. 2003. *Separate and Unequal: Homer Plessy and the Supreme Court Decision that Legalized Racism.* Gretna, LA: Pelican Press.

Fireside presents a powerful account of the *Plessy v. Ferguson* decision. His book combines judicial records with historical photographs to provide a richly evocative portrait of Jim Crow-era Louisiana. His book presents a history less well known but every bit as explosively influential as that of Rosa Parks.

Flores, Lori. 2016. *A Grounds for Dreaming: Mexican Americans, Mexican Immigrants, and the California Farm Workers Union.* New Haven, CT: Yale University Press.

Flores's book provides a sweeping and critical history of how Mexican Americans organized for their rights in the decades leading up to Cesar Chavez and the UFW. It looks at the U.S.-born, the Bracero workers, and undocumented workers and how they confronted and interacted with one another. It is an incisive study of labor, migration, gender, citizenship, and class and how those factors intertwine to impact the civil rights challenges faced by Mexican Americans.

Frank, Barney. 2015. *Frank: A Life in Politics from the Great Society to Same-Sex Marriage.* New York: Farrar, Strauss and Giroux.
Frank relates his journey from Boston's city politics to the U.S. Congress and his four-decade stellar career. His book is a guide to how political change really happens and how to rebuild trust in an active government. It is a call to arms for the successful use of the elective-office approach to policy change to protect and expand civil rights.

Gans, Marshall. 2009. *Why David Sometimes Wins: Leadership, Organization, and Strategy in California's Farmworkers Movement.* New York: Oxford University Press.
This book tells the story of Cesar Chavez and the UFW and how and why they succeeded. It offers insights from a longtime movement organizer and scholar about turning short-term advantage into long-term gain. It is an authoritative and important contribution to learning about the movement's struggles and successes.

Giddings, P. J. 2008. *Ida: A Sword Against Lions: Ida B. Wells and the Campaign against Lynching.* New York: Amistad/Harper Collins.
Giddings's book is a sweeping narrative about Ida Wells, her struggle against lynching, and a nation riven by race. Meticulously researched, it is a compelling biography of the progressive luminary.

Ginsburg, Ruth Bader. 2018. *My Own Words*. New York: Simon and Schuster.

> This is a witty, engaging, serious, and playful collection of Ginsburg's writings and speeches covering a wide range of topics. She demonstrates the value of looking beyond U.S. shores when interpreting the constitution. It is a fascinating glimpse into the life on one of the United States' most influential women.

Goodwin, Doris Kearns. 2005. *Team of Rivals: The Political Genius of Abraham Lincoln*. New York: Simon and Schuster.

> Goodwin illuminates Lincoln's political genius. The book follows his career from a one-term congressman and prairie lawyer to the presidency and his prevailing over rivals to become one of the greatest of U.S. presidents.

Gould, Lewis. 2003. *Grand Old Party: A History of the Republican Party*. New York: Random House.

> In this comprehensive history of the Republican Party, Gould traces the evolution of the GOP from its emergence as an antislavery coalition in the 1850s to its role in the Bush years. It concludes with an assessment of the party's historical legacy.

Gould, Lewis. 2010. *1968: The Election that Changed America*. Chicago, IL: Ivan R. Dee.

> Gould's book is a detailed narrative of the 1968 election and how Nixon came to win the presidency. It explores how events and issues shaped national affairs in the two decades that followed.

Green, Michael S., and Scott L. Stabler, eds. 2015. *Ideas and Movements that Shaped America: From the Bill of Rights to "Occupy Wall Street,"* 3 vols. Santa Barbara, CA: ABC-CLIO.

> This three-volume set covers movements and bold ideas and beliefs from the Bill of Rights to Occupy Wall Street

and how they shaped the nation. It provides entries with sources that improve the readers' understanding of the American experience.

Gregory, Raymond. 2014. *The Civil Rights Act and the Battle to End Workplace Discrimination.* Lanham, MD: Rowman and Littlefield.
Gregory provides a history of civil rights and workplace discrimination in America. His book outlines positive ways forward as our society and the nation diversifies and redefines what it means to be respectful of citizens' most inalienable, protected, and sacred rights.

Gutzman, Kevin. 2007. *The Politically Incorrect Guide to the Constitution.* Washington, D.C.: Regnery Publishing.
Gutzman's book argues that there is little relationship between the constitution as ratified by the original states and the constitutional law imposed by judges since then. He argues that the Supreme Court interpreted the Fourteenth Amendment to twist the use of the Bill of Rights.

Hacker, Andrew. 2003. *Two Nations: Black and White, Separate, Hostile, Unequal.* New York: Scribner.
Hacker's book explains the origins and meaning of racism and clarifies conflicting theories of equality and inferiority. His book paints a stark picture of racial inequality in the United States and explores controversial policies that cause the gap between the races.

Hagedorn, Sara L., and Michael C. LeMay. 2019. *The American Congress: A Reference Handbook.* Santa Barbara, CA: ABC-CLIO.
The book thoroughly examines the operations and politics of the U.S. Congress. It guides readers to their own assessment of congressional politics, presents the major functions of congress, and examines how they evolved. It provides readers with the bases for future reading and

study of the subject. It demonstrates the important role Congress plays in setting, protecting, or at times reducing civil rights policy and law.

Halbrook, Stephen P. 1989. *A Right to Bear Arms: State and Federal Bills of Rights and Constitutional Guarantees.* New York: Greenwood Press.

Halbrook explains the origins of the right to bear arms using original sources, such as period newspapers, constitutional convention debates, and writings of the framers of state constitutions. He accounts for changes in the bill of rights and how they affect the right to bear arms.

Hall, Kermit, and James Ely, eds. 2009. *The Oxford Guide to United States Supreme Court Decisions.* New York: Oxford University Press.

The editors offer a collection of insightful accounts by eminent legal scholars of landmark cases before the Supreme Court from *Marbury v. Madison* to the Dred Scott decision to *Brown v. Board of Education* and *Roe v. Wade.* It includes more than 400 cases, including more than 50 new landmark rulings, such as *Gonzales v. Planned Parenthood.*

Hannah-Jones, Nikole. 2012. *Living Apart: How the Government Betrayed a Landmark Civil Rights Law.* New York: Open Road Media.

This book offers a riveting view of the interworking of the U.S. government's policy role in housing segregation, and its failures to uphold laws meant to prevent it. It investigates the failure to fight housing segregation since the Nixon Administration. It faults both chambers of Congress, the Courts, and the Department of Housing and Urban Development. It details how and why repeated attempts to create integrated neighborhoods have floundered.

Hartman, Thom. 2004. *Unequal Protection: The Rise of Corporate Dominance and the Theft of Human Rights*. Emmaus, PA: Rodale Books.

> Hartman tells a startling story that changes the readers' understanding of American history. He uncovers original eyewitness accounts of the Boston Tea Party and shows it was provoked by specific actions of the East India Tea Company and the commercial interests of the British elite. He then describes the history of the Fourteenth Amendment and shows how corporate lawyers used it to extend business rights far more than those of the freed slaves. He proposes specific legal remedies to the excessive power of corporate America.

Head, Tom. 2009. *Civil Liberties: A Beginner's Guide*. London: Oneworld Publications.

> This book weaves history, philosophy, and practical advice for activists in this thought-provoking guide to civil liberties.

Hitchcock, William. 2018. *The Age of Eisenhower: America and the World in the 1950s*. New York: Simon and Schuster.

> In his definitive account of the Eisenhower presidency, Hitchcock draws on extensive declassified materials and a trove of unpublished documents. It is an eye-opening reevaluation of Eisenhower and his presidency.

Holzer, Harold, and Sara Vaughn Gabbard, eds. 2007. *Lincoln and Freedmen: Slavery, Emancipation, and the Thirteenth Amendment*. Carbondale: Southern Illinois University Press.

> A comprehensive book, it presents Lincoln's responses to slavery as a politician, president, writer, orator, and commander in chief. A collection of essays, the book explores slavery as a constitutional issue from the founders' original intent to Lincoln's decision to issue the Emancipation Proclamation. It offers a rare view of how Lincoln's views played a vital role in emancipation.

Horne, Gerald. 2010. *W.E.B. Du Bois: A Biography.* Westport, CT: Greenwood Press.

> The author provides a new interpretation of the life of W.E.B. Du Bois, providing a comprehensive overview of his life and times. It uses an interdisciplinary approach and traces his radicalization over time with the effects of the Cold War and anti-communism on his philosophy.

Hudson, David L., Jr. 2015. *Teen Legal Rights*, 3rd ed. Santa Barbara, CA: Greenwood Press.

> Hudson's book examines all aspects of teens' legal rights—at school, work, and home. It simplifies the laws, rights, and constitutional implications affecting teens today.

Issacharoff, Samuel, Pamela Karlan, Richard Pildes, and Nathaniel Persily. 2016. *The Law of Democracy: Legal Structures of the Political Process*, 5th ed. New York: Foundation Press.

> This book offers a systematic account of the legal construction of American democracy. It covers the Voting Rights Act, campaign finance, and political corruption issues. It examines the struggle over gerrymandering, the relationship of the states to political parties, and the tensions between majority rule and minority civil rights.

Johnson, Brian. 2008. *W.E.B. Du Bois: Toward Agnosticism, 1868–1934.* Lanham, MD: Rowman and Littlefield.

> Johnson's book describes Du Bois's evolution of religious views and traces his mounting skepticism through his earliest experiences of sociological training in Berlin. It culminates with his writings in *The Crisis.* Johnson shows the later Du Bois as a scientifically oriented agnostic who did not adhere to any religious orthodoxy.

Johnson, John W. 2005. *Griswold v. Connecticut: Birth Control and the Constitutional Right to Privacy.* Lawrence: University Press of Kansas.

Johnson's book is a comprehensive exploration of the *Griswold* case and its impact on U.S. law and society. He explores the origins of the case, provides a detailed narrative of the case, and examines its impact on same-sex relations. Johnson show how the case illuminates one state's struggle to establish the right to limit birth control and the national debate over privacy. He reveals *Griswold* as a multifaceted decision. His book is a deft and incisive analysis of the case and its impact and import.

Johnson, Troy. 2007. *Red Power: The Native American Civil Rights Movement*. New York: Chelsea House.
This book is one in a series of landmark events in Native American history. It examines the Red Power movement within the broader context of the Native American struggle for civil rights.

Jones, Robert P. 2016. *The End of White, Christian America*. New York: Simon and Schuster.
Jones's book deftly shows how the demise of white Christian America holds promise and peril for those concerned about racial justice and the future of race relations. The book uses a nonpolemic approach that offers insights into a changing nation that remains spiritual and religious in its core beliefs.

Joselin, Katherine. 2004. *Jane Addams: A Writer's Life*. Champaign: University of Illinois Press.
This book is an expansive, revealing, and refreshing reexamination of Jane Addams and her efforts towards progressive policies and social reform. Joselin argues persuasively that Jane Addam's power as a public figure stems from the success of her books and essays, and shows Addams to be an impressive literary woman.

Kanefield, Teri. 2016. *Free to Be Ruth Bader Ginsburg: The Story of Women and Law.* New York: Amazon Publishing.

> Kanefield mixes social and legal history to provide a moving and intimate biography of Justice Ginsburg. Her book captures a turbulent era and how Justice Ginsburg defied expectations to become one of the most powerful women in America.

Keck, Thomas M. 2004. *The Most Activist Supreme Court in History: The Road to Modern Judicial Conservatism.* Chicago, IL: University of Chicago Press.

> Keck astutely analyzes the Rehnquist Court and how its decisions related to broader tends in political and social change. It delves into the relationship between constitutional decision making and the political and social forces that influence the process.

Keppel, Ben. 2016. *Brown v. Board and the Transformation of American Culture.* Baton Rouge: Louisiana State University Press.

> Keppel tracks the *Brown* decision and its impact on race, class, and ethnicity. He focuses on three cultural "first responders" to track the impact of the decision: Robert Cole, Bill Cosby, and Joan Ganz Cooney. Keppel shows how their pioneering work provided new codes of conduct and guided America through the growing pains of becoming a truly pluralistic nation.

Kerstein, Andrew. 2006. *A. Philip Randolph: A Life in the Vanguard.* Lanham, MD: Rowman and Littlefield.

> Kerstein's book explores the significance and accomplishments of Randolph as a labor and a civil rights leader. He shows how Randolph's political philosophy and his involvement in the labor and the civil rights movements shaped his quest to improve the lives of American workers.

Keyssar, Alexander. 2009. *The Right to Vote: The Contested History of Democracy in the United States*, 2nd ed. New York: Basic Books.

> Keyssar's book is a widely acclaimed account of the evolution of suffrage from the American Revolution through to 2000. This revised edition updates the story to 2008 and the election of President Barack Obama. It is a sweeping interpretation of American political history viewed through the lens of voting rights that serve to underpin so many other basic civil rights.

Knight, Louise. 2010. *Jane Addams: Spirit in Action*. New York: W. W. Norton.

> In this landmark biography of Jane Addams, Knight shows the boldness, creativity, and tenacity of Addams and how she put her ideas of democracy into action. Knight details her work as a grassroots organizer, and partner to trade unions, women, immigrants, and African Americans seeking social justice. In this powerful portrait, Addams emerges as the cofounder of the NAACP and a leader for international peace and the winner of the Nobel Peace Prize.

La Beau, Bryan. 2017. *A History of Religion in America*. Abington, UK: Routledge Press.

> LaBeau's two-volume book provides a comprehensive history of religion in America from the end of the Civil War to post-9/11 America. It explores every major religious group and examines a multiplicity of topics, such as: the aftermath of the Civil War, immigration's impact on American religion, the rise of the social gospel, the fundamentalist response to the social gospel movement, religion during the Cold War era, the 1960s counterculture, and religion in post-9/11. He shows how various religious denominations have had negative or positive impact on

civil rights and the freedom of religion issues arising from the Establishment and Free Exercise clauses.

LaFave, Wayne. 2012. *Search and Seizure.* St. Paul, MN: Thomson/West.
> This basic text covers search and seizure and the Fourth Amendment in great detail and explores its ramifications on U.S. society.

LaFave, Wayne, Jerold Israel, Nancy King, and Orin Kerr. 2017. *Criminal Procedure*, 6th ed. St. Paul, MN: West Publishing.
> This basic text examines the law governing criminal justice processes from the initial investigation to post-appeal collateral attacks. It emphasizes basic issues, and leading Supreme Court opinions are given in-depth treatment.

Laughlin, Kathleen, and Jacqueline Castledine, eds. 2010. *Breaking the Wave: Women, Their Organizations, and Feminism, 1945–1985.* Abington, UK: Routledge.
> The authors review the long history of feminism, both as expressed in the political mainstream and in leftist politics and the impact of sexual politics. The many contributed essays to the volume cover virtually every feminist organization up to the late 1980s.

Lee, Erika. 2020. *The Making of Asian America.* New York: Simon and Schuster.
> Lee's powerful new book examines the rich, complicated histories of Asians in the United States and how generations of Asian immigrants and their U.S.-born descendants have made and remade Asian American life. It covers the Japanese American incarceration during World War II. It looks at the arrival of new refugees today and details their community activism and how they are now held as America's "model minority." It provides an eye-opening understanding of America itself.

LeMay, Michael C. 2006. *Guarding the Gates: Immigration and National Security.* Santa Barbara, CA: Praeger Press.

The book discusses how immigration and national defense policies are interwoven. It provides readers with the historical record to assess pros and cons of policy today. It examines the Department of Homeland Security and how the establishment of the DHS and the manner in which it enforces its policies raises many civil rights concern as it attempts to secure "Fortress America."

LeMay, Michael C. 2009. *The Perennial Struggle*, 3rd ed. Upper Saddle River, NJ: Prentice Hall.

This is a comprehensive examination of the struggle by ethnic, ideological, racial, and religious minority groups in America to cope with discrimination to achieve their civil rights. It distinguishes three overall coping strategies that each use one of two tactical approaches. It covers a multiplicity of groups from the founding to post-2000 events. It describes how groups use activism, laws, and court cases to secure their rights.

LeMay, Michael C., ed. 2013. *Transforming America: Perspectives on U.S. Immigration, Vols. 1, 3.* Santa Barbara, CA: Praeger Press.

This three-volume set collects essays by thirty scholars to examine how immigrant groups throughout American history have shaped and reshaped American society. Volume 3 focuses on 1945 to date. The essays are multidisciplinary.

LeMay, Michael C. 2018a. *Religious Freedom in America: A Reference Handbook.* Santa Barbara, CA: ABC-CLIO.

This volume explores the issue of religious freedom as guaranteed by the First Amendment from the founding to current events. It examines a wide variety of religious groups and how they used activism, law, the courts, and politics to secure their rights.

LeMay, Michael C. 2018b. *U.S. Immigration Policy, Ethnicity, and Religion in American History.* Santa Barbara, CA: ABC-CLIO.
This book explores the interrelationships between ethnicity, religion, and immigration policy throughout American history. It show how each are inextricably linked and influence each other as well as American society and historical political development.

LeMay, Michael C. 2019. *Immigration Reform: A Reference Handbook.* Santa Barbara, CA: ABC-CLIO.
This book focuses on how immigration policy reform is achieved and the impact it has on American society and on civil rights policy in particular. It examines ethnic and racial groups and explores in-depth the interrelationship between immigration reform politics and civil rights policy concerns.

Lewis, David. 2009. *W.E.B. Du Bois: A Biography.* New York: Henry Holt.
This biography of W.E.B. Du Bois won a Pulitzer Prize. It tracts his fifty-year career and show how Du Bois changed forever the way Americans think about themselves.

Lipset, Seymour Martin, and Gary Marks. 2000. *It Didn't Happen Here: Why Socialism Failed in the United States.* New York: W. W. Norton.
This book explores why socialism failed to play a significant role in the United States. The authors explore various explanations for this phenomenon of American political exceptionalism. It shows how the expansion of rights was an important factor in the failure of socialism to take hold in the United States even during the Great Depression era, when socialism expanded in much of the other industrial nations of the West.

Long, Carolyn. 2006. *Mapp v. Ohio: Guarding against Unreasonable Search and Seizures.* Lawrence: University Press of Kansas.

Long follows the police as they raid Mapp's home. She chronicles the events that led to the landmark ruling in *Mapp v. Ohio*. She discusses the controversies it created and assesses its impact on police behavior and subsequent prosecutions and convictions of the accused. The book illuminates one of the keystone decisions of the Warren Court's criminal procedure revolution.

Lynch, Frederick. 2011. *One Nation under AARP: The Fight over Medicare, Social Security, and America's Future.* Berkeley: University of California Press.

Lynch's book provides a fresh and even-handed account of the AARP, the political lobby that sets the national agenda on Medicare and Social Security. She describes how AARP harnesses the 78 million baby boomers as the largest-ever senior voting bloc. The book analyzes hundreds of documents.

Mack, Kenneth. 2012. *Representing the Race: The Creation of the Civil Rights Lawyer.* Cambridge, MA: Harvard University Press.

Mack uses law, biography, history, and race relations to examine the first era of civil rights lawyering. In its engaging style, the book brings its subject dynamically alive, featuring both famous and historically forgotten lawyers.

Marable, Manning. 2005. *W.E.B. Du Bois: Black Radical Democrat.* Boulder, CO: Paradigm Publishers.

This book is a solid biography of the most gifted black intellectual of his time. The focus of the book is on the writings of Du Bois—his books, essays, and articles.

Marger, Martin. 2014. *Race and Ethnic Relations*, 10th ed. Belmont, CA: Wadsworth.

This is the tenth edition of a classic text on race and ethnic relations. The book tackles a diversity of issues from an American and a global perspective. It has an expansive coverage of race and ethnic relations in a unique comparative approach, with current statistics, figures, maps, and numerous citations. The tenth edition has a new chapter on Arab Americans.

Marquez, Benjamin. 2003. *Constructing Identities in Mexican-American Political Organization: Choosing Sides, Taking Sides.* Austin: University of Texas Press.

Marquez explores the formation of group identity and whether Mexican Americans seek to assimilate or separate. The book provides a broad cross-section of groups to shed light on the process of political identity formation through the use of identity politics.

Marshall, Thurgood, and Mark Tushnet, ed. 2001. *Thurgood Marshall: His Speeches, Writings, Arguments, Opinions, and Reminiscences.* Chicago, IL: Lawrence Hill Books.

The book uses Marshall's speeches, writings, arguments, opinions (both majority and dissenting), and reminiscences to illuminate Justice Marshall and his impact on civil rights law and jurisprudence.

Mayer, Kenneth R. 2001. *With the Stroke of a Pen: Executive Orders and Presidential Power.* Princeton, NJ: Princeton University Press.

Mayer's book is an in-depth study of executive orders from Jefferson to Bush and how presidents have used them to wield their influence on civil rights and foreign policy. Mayer describes a presidential office that is more powerful and active that that typically depicted in political science literature.

McClurg, Andrew J., David B. Kopel, and Brannon P. Denning, eds. 2002. *Gun Control and Gun Rights: A Reader and Guide.* New York: New York University Press.

This book is a collection essays by scholars to provide a perspective on both sides of the U.S. gun debate. It provides a balanced gun policy reader. The book draws on a variety of sources and perspectives, and it raises a number of provocative questions concerning this hotly contested civil rights issue.

McPherson, James M., and James K. Hogue. 2010. *Ordeal by Fire: The Civil War and Reconstruction.* New York: McGraw-Hill.

Presenting up-to-date scholarship, this book tells the story of the Civil War and Reconstruction eras. It describes the social, economic, political, and ideological conflicts that led to the war as the transitional and transformational event in U.S. history.

Meacham, Jon. 2012. *Thomas Jefferson: The Art of Power.* New York: Random House.

This superb biography by the Pulitzer prize–winning historian brings to vivid life the extraordinary man and his remarkable times. Jefferson's genius, in Meacham's view, is that he was both a political philosopher and political maneuverer, thereby demonstrating the art of power. The book demonstrates Jefferson's important impact on the development and the impact of the Bill of Rights and securing the foundation of the fundamental rights of citizens.

Mead, Rebecca. 2004. *How the Vote Was Won: Woman Suffrage in the Western United States, 1868–1914.* New York: New York University Press.

Mead shows that Western suffrage came about as a result of the unsettled state of regional politics and the complex nature of Western race relations. She details the broad alliances between suffragists and farm-labor progressive reformers.

Melzer, Scott. 2009. *Gun Crusaders: The NRA's Culture Wars.* New York: New York University Press.

> Melzer provides an insider's look at the NRA and its culture war. The book presents a rich analysis of NRA materials, leader's speeches, and in-depth interviews of rank-and-file NRA members. Melzer focuses on how the NRA constructs and perceives threats to gun rights as one more attack in a liberal cultural war.

Miller, Mark. 2009. *The View of the Courts from the Hill: Interactions between Congress and the Federal Judiciary.* Charlottesville: University of Virginia Press.

> Miller traces the evolution of interactions between Congress and the federal courts. He raises an alarm over the recent threat to judicial independence from congressional interference that he argues has reached dangerous heights. He attributes the emerging threat to the religious right and conservative members of Congress who act as their allies and promote their agenda.

Moore, Louis. 2017. *We Will Win the Day: The Civil Rights Movement, the Black Athlete, and the Quest for Equality.* Santa Barbara, CA: Praeger Press.

> Moore provides a history of activist African American athletes and their role within the Black community. He profiles a series of athletes who pave the way for integration in their respective sports.

Moye, J. Todd. 2013. *Ella Baker: Community Organizer of the Civil Rights Movement.* Lanham, MD: Rowman and Littlefield.

> Moye provides a compelling biography of Ella Baker with an emphasis on grassroots community organizing. It is a concise, readable, and current examination of Baker's life and her profound impact on the civil rights struggle as an agent of social change across a wide variety of social issues.

Murdoch, Joyce, and Deb Price. 2002. *Courting Justice: Gay Men and Lesbians v. the Supreme Court*. New York: Basic Books.
>   This book offers a compelling look at the Supreme Court's handling of gay and lesbian challenges to apply equal protection to them. The authors' interviews of friends, relations, and former clerks to Supreme Court justices provide an inside look at individual rulings. The book is carefully researched, and it advocates for an inspiring new perspective on the gay rights movement.

Newton, Jim. 2006. *Justice for All: Earl Warren and the Nation He Made*. New York: Riverhead Books.
>   Newton's book provides a solid biography of Chief Justice Earl Warren. It assesses his impact on the Supreme Court and describes his ultimate legacy on American jurisprudence that is centered on the expansion of civil rights and liberties.

Nez, Chester. 2012. *Code Talkers: The First and Only Memoir by One of the Original Navajo Code Talkers*. New York: Dutton Caiber/Penguin Random House.
>   The book offers a compelling, firsthand account of the experiences and the impact of the Code Talkers on World War II. Their contributions did much to change the view that U.S. society had of Native Americans and advanced their struggle to secure their civil rights and basic citizenship rights.

Ng, Wendy. 2001. *Japanese American Internment during World War II: A History and Reference Guide*. Westport, CT: Greenwood Press.
>   Ng's book is a thorough study of the internment experience. It details its historical background and assesses its effects of the policy on Japanese Americans and, ultimately, on the nation.

Nussbaum, Martha. 2010. *From Disgust to Humanity: Sexual Orientation and Constitutional Law*. New York: Oxford University Press.

Nussbaum's book combines rigorous analysis of the leading constitutional cases on sexual orientation with a philosophical reflection about the underlying concepts of privacy, respect, discrimination, and liberty. She discusses issues from nondiscrimination and same-sex marriage to "public sex" and the recent landmark decisions of state and federal courts that are shifting toward what she labels a "humanity-centered" vision.

Obermayer, Herman. 2009. *Rehnquist: A Personal Portrait of the Distinguished Chief Justice of the United States.* New York: Oxford University Press.

Obermayer, a longtime friend of Chief Justice William Rehnquist, provides a personal tribute to the late chief justice. It is a portrait designed to enhance the legacy of the chief justice who was among the Court's most influential.

O'Brien, David H. 2017. *Constitutional Law and Politics: Civil Rights and Civil Liberties*, Vol. 2. New York: W. W. Norton.

O'Brien's book is a solid text that treats the intertwining aspects of law and politics. It describes how the court weaves through both. It discusses the origins of constitutional clauses, covers numerous case opinions, and provides a fuller understanding of constitutional law's strengths and weaknesses.

Ogletree, Charles. 2004. *All Deliberate Speed: Reflections on First Half Century of Brown v. Board of Education.* New York: W. W. Norton.

The author provides a measured blend of personal memoir, exacting legal analysis, and studied insight into the *Brown* case. The book offers an eyewitness account of the legacy of the *Brown* decision and its impact on five decades of race relations in the United States.

Orozco, Cynthia. 2009. *No Mexicans, Women, or Dogs Allowed: The Rise of the Mexican Civil Rights Movement.* Austin: University of Texas Press.

> Orozco's book offers a detailed history of the League of United Latin American Citizens (LULAC), placing it in its twentieth-century context. She examines the realities of the organization's early activism. She uses oral histories to probe LULAC's origins, and against the backdrop of the Mexican Revolution, World War I, gender discrimination, and severe racial segregation, she recasts LULAC at the forefront of civil rights movements in America.

Patterson, James T. 2001. *Brown v. Board of Education: A Civil Rights Milestone and Its Troubled Legacy.* New York: Oxford University Press.

> Patterson's book is a thorough examination of the *Brown* decision, its historical background, and a sober-minded assessment of its troubled legacy.

Powe, Lucas. 2000. *The Warren Court and American Politics.* Cambridge, MA: Harvard University Press.

> Chief Justice Earl Warren led the Supreme Court during its most revolutionary and controversial period in American history. Powe looks at the Supreme Court in a wide political environment to argue the Warren Court functioned as a partner in Kennedy-Johnson liberalism, imposing national liberal values on groups that were outliers: the White South, rural America, and areas of Roman Catholic dominance. He offers a learned and lively narrative to discuss more than 200 significant rulings which changed the balance of American legislatures, gradually eliminating anti-communism in domestic security programs, reformed basic criminal procedures, banned school-sponsored prayer, and shaped new law on pornography.

Ransby, Barbara. 2003. *Ella Baker and the Black Freedom Movement: A Radical Democratic Vision.* Chapel Hill: University of North Carolina Press.

> Ransby chronicles the life of Ella Baker and her long career as a civil rights organizer, an intellectual, and a teacher. Her book reveals Baker as a complex figure whose radical democratic world view compelled her to empower the Black poor and to emphasize a group-centered, grassroots leadership of the civil rights movement that set Baker apart from most of her political contemporaries.

Rawn, James. 2010. *Root and Branch: Charles Hamilton Houston, Thurgood Marshall, and the Struggle to End Segregation.* New York: Bloombury Press.

> James Rawn provides a riveting story of two fiercely dedicated lawyers, Charles Hamilton Houston and Thurgood Marshall, and details their epic fight from county courthouses to the United States Supreme Court and, in doing so, laid the legal foundation of the civil rights movement.

Raymond, Emilie. 2006. *From My Cold Dead Hands: Charlton Heston and American Politics.* Lexington: University Press of Kentucky.

> Raymond's book is not a comprehensive biography of Charlton Heston. It only briefly touches on his personal life and acting career. Raymond focuses on Heston's affiliations, especially the NRA, and how he evolved from a Democratic civil rights marcher to the increasingly right-wing stance of his politics. She shows how Heston made the NRA a bigger and stronger organization.

Reeves, Richard. 2015. *Infamy: The Shocking Story of the Japanese American Internment in World War II.* New York: Henry Holt.

> Meticulously documented, Reeve's book shows that the decisions that forced the relocation and internment

during World War II were racially biased. He shows how an overblown fear about national security can lead to shameful consequences. The failures in civil rights protections of that period offer lessons for today. Reeve's book is an engaging and comprehensive examination of what has been an overlooked era of American history, and a stain on the nation's civil rights and liberties record.

Robertiello, Gina, ed. 2017. *The Use and Abuse of Police Power in America: Historical Milestones and Current Controversies.* Santa Barbara, CA: ABC-CLIO.

Robertiello's book is a timely investigation of law enforcement and how it carries out its public safety and crime fighting mandates. It details two points that influenced the evolution of police powers, and offers a critical perspective on contemporary trends in law enforcement attitudes and practices. It is especially relevant for the current efforts to reform police and address racism within police departments and their operations in light of the Black Lives Matter movement and the police reform movement sparked by the homicide of George Floyd at the hands (and knee) of Minneapolis police.

Roydhouse, Marion W. 2017. *Votes for Women! The American Woman Suffrage Movement and the Nineteenth Amendment: A Reference Guide.* Santa Barbara, CA: Greenwood Press.

The book is a detailed account of the long and often bumpy road to suffrage for women, from the Seneca Falls convention to adoption and ratification of the Nineteenth Amendment. It is an even-balanced story of the women's suffrage movement and its leaders. It explores their sometimes difficult relationships with the abolition and temperance movements.

Rutherglen, George. 2013. *Civil Rights in the Shadow of Slavery: The Constitution, Common Law, and the Civil Rights Act of 1865.* New York: Oxford University Press.

Rutherglen's book recounts the history of the first civil rights act. It offers a reassessment of its deep and continuing influence on constitutional and statutory protections of civil rights. It describes the debates over the act that dealt with controversies like the scope of federal protection versus private discrimination, and to the remedies available to victims of civil rights violations that have been at the center of almost all subsequent controversies in courts and legislatures since 1866.

Samito, Christian. 2015. *Lincoln and the Thirteenth Amendment.* Carbondale: Southern Illinois University Press.

Samito examines how Lincoln's opposition to amending the Constitution shaped his political views before he became president, and how constitutional arguments overcame his objections, leading him to support enactment of the Thirteenth Amendment in 1864. Samito shows how Lincoln came to support the amendment to abolish slavery because it worked within the constitutional structure to preserve key components of American constitutionalism in the face of Radical Republican schemes. He provides an authoritative historical treatment of the amendment, and his book closes with a lively discussion of how the Thirteenth Amendment applies to current events. He demonstrates how the constitutional change that Lincoln helped bring about continues to be relevant today.

Sargent, Frederic. 2004. *The Civil Rights Revolution: Events and Leaders, 1955–1968.* Jefferson, NC: McFarland Publishing.

Sargent's book describes apartheid in the United States that prevailed before *Brown.* It covers fifty-four confrontations in the struggle for civil rights. It profiles sixty civil rights leaders. Finally, it discusses six important civil rights laws and assesses the general accomplishments of the civil rights struggle.

Schwartz, Herman, ed. 2003. *The Rehnquist Court: Judicial Activism of the Right*. New York: Hill and Wang.

> The book presents essays by seventeen distinguished legal scholars. They evaluate the Rehnquist Court and its legacy of judicial activism by the political right.

Shaw, Randy. 2008. *Beyond the Fields: Cesar Chavez, the UFW, and the Struggle for Justice in the 21st Century*. Berkeley: University of California Press.

> Shaw's book presents a compelling biography of Chavez and a detailed discussion of the UFW during its heyday in the 1960s and 1970s. Shaw describes how the UFW became the era's leading incubator of young activist talent who went on to play critical roles in progressive campaigns. He details how UFW volunteers and staff were dedicated to furthering economic justice and bringing about social change.

Silkey, Sarah. 2015. *Black Woman Reformer: Ida B. Wells, Lynching, and Transatlantic Activism*. Athens: University of Georgia Press.

> Silkey's book is an excellent biography of Ida B. Wells. It explores here antilynching campaign as a focus to understand the broader context of nineteenth-century transatlantic reform. It is based on extensive archival research in the United States and Britain.

Smith, Steven S., and Jason M. Wielen. 2006. *The American Congress*, 8th ed. Cambridge, UK: Cambridge University Press.

> The book provides an insightful and comprehensive treatment of congressional politics. It covers the major features of Congress, such as its party and committee systems, its leadership, and voting and floor activity. It has discussions of the functions that presidents, the courts, and interest groups have in congressional policy making, including policy focused on civil rights.

Spring, Joel. 2018. *The American School: From the Puritans to No Child Left Behind*, 10th ed. New York: McGraw-Hill.

Springs new edition of a classic history of American education is comprehensive—from the seventeenth century to today's global capitalism. It characterizes and interprets each historical period in concise style. It provides an interesting chapter that links the religious colonial Puritans' fundamentalist ideas to the Trump administration and the influence on it of the Alt-right.

Squires, Gregory. 2017. *The Fight for Fair Housing: Causes, Consequences, and Future Implications of the 1968 Federal Fair Housing Act.* London and Philadelphia, PA: Routledge Press.

Squires' book examines the Fair Housing Act of 1968 that was enacted in a time of turmoil, conflict, and even conflagration in cities across the nation. His book describes what happened to enable enactment of the law, why, and what remains to be done. It has contributions from fair housing activists and scholars to analyze its passage, its consequences, and its implications for the future.

Stern, Kenneth. 2002. *Loud Hawk: The United States versus the American Indian Movement.* Norman: University of Oklahoma Press.

Stern's book is an eye-opening and detailed story of governmental abuse of power, constitutional violations, perjured testimony, suppression of evidence, and fabrication of evidence. It details the FBI's counter intelligence program against AIM. It is a clear and concise telling of the events leading up to the case and the problems of the Pine Ridge reservation.

Stewart, Chuck. 2018. *Documents of the LGBT Movement.* Santa Barbara, CA: ABC-CLIO.

This book presents and discusses documents of pivotal moments in the LGBT rights movement from the First

People, through the influx of European settlers, on to the slave trade from Africa, to the modern era. It demonstrates why the LGBTQ rights movement is at the forefront of current civil rights struggles.

Stooksbury, Kara E., John M. Scheb II, and Otis W. Stephens Jr., eds. 2017. *Encyclopedia of American Civil Rights and Liberties: Revised and Expanded Edition,* 4 vols. Santa Barbara, CA: ABC-CLIO.

This four-volume set is a timely, revised edition using the encyclopedia format. It is a comprehensive discussion of American civil rights and liberties. The new edition deals with such topics as gay marriage and government surveillance. The set has 700 entries and covers key constitutional provisions, important Supreme Court decisions, social movements and advocacy groups, historical figures, and relevant legal doctrines.

Strum, Philippa. 2010. *Mendez v. Westminster: School Desegregation and Mexican American Rights.* Lawrence: University Press of Kansas.

Strum expertly describes the 1947 *Mendez* case in which segregation in education was first successfully challenged in federal court, preceding the better known *Brown* decision. The book weaves together narrative and analysis with personality portraits of those involved in the case to provide voices of all the protagonists. It highlights how Mexican Americans took the lead to secure their civil rights and overcome the racism of school boards.

Stuart, Gary L. 2004. *Miranda: The Story of America's Right to Remain Silent.* Tucson: University of Arizona Press.

Stuart tells the inside story of the *Miranda* case. He unravels its complex history and analyzes the competing social issues of the case. He assesses its aftermath. Stuart updates the story with the Supreme Court's *Dickerson* decision

(2000) and the implications for cases in the wake of the 9/11 attacks. He concludes with offering observations on the Miranda case's impact on law enforcement and the civil rights of the accused.

Stuhler, Barbara. 2003. *For the Public Record: A Documentary History of the League of Women Voters.* Washington, D.C.: Pogo Press.

Stuhler's book is a concise documentary history of the League of Women Voters. It employs interviews of members of the LWV to tell in their own words the compelling story of the political, but nonpartisan, women of the twentieth century. It describes their work for good government and demonstrates the importance of an informed and active citizenry.

Theohans, Jeannie. 2015. *The Rebellious Life of Rosa Parks.* Boston, MA: Beacon Press.

This book won multiple awards. It is quite simply, the definitive biography of Rosa Parks and details her extraordinary life and impact on the civil rights movement, but also on social change in American society.

Thomas, William H., Jr. 2008. *Unsafe for Democracy: World War I and the U.S. Justice Department's Covert Campaign to Suppress Dissent.* Madison: University of Wisconsin Press.

Historian Wayne Thomas examines the Department of Justice's use of the Espionage Act of 1917 and the Sedition Act of 1918 to suppress dissent. He details how, during World War I, the DOJ targeted isolationists, pacifists, immigrants, socialists, labor organizers, African Americans, clergymen, the unemployed, the mentally ill, college students, and schoolteachers. He analyzes documents that show that in case after case, they used threats and warnings to frighten war critics and silence dissent. Thomas' book is especially relevant today as the DOJ and DHS once again attempt to silence dissent over police abuse of power.

Tushnet, Mark. 2005. *A Court Divided: The Rehnquist Court and the Future of Constitutional Law.* New York: W. W. Norton and Company.

Tushnet examines the Rehnquist Court, arguing that the Court has always followed election returns. He notes that the Warren and Burger Courts never got far out of line with the national political consensus. Tushnet shows the Rehnquist Court reflected the 1980s and 1990s and the rise of conservatism. He shows how the Court followed Congress's lead, striking down several symbols of the New Deal regulatory state. The Court sided with more liberal positions at the margins of the social cultural wars—on gay rights, affirmative action, and early term abortions. As Tushnet notes, in the arena of politics, economic conservatives were winning and cultural conservatives were losing.

Tushnet, Mark V. 2007. *Out of Range: Why the Constitution Can't End the Battle over Guns.* Oxford and New York: Oxford University Press.

Constitutional scholar Mark Tushnet takes on the vexing question of guns and the Constitution. He examines competing interpretations of the Second Amendment: strict originalists and the more eclectic approach. On balance, Tushnet supports a more collective view that allows for greater government regulation. He shows how the dispute over guns has become part of the culture war and concludes that no amount of meaning of the Constitution and no amount of evidence would persuade people that they are "wrong."

Tushnet, Mark V. 2008. *Dissent: Great Opposing Opinions in Landmark Supreme Court Cases.* Boston, MA: Beacon Press.

The distinguished Supreme Court scholar explains sixteen influential cases throughout the Court's history. He offers a sense of what could have developed if the dissents instead of the majority opinions had won the case.

Uviller, H. Richard, and William Merkel. 2002. *The Militia and the Right to Bear Arms, or, How the Second Amendment Fell Silent.* Durham, NC: Duke University.

The authors examine the historical development of the Second Amendment and demonstrate that the militia envisioned by the founders has long since disappeared and contend that the constitutional right to bear arms has evaporated with the universal militia of the eighteenth century. Their book espouses a centrist position of the polarized arena of Second Amendment interpretation.

Vile, John. 2014. *Essential Supreme Court Decisions: Summaries of Leading Cases in U.S. Constitutional Law*, 16th ed. Lanham, MD: Rowman and Littlefield.

John Vile's book has become a standard study of the most important Supreme Court cases in United States constitutional law. His book includes every facet of constitutional law, including powers and privileges of the three branches of the national government, federalism, war powers, and extensive briefs on civil rights and civil liberties. This new edition is revised and updated and it covers cases based on years, by Supreme Court Chief Justices who presided over the cases, and by type of cases.

Vile, John R. 2015a. *Encyclopedia of Constitutional Amendments, Proposed Amendments, and Amending Issues, 1789–2015*, 4th ed., 2 vols. Santa Barbara, CA: ABC-CLIO.

In this fourth and updated edition, Vile presents a comprehensive review of constitutional amendments and proposed amendments, and he discusses the critical issues they have dealt with from 1789 to the present. He covers each of the twenty-seven amendments, as well as essays on proposed ones, and outlines proposals for more radical changes to the U.S. Constitution.

Vile, John R. 2015b. *Founding Documents of America: Documents Decoded.* Santa Barbara, CA: ABC-CLIO.
Vile offers historic documents key to the foundation of the national government with introductions that supply the background information and analysis that highlight key provisions and provide historical context. He covers the Declaration of Independence, the Constitution, the Bill of Rights, private diary entries, and political polemics organized chronologically into four sections. The book covers more than fifty primary source documents.

Wainwright, Susan, ed. 2019. *In Defense of Justice: The Greatest Dissents of Ruth Bader Ginsburg.* Fairhope, AL: Mockingbird Press.
Wainwright's book features the greatest dissents of Justice Ginsburg presented in a non-lawyer style that makes it accessible and gives RBG's admirers an approach to her life's work. RBG is renowned for her fiery dissents. Each dissent presented is prefaced with an explanation of the case to aid the lay reader for approaching the legal prose. The book highlights Justice Ginsburg at the zenith of her passion to persuade future generations of the Court's error.

Walker, Craig. 2018. *Ethel Percy Andrus: One Woman Who Changed America.* Washington, D.C.: AARP Press.
Walker's book is the first comprehensive history of Ethel Andrus, the founder of the AARP. Andrus emerges from the book as a teacher, principal, and fighter for the quality of life of the nation's seniors, advocating for affordable group health care, a discount drug purchasing plan, and travel services.

Wallis, Jim. 2016. *America's Original Sin: Racism, White Privilege, and the Bridge to a New America.* Grand Rapids, MI: Brazos Press.
Wallis calls racism America's original sin and his book offers a prophetic call to action in overcoming racism so ingrained in society. His book shows how people of faith can overcome embedded racism and create grassroots change to bridge to a multiracial church and a new America. It is particularly relevant to the current reform efforts to address police abuse of power and systemic racism in the judicial and criminal justice systems.

Weisberg, Stuart. 2009. *Barney Frank: The Story of America's Only Left-Handed, Gay, Jewish Congressman.* Amherst: University of Massachusetts Press.
This lively biography of Barney Frank documents his life and career, capturing Frank's delightful quirkiness, irreverence, and complexity. He also describes Frank's gruff exterior, impatience, and aversion to wasting time. Weisberg's biography shows Frank as a superb legislator and pragmatic politician. He highlights Frank's dedication to an unabashedly liberal agenda. Frank's depth of intellect and sense of humor made him one of the most influential and colorful figures in Washington.

White, Deborah. 2012. *Freedom on My Mind.* Boston, MA: St. Martin's Press.
In this book, award-winning scholars have collaborated to offer an innovative new African American history. It weaves narrative with carefully selected primary sources. It focuses on the diversity of the Black experience. Each chapter has two themed sets of written documents guiding students through the analyzing of sources.

Wilhelm, Cornelia. 2011. *The Independent Order of B'nai B'rith and True Sisters Pioneers of a New Jewish Identity, 1843–1914.* Detroit, MI: Wayne State University Press.

The book examines B'nai B'rith and its closely related organization, the Independent Order of True Sisters. It finds their German Jewish social and intellectual context to explore "civic Judaism." It details the founding, growth, and evolution of both organizations using extensive archival research.

Wilson, Harry L. 2017. *Gun Politics in America: Historical and Modern Documents in Context*, 2 vols. Santa Barbara, CA: ABC-CLIO.

Wilson's two-volume book covers the history of firearms and gun control in America. It presents original documents and places them in the social and political context in which they were written. It helps readers understand the cultural and political development that brought the nation to its current stalemate over guns and gun policy.

Winkler, Adam. 2011. *Gunfight: The Battle over the Right to Bear Arms in America.* New York: W. W. Norton.

Winkler's book is an intentionally provocative history of how guns—not abortion, race, or religion—are at the heart of America's cultural divide. He uses the 2008 decision of *District of Columbia v. Heller* as a springboard for his historical narrative.

Wolbrecht, Christina, and Rodney E. Hero. 2005. *The Politics of Democratic Inclusion.* Philadelphia, PA: Temple University Press.

The authors contribute to our understanding of the processes and mechanisms by which underrepresented groups have or have not achieved political incorporation. They collect essays from contributors that trace the issue of inclusion from colonial times to the present. They give particular emphasis to the institutions, processes, rules, and the context of the American political order encourage, mediate, or hamper the representation and incorporation of disadvantaged groups.

Woods, Randall. 2006. *LBJ: Architect of American Ambition.* New York: Free Press.

> Distinguished historian Woods offers a wholesale reappraisal and sweeping authoritative account of LBJ. He used thousands of newly released documents, White House tapes, and extensive interviews with key aides to bring crucial new evidence to bear on key aspects of the man and the politician.

Zentner, Scot, and Michael LeMay. 2020. *Party and Nation: Immigration and Regime Politics in American History.* Lanham, MD: Lexington Books.

> This book blends three topics: a history of American political development, a history of American political parties, and a history of the politics of immigration. It covers these themes, noting how they intertwine and influence one another, from the founding to current politics. It takes into account diverse viewpoints. It analyzes such critical elections as 1800, 1860, and 1932 to illustrate the theme of regime politics.

Zotti, Priscilla H. M. 2005. *Injustice for All: Mapp v. Ohio and the Fourth Amendments.* New York: Peter Lang.

> Using original documents and extensive interviews, this book details the historical, legal, and political significance of the most famous and impactful Fourth Amendment case on search and seizure jurisprudence: *Mapp v. Ohio.*

Scholarly Journals

American Journal of Legal History was established in 1957. It is a peer-reviewed and edited legal periodical that is published quarterly. Since 2015, it has been published by Oxford University Press. It publishes scholarly articles on all aspects and periods of legal history in both a print and an online format. Each issue regularly features book reviews. Since its relaunch in 2016, it has published contributions of a comparative, international or transnational nature. The journal is edited by

Professors Al Brophy (University of North Carolina School of Law, Chapel Hills) and Stefan Vogenauer (Max Plank Institute for European Legal History, Frankfurt).

American Journal of Sociology was established in 1895 and is the oldest academic journal of sociology in the United States. It is attached to the Department of Sociology at the University of Chicago and is published bimonthly. It is a leading voice in all areas of sociology, with an emphasis on theory building and innovative methods, and is open to interdisciplinary contributions from anthropologists, economists, educators, historians, and political scientists. It publishes book reviews and commissioned book review essays.

Columbia Law Review has been published since 1901 and is a leading publication of legal scholarship. It is published in eight issues a year. It receives some 2,000 submissions per year and publishes twenty to twenty-five manuscripts annually. It has an online supplement, *Columbia Law Review Online*, since 2008. It is edited by Columbia University Law School.

Emory International Law Review is a leading journal of international legal scholarship known for its excellence in scholarship, legal research, analysis, and professionalism. It publishes articles on a vast array of topics from human rights to international intellectual property issues. It is published quarterly.

Emory Law Journal was founded in 1952 as the *Journal of Public Law*. It has been publishing academic, professional, and student-authored legal scholarship on the full range of legal subjects since 1978. It publishes six issues annually.

Georgetown Journal of Legal Ethics was founded in 1987. It is published quarterly. It publishes interdisciplinary scholarship related to the future of the legal profession, issuing cutting-edge articles on ethical issues from diverse practical areas.

Georgetown Law Review is headquartered at Georgetown University Law School in Washington, D.C. It has published more than 500 issues since its inception in 1912. It employs one hundred law students. It publishes its *Annual Review of Criminal Procedure* with articles across the full spectrum of legal issues and cases.

Harvard Law Review publishes eight regular annual issues of various legal articles by professors, judges, practitioners, and law students, as well as leading case summaries. It is run by an independent student group at Harvard Law School. It also publishes an *Online Harvard Law Review Forum*. One of the nation's oldest law reviews, it has been published since 1887. It is one of the most prestigious law reviews and its alumni include President Barack Obama, seven Supreme Court justices, and a host of federal court judges and other high-level federal government officials.

Hastings Law Journal has been published since 1949. It is the flagship law review of the University of California-Hastings. It is published six times per year. Its scholarly articles span a wide variety of legal issues and are written by experts in the legal community. It also publishes an occasional law symposium issue. It is run by ninety student members, and it reaches a large domestic and international audience.

Michigan Law Review publishes eight issues annually, seven of which comprise articles by legal scholars and practitioners and notes by law students. One issue is devoted to book reviews. The review publishes important judicial decisions and legislative developments. It has been published by the University of Michigan Law School since 1902. In 2016, it was ranked as the sixth-best law journal.

Northwestern University Law Review was founded in 1906 as the *Illinois Law Review*. It is published quarterly in print and online. It features articles on general legal scholarship. It is student operated with articles written by professors, judges, and legal practitioners, as well as student pieces. It hosts special symposium issues annually, such as *Ordering State-Federal Relations through Preemption Doctrine* (2007).

Notre Dame Law Review was founded in 1925, known as the *Notre Dame Lawyer* until 1982. It is student edited and fosters scholarly discourse within the legal community mindful of its Catholic tradition. It is published quarterly and has an annual symposium issue on Federal Courts, Practice, and Procedure as a forum exploring civil practice and procedures in the federal courts.

Review of Politics publishes articles primarily on political theory, interpretive studies of law, and historical analysis on all aspects of politics, institutions, and techniques; literary reflections on politics; and constitutional theory and analysis. It has been published quarterly since 1939 and is published by Cambridge University Press for the University of Notre Dame.

Stanford University Law Review is published both in print (since 1948) and online (since 2011). It fosters intellectual discourse among student members and contributes to legal scholarship by addressing important legal and social issues. It is published in six issues per year and its articles are contributed by *Law Review* members, other Stanford Law School students, professors, judges, and practicing attorneys.

Supreme Court Review is published by the University of Chicago Law School since it first appeared in 1910. It provides a sustained and authoritative survey of the Court's most significant decisions. It provides an in-depth critique of the Supreme Court and its work and on the ongoing reforms and interpretations of U.S. law. It is written by and for legal academics, judges, political scientists, journalists, and sociologists. It is published annually in the spring.

University of California Law Review is the preeminent legal publication of the University of California, Berkeley School of Law. It was founded in 1912. It is published six times annually, covering a wide variety of topics of legal scholarship. It is edited and published entirely by students at Berkeley Law. It publishes research by the Berkeley Law faculty, centers, students, judges, and legal practitioners.

University of Chicago Law Review was founded in 1933. It is edited by the Law School's students and is one of the most prestigious and often-cited law reviews. Its authors include a host of Supreme Court justices, federal court judges, state supreme court judges, and preeminent legal scholars. It is published quarterly.

University of Minnesota Law Review has been published since 1917. It is solely student-edited, and its board of student editors number thirty-nine. It is published quarterly and covers the entire range of legal issues. It also publishes an annual Symposium issue.

University of Pennsylvania Journal of Constitutional Law provides a forum for the interdisciplinary study of and analysis of constitutional law. It cultivates legal scholarship, promotes critical perspectives, and reinvents the traditional study of constitutional law. It has twenty student editors and has been published quarterly since 1998.

University of Pennsylvania Law Review is a law review focusing on a wide range of legal issues. It was founded in 1852 and published its 168th volume in seven issues in the 2019–2020 academic year. It serves the legal profession, the bench, the bar, and the legal academy by providing a forum for publication of legal research. From about 2000 submissions, it selects twelve articles in each volume and is cited with such peer organizations as Columbia, Harvard, and Yale.

University of Virginia Law Review has been one of the most prestigious publications in the legal profession for more than one hundred years. It was begun in 1913. The Virginia Law

School was founded by Thomas Jefferson in 1819. The *Review* is published eight times annually. It covers law-related issues by and for judges, practitioners, teachers, legislators, students, and others interested in the law.

Yale Law and Policy Review has been published since 1982. It is published bi-annually and features legal scholarship and policy proposals contributed by lawmakers, judges, practitioners, academics, and students. It publishes an online companion titled *Inter-Alia.*

Yale Law Journal has been published since 1891. It has been at the forefront of legal scholarship and shapes discussion of the most important and relevant legal issues through rigorous scholarship. It is published eight times per year, and its online companion has been published since 2005. It is one of the most widely cited law reviews in the nation.

Films

The Butler. 2013. IMDb. 2 hours, 12 minutes in color. This biography of Cecil Gaines, the White House butler who served eight presidents features the civil rights movement, Vietnam, and other major events affecting American society. Follow Through Productions.

Cesar Chavez. 2014. IMDb. 102 minutes, color. This biopic follows Chavez from organizing the UFW to his death. It is historically accurate.

The Feeling of Being Watched. 2018. IMDb. 1 hour 26 minutes. A journalist uncovers a FBI terrorism surveillance probe in Chicago and its impact on the community. 7.2 rating.

Hacksaw Ridge. 2016. IMDb. 2 hours 19 minutes, color. 8.1 rating, and 2 Oscars winner. This is the true story of Medal of Honor winner Desmond Doss, a CO U.S. army medic who saved between fifty and one hundred men without carrying a gun.

Harriet. 2020. IMDb. 2 hours 5 minutes, in color. The extraordinary biopic of Harriet Tubman starring Cynthis Erivio as Tubman rates 7.0 of 10. Distributed by Perfect World Pictures, it is a Martin Chase Production.

I Am MLK, Jr. 2018. IMDb, 1 hour 35 minutes, in color. This feature length biopic focuses on his 12 years as the USA's leading civil right activist. It has a five star rating.

LBJ. 2016. IMDb. 1 hour 38 minutes, in color. This biopic stars Woody Harrelson as LBJ, and follows his rise from Congressman to the White House. Acacia Film Entertainment, Castle Rock Entertainment, and Savvy Media Holdings production. It is rated 7.3/10 on IMDbPro.

Loving. 2016. IMDb. 2 hours 3 minutes, in color, 7.5 rating. The true story of the Lovings, their interracial marriage that ended with the historic 1967 Supreme Court decision.

Milk. 2008. IMDb. 2 hours 8 minutes, in color, 7.5 rating. The story of Harvey Milk, California's first openly gay elected official, starring Sean Penn. It won two Oscars.

Naz and Maalik. 2015. IMDb. 1 hour 26 minutes, color, rated 5.7. The story of two closeted Muslim teens, their struggle to come clean about their sexuality, and coming into the crosshairs of the War on Terrorism.

Selma. 2014. 127 minutes, color. It follows MLK and his movement from Selma to Montgomery, culminating in President Lyndon Johnson's signing of the Voting Rights Act of 1965. It won the NAACP Image Awards for Outstanding Actor (David Oyelowo) and Outstanding Picture. Distributed by Paramount Pictures, rated 8.7/10 on Rotten Tomatoes system and 7.5/10 on IMDb.

1649 Maryland Colony adopts Maryland Act of Tolerance, allowing for some freedom of religious affiliation but the colony has an established religion.

1689 English Bill of Rights enacted. It is a precedent for United States Bill of Rights.

1776 Declaration of Independence written, and signed on July 4. George Mason drafts Virginia's Declaration of Rights that later become a model for the Bill of Rights.

1777 Articles of Confederation drafted without Bill of Rights.

1781 Articles of Confederation ratified without Bill of Rights. It establishes a weak central government.

1787 Second Constitutional Convention is held to revise the Articles of Confederation. It results in proposing the new Constitution.

1789 The Constitution is ratified; a new government begins which drafts Bill of Rights amendments. Ten of the twelve proposed amendments are adopted.

1791 The Bill of Rights—comprising the first 10 Amendments— is ratified.

1801 Thomas Jefferson begins his presidency. Democratic-Republican Party created. The Second Great Awakening revival

---

A protestor wears a Black Lives Matter face mask and hugs her son, dressed as a superhero, at a Black Lives Matter rally on June 14, 2020. (Dave Cooil/ Dreamstime.com)

movement begins and spreads (1820–1870), especially along the frontier region.

1803   Louisiana Purchase adds territory and Catholics to the U.S. population. *Marbury v. Madison* decision handed down; establishes judicial review power.

1812   War with England, at the time often called "Madison's war."

1820   Missouri Compromise enacted.

1823   Mormon Church begins in New York.

1826   Thomas Jefferson dies.

1830   Indian Removal Act passed; President Jackson begins removal of tribes, especially the Cherokee. Thousands die on the Trial of Tears.

1836   Mormons move to Kirtland, Ohio. James Madison dies.

1838   Governor Lilburn Boggs issues extermination order against the Mormons. Mormons move to Nauvoo.

1844   Seventh-day Adventist Church is founded.

1848   Treaty of Guadalupe Hidalgo signed. Irish potato famine brings wave of immigrants/Catholics to the United States and spurs anti-Catholic discrimination. California gold rush begins bringing thousands of Chinese immigrants to West Coast. Anti-Chinese sentiment and discrimination begins. Seneca Falls Convention held, and Women's Suffrage Movement begins.

1849   Order of Star Spangled Banner/Know Nothing Party begins. Anti-Catholicism and discrimination rise sharply. Supreme Court rules on *Luther v. Borden* decision.

1850   Missouri Compromise regarding entry of slave states and free states passed.

1854   Republican Party established with an antislavery platform.

1857   *Dred Scott* decision made. Rules "slaves" are property and must be returned to owners.

1858   Union troops occupy Utah until 1862 to control Mormons there.

1860   President Abraham elected; Civil War begins.

1861   Lincoln suspends writ of habeas corpus.

1862   Homestead Act passed; Transcontinental Railroad construction begins; Morrill Anti-Bigamy Act signed.

1863   President Lincoln issues Emancipation Proclamation order freeing slaves in 10 Confederate States; Lincoln gives his famous Gettysburg Address.

1864   Lincoln is re-elected; Reconstruction Era (1864–1877) begins.

1865   Civil War ends; on December 6, the Thirteenth Amendment is ratified. President Abraham Lincoln assassinated on April 15.

1866   Civil Rights Act enacted on April 6.

1868   Fourteenth Amendment is ratified.

1869   National Women's Suffrage Association is founded.

1870   Fifteenth Amendment is ratified. The first wave of Hasidic Jews arrives.

1871   National Rifle Association is founded.

1872   Jehovah's Witnesses Church is founded.

1873   Slaughter House cases are ruled on by the Supreme Court.

1875   Civil Rights Act of March 3, 1875 enacted—aka "the Enforcement Act."

1876   *United States v. Cruikshank* decision regarding Second Amendment's right to bear arms.

1877   Post-Reconstruction Era begins (1877–1890).

1879   *Reynolds v. Sims* upholds polygamy laws against Mormons.

1886 *Presser v. Illinois* Second Amendment decision handed down.

1890 *Davis v. Beason* ruling again upholds bigamy laws against the Mormons. Mormon Manifesto issued by LDS President Woodruff announcing end of practice of polygamy. Progressive Era (1890–1920) begins.

1894 *Miller v. Texas* ruling on Second Amendment.

1896 *Plessy v. Ferguson* decision establishes "separate-but-equal" doctrine, legally justifying segregation and spurring use of Jim Crow laws throughout the South. William McKinley elected president, beginning the Progressive Era.

1897 *Robertson v. Baldwin* decision regarding Second Amendment.

1898 Spanish American War. United States acquires new territory, new citizens.

1905 *Lochner v. New York* rules New York's labor law violates Fourteenth Amendment. *Rooney v. North Dakota* rules private execution does not violate ex-post-factor clause regarding capital punishment. *Beavers v. Haubert* decision regarding Sixth Amendment rights to fair trial handed down.

1909 National Association for the Advancement of Colored People is founded.

1910 The Urban League is founded.

1914 *Weeks v. United States* case decided, holds warrantless seizure unconstitutional. Marcus Garvey founds the Universal Negro Improvement Association, promoting black separatism.

1917 The Espionage Act is passed. The United States enters World War I.

1918 The Sedition Act is passed.

1919 Attorney General Palmer uses "Red Scare" raids to round up radical Socialists and Communists. *Schenck v. United*

States upholds convictions of Socialists under the Espionage Act. Several hundred deported to Russia.

1920   The Nineteenth Amendment is ratified. The American Civil Liberties Union is founded. The League of Women Voters is founded.

1922   *Leser v. Garnett* upholds the constitutionality of Nineteenth Amendment. The Cable Act of September 22 passed granting citizenship to women when their husband is naturalized and also stripping citizenship from women who marry foreigner who cannot become a citizen. *Ozawa v. United States* rules law banning Japanese immigrants (Issei) from naturalization is constitutional.

1923   Court holds in *United States v. Bhagat Singh Thind* that citizenship being open only to "free white person" means individual who looks white; East Indians are therefore not white and cannot naturalize.

1924   *Hester v. United States* decided, establishes the open fields doctrine. In recognition of their service in World War I, Congress enacts Act of June 4, "Citizenship for Non-citizen Indians."

1925   *Gitlow v. New York* sets "clear and present danger" test.

1926   Eugene Debs dies.

1928   *Olmstead v. United States* finds wiretaps constitutional.

1929   Japanese American Citizens League is founded. League of United Latin American Citizens is founded. *United States v. Schwimmer* decides that a woman who refuses to swear oath because of pacifism can be denied citizenship. New York passes law requiring literacy test for new voters. The stock market crash leads to the Great Depression (1930–1941) and FDR's New Deal's emphasis on economic rights.

1931   Act of March 3 restores citizenship of women lost when married to a foreign man or for residence abroad as per the Cable Act of 1922. Civil rights icon Ida B. Wells dies.

1932 *Blockburger v. United States* sets standards regarding double jeopardy.

1934 National Firearms Act is passed. Nation of Islam is founded.

1935 Act of June 24 allows for naturalization of aliens who were veterans of World War I, explicitly according citizenship to Asian veterans.

1936 Repatriation of native-born women who lost citizenship by marriage.

1939 *United States v. Miller* decided regarding Second Amendment's right to bear arms. World War II breaks out in Europe.

1940 *Chambers v. Florida* holds compelled confessions are inadmissible.

1941 Pearl Harbor attacked; United States enters World War II.

1942 Japanese Americans relocated and internship camps opened, by Executive Order 9066, and Act of March 21, 1942. 120,000 incarcerated. The Congress of Racial Equality is founded.

1943 *Hirabayashi v. United States* upholds constitutionality of relocation order by virtue of "military necessity." Chinese Exclusion Act repealed, and China is given quota. Chinese immigrants are able to naturalize.

1944 *Korematsu v. United States* ruled excluded zones order is constitutional. *Ex parte Mitsuye Endo* rules Endo and others cannot be detained in internment camps, National Congress of American Indians is founded. *Ashcraft v. Tennessee* rules extorted confession is inadmissible.

1945 *Girouard v. United States* reverses Schwimmer and rules a conscientious objector is allowed to be admitted despite refusal to swear oath.

1947 Community Service Organization is founded. *Francis v. Resweber* rules execution after a failed attempt is not cruel and unusual punishment.

1949   *Brinegar v. United States* sets reasonableness test regarding probable cause.

1950   Mattachine Society is founded. *Johnson v. Eisentager* rules Court has jurisdiction over German war criminals.

1952   McCarran-Walter Act is passed; it allows Issei to be naturalized.

1953   *Burns v. Wilson* allows military courts to question suspects without informing them of their rights. Earl Warren appointed Chief Justice of Supreme Court.

1954   *Brown v. Board of Education* overturns *Plessy*; rules segregation of public school is unconstitutional, and "desegregation" movement begins.

1955   *United States v. Provoo* rules on fair trial clause. Daughters of Bilitis is founded.

1957   Montgomery Alabama bus boycott starts, and Montgomery Improvement Association begins. Southern Christian Leadership Council is founded by MLK, Ralph Abernathy, Ella Baker and others; President Eisenhower sends troops to protect Little Rock, Arkansas high school desegregation students. Eisenhower signs the Civil Rights Act of August 9, aka the Eisenhower Civil Rights Act. *United States v. Pollard* rules on Fair Trial clause of Sixth Amendment.

1958   The American Association of Retired Persons is founded.

1960   The Student Nonviolent Coordinating Committee is founded. The Civil Rights Act of May 6, 1960 is enacted banning the poll tax and setting up conditions for federal voter registration efforts.

1961   The National Indian Youth Council is founded. The Supreme Court decides *Mapp v. Ohio* case regarding unreasonable search and seizure; it sets the exclusionary rule.

1962   The United Farm Workers begun by Cesar Chavez and Dolores Huerta. *Fong Foo v. United States* rules on double jeopardy case.

1963   The Association Federale de Mercedes begins. The Supreme Court decides *Gideon v. Wainwright* on need to provide counsel to indigent person. On November 22, President John F. Kennedy is assassinated. On February 21, Malcolm X is assassinated. Civil rights icon W.E.B. Du Bois dies.

1964   Act of July 2, 1964 passed—aka the Equal Employment Opportunity Act.

1965   Civil Rights Act of August 6 enacted; Voting Rights Act. *Griswold v. Connecticut* holds Connecticut's "Comstock" law is unconstitutional.

1966   The Black Panther Party is founded. *Miranda v. Arizona* decision sets test of "Miranda warnings" for police on arrest of suspect being read his rights. The Crusade for Justice starts in Colorado. *United States v. Ewell* decided regarding fair trial rules.

1967   *Afroyim v. Rusk* rules that a citizen may have dual citizenship with USA and Israel. *Katz v. United States* rules on and establishes the Katz test for reasonable grounds for expectation of privacy. The Mexican American Youth Organization is founded. *Klopfer v. North Carolina* rules on fair trial constraints of Sixth Amendment. *Loving v. Virginia* holds Virginia's interracial marriage ban is unconstitutional; it sets precedent for same-sex marriage. *Warden v. Hayden* rules "mere evidence" may be seized. *Berger v. New York* rules electronic eavesdropping without a warrant is unconstitutional.

1968   *Terry v. Ohio* holds police may stop if there is reasonable suspicion person is armed. The Mexican American Legal Defense and Education Fund is founded. The National Council of La Raza begins. The American Indian Movement begins. Civil Rights Act of April 11, the Fair Housing and Indian Civil Rights Act, is passed. President Lyndon Johnson issues proclamation committing U.S. law to UN's Protocol and Convention on Status of Refugees, giving refugees increased civil rights. The Omnibus Crime Control and Safe Streets Act is passed. *Bumper v. North Carolina* rules on consent if warrant is invalid. On April 4, Martin Luther King, Jr. is assassinated. On June 5, former Attorney General, Senator, and presidential candidate Robert F. Kennedy is assassinated.

1969   *Smith v. Hooey* issues rules of fair trial constraints of Sixth Amendment.

1970   Twenty-Sixth Amendment is ratified. *Dickey v. Florida* and *Chambers v. Maroney* cases are decided.

1971   *Coolidge v. New Hampshire* sets automobile exception to Fourth Amendment's search and seizure prohibitions. *United States v. Marion* regarding Sixth Amendment's requirements for a fair trial decided. The National Women's Political Caucus is established. The Southern Poverty Law Center is established.

1972   *Baker v. Wingo* decision on Sixth Amendment Fair Trial clause. *U.S. v. Cody* rules on Second Amendment case. *Adams v. Williams* and *United States v. District Court* cases are decided.

1973   Court decides *Roe v. Wade,* ruling right to privacy means abortion is legal. *Braden v. 30th Circuit* and *Strunk v. United States* decisions rendered regarding condition for a fair trial rights of Sixth Amendment. *Schneckloth v. Bustamente* decided. President Lyndon B. Johnson dies.

1974   The Asian American Legal Defense and Education Fund is established. *United States v. Matlock* holds police may search if consent given by third party. *United States v. Calandra* and *United States v. Kahn* decided. Chief Justice Earl Warren dies.

1976   *Woodson v. North Carolina* rules state laws providing for mandatory death penalty are unconstitutional. *United States v. Watson* decided; *South Dakota v. Opperman* decided.

1977   *United States v. Lovasco* decided regarding Sixth Amendment's Fair Trial clause; *Nixon v. Administrator of General Service* decided.

1978   *Zucher v. Stanford* decided; *Mincey v. Arizona* decided. Human Rights Watch is founded. *Regents of University of California v. Bakke* holds fixed racial quotas unconstitutional but affirmative action plans are constitutional if the affirmative action plans are but one of several factors being considered.

1979 *Smith v. Maryland* holds use of pen register was not a search. *Delaware v. Prouse* decided.

1980 *Lewis v. United States* decision on Second Amendment rights issued. *United States v. Mendenhall* case decided; *Godfrey v. Georgia* rules on aggravating factors in death penalty cases decided. The American Arab Anti-Discrimination Committee is founded, as is the Arab American Political Action Committee.

1982 Supreme Court decides *United States v. McDonald*; *United States v. Ross*; and *Washington v. Chrisman*.

1983 *Illinois v. Gates*; *Michigan v. Long* decisions handed down, as is *Florida v. Royer* on seizure of person and probable cause.

1984 Supreme Court rules on series of cases on states search and seizure: *Oliver v. United States*; *Florida v. Meyers, Walter v. Georgia*; *Hudson v. Palmer, United States v. Leon, Massachusetts v. Sheppard*; and in *Spaziano v. Florida* regarding judge v. jury deciding on aggravating factors in death penalty case.

1985 *New Jersey v. T.L.O.* and *California v. Carney* cases decided.

1986 *United States v. Loud Hawk* decided on Sixth Amendment fair trial clause. *Bowers v. Hardwick* rules on right of privacy to engage in homosexual activity. *California v. Greenwood* holds warrantless search of garbage is constitutional. *New York v. Class* and *California v. Ciraolo* cases decided. Firearm Owner Protection Act passed.

1987 *Sumner v. Shuman* holds death penalty cannot be mandatory even if prisoner is already serving life sentence without parole. ACT UP is founded.

1989 *Skinner v. Railway Labor Executives' Association* case decided.

1990 *United States v. Verdugo-Urquirdez* Second Amendment case decided. *Illinois v. Rodriquez* upholds warrantless search with third-party consent. *Walton v. Arizona* rules judge's finding of aggravating factors in death penalty is constitutional. It is overruled in 2002 by *Ring v. Arizona.*

1991   Civil Rights Act of November 21—aka Equal Opportunity Act—passed.

1992   *Casey v. Planned Parenthood* and *Dogget v. United States* and *United States v. Felix* cases are decided.

1993   Brady Handgun Violence Protection Act is passed. Civil Rights Act of May 20, the National Voter Registration Act is passed. On April 23, Cesar Chavez dies. Justice Thurgood Marshall dies.

1994   Violent Crime Control and Law Enforcement Act is passed.

1995   *Harris v. Alabama* upholds law allowing judge to impose death penalty making jury recommendation non-binding even if it calls for life imprisonment. American Association of People with Disabilities is founded.

1996   *Ohio v. Robinette* upholds police search of car at traffic stop.

1997   *Chandler v. Miller* decides on Georgia law requiring drug test to run for office.

2002   *Florida v. J. S.* upholds use of stop and frisk based on anonymous tip. *United States v. Drayton* rules on consent and search on public bus. *Atkins v. Virginia* holds the execution of a mentally retarded offender is unconstitutional.

2003   Transgender Education Association is founded. *Sell v. United States* rules on Sixth Amendment fair trial factors. *Lawrence v. Texas* holds law banning homosexual activity between consenting adults in private is unconstitutional.

2004   *Hiibel v. 6th Judicial District of Nevada* rules that a "terry stop" ID requirement did not violate the Fifth Amendment. *Rasul v. Bush* decides that foreign nationals detained at Guantanamo Bay could petition federal courts for writ of habeas corpus review. *Hamadi v. Rumsfeld* holds U.S. citizens charged as enemy combatants have the right to due process to challenge their enemy combatant status.

2005   *Roper v. Simmons* holds death penalty for offender under eighteen at time of crime is unconstitutional. *Kelo v. City of New London* rules "taking clause" of Fifth Amendment on eminent domain seizure is legal even for private owner to another private owner. Congress enacts the Protection of Lawful Commerce in Arms Act. Civil rights icon Rosa Parks dies. Chief Justice William Rehnquist dies.

2008   *District of Columbia v. Heller* rules the D.C. handgun ban unconstitutional. *Kennedy v. Louisiana* rules death penalty unconstitutional for child rape with non-homicidal crimes against the person.

2009   *Vermont v. Brillon* case decided on Sixth Amendment fair trial clause. On August 22, Senator Edward "Ted" Kennedy, leading civil rights advocate in the Senate, dies.

2010   Supreme Court deems that the City of Chicago gun law is unconstitutional in *McDonald v. City of Chicago*. In *Ontario v. Quon* Court rules on right to privacy and electronic communication within a government workplace. Court rules on cases on Sixth Amendment right to fair trial in *Berghuis v. Smith*, and *Thaier v. Haynes*.

2011   *Bond v. United States* holds that individuals have standing to raise Tenth Amendment challenges to federal laws.

2012   In *United States v. Jones* Court holds that the use of a GPS tracking device is a "search" and warrant is required. *Smith v. Cain* Sixth Amendment rule on fair trial clause.

2013   In *Maryland v. King* Court holds that use of cheek swab in comparable to finger printing and is reasonable search under the 4th Amendment.

2014   The National Center for Civil and Human Rights established.

2016 In *Hurst v. Florida* Court holds law giving judge authority to decide facts relating to sentencing violates Sixth Amendment requiring jury to determine aggravating factors in death penalty case.

2018 *Carpenter v. United States* rules that cell-site location information requires a warrant be issued on probable cause to comply with privacy of historical cellphone location records. Trump administration issues zero-tolerance policy. DOJ Announces separation of children from parents during detention, and announces policy to deny protection for gender-based or gang violence as basis for claiming asylum. Trump administration changes definition of "public charge," issues new rules regarding asylum.

2019 Trump issues new orders on asylum; Trump issues executive order 9844 declaring national emergency at U.S. Southern border, then vetoes a joint resolution terminating the national emergency act.

2020 January—COVID-19 pandemic outbreak threatens to end "birth tourism," wherein women from Mexico and Central America travel to the United States to have a child born in a U.S. hospital, making the child a U.S. native-born citizen; Court issues injunction regarding prohibition of refugee resettlement; March to April many states order "shut-down"; May—George Floyd killed and his death launches movement to reform police and address systemic racism; July—states order mask wearing in public, social distancing, and Representative John Lewis and C. T. Vivian, civil rights icons, die; Trump issues executive action excluding counting aliens in 2020 census, suspends entrance of aliens following coronavirus outbreak; Trump sends federal troops to Portland and tear gasses protestors in Washington, D.C., and Portland; orders same troops to Cleveland, Detroit, and Milwaukee; troops, with no name tags or unit identification and wearing military uniforms sweep up people on streets into unmarked vans without citing probable cause; Supreme Court decides Florida case upholding law that bars ex-felons from voting if they have unpaid fines; Court rules in *Altitude Express v. Zarda,* and *Bostock v. Clayton County* upholding Civil Rights Act of 1964 that "sex" includes sexual orientation; in *Babb v. Wilkie* Court upholds Age Discrimination in Employment Act of 1967 ruling that personnel actions must be untainted by any consideration of age; in *Colorado Department of State v. Baca* Court upholds Colorado law prohibiting so-called "faithless" electors; in *DHS v. Regents of UCA* court rules DHS's decision to rescind DACA was "arbitrary and capricious"; in *Espinoza v. Montana Department of Revenue* Court rules Montana withholding funds for education that excludes religious education options violates Free Exercise Clause; in *June Medical Services LLC v. Russo* Court reverses appeals court upholding Louisiana law requiring admissions privileges at local hospital in order to perform abortions; in *Kahler v. Kansas* Court rules Kansas may abolish certain uses of insanity defense, in *McGirt v. Oklahoma* Court rules certain parts of Oklahoma are in Indian reservation; in *McKinney v. Arizona* Court rules state appellate courts may reweigh aggravating and mitigating circumstances in habeas corpus review in death penalty cases; in *Our Lady of Guadalupe School v. Morrisy-Berru* Court rules free exercise clause prevents civil courts from adjudicating employment discrimination claims against religious employers when employee carried out important religious functions; in *R.G. and G.R. Harris Funeral Homes Inc. v. EEOC,* Court upholds Civil Rights Act of 1964 with respect to prohibition of discrimination of transgender employee on basis of transgender status.n is appointed by President Jimmy Carter to head the EEOC. She is the first woman to head it.

Ageism   Prejudice or discrimination against a particular age group, in the United States, especially the elderly.

Amicus curiae   Latin for "friend of the court," this is a legal brief submitted by a person or group who is not a party to the legal dispute or case but who argues a particular legal position for the court's consideration. Most Supreme Court cases that are challenging government action on constitutional grounds have amicus briefs associated with them.

Appellant/appellee   The two parties to an appeal case. An appeal is a procedure by which an appellant (a person or entity) seeks review of a lower court's ruling. Appellee is the respondent to an appeal.

Arguendo   A Latin phrase sometimes used in Supreme Court opinions meaning "for the sake of argument."

Articles of Confederation   The confederal government (1781–1789) created by the Second Constitutional Congress to replace British rule. It was replaced by the U.S. Constitution in 1789. It had no Bill or Rights.

Ascribed status   One assigned at birth or assumed involuntarily later in life, often based on biological factors that cannot be changed through individual effort or achievement.

Ashkenazi   A Hebrew word that refers to Germany. Ashkenazi Jews are those from Eastern Europe, in contrast with

Sephardic Jews from the Mediterranean Sea area, such as Spain, Portugal, the Middle East, and Northern Africa.

Bill of Rights   A bill or declaration of rights delineated as fundamental rights and consisting of the first ten amendments to the 1789 Constitution of the United States.

#BlackLivesMatter   A phrase and motto referring to the social movement advocating the reform of police departments regarding abusive and excessive use of force against people of color, and calling for reforms addressing systemic racism.

B'nai B'rith   Hebrew, meaning Children of the Covenant. It is a Jewish service organization that combats anti-Semitism and bigotry that began in 1843.

Certiorari   A writ or order by which a higher court reviews the decision of a lower court.

Citizenship   The legal concept identifying a member of a society tied to the right to vote, to be eligible to hold political offices, and other fundamental rights contained in the Bill of Rights.

Civil liberties   The basic freedoms contained in the first amendment; such as freedom of religion, speech, press, assembly and to petition the government that together form the cornerstone of democracy.

Civil rights   The rights of citizens to political and social freedom and equality; ensuring peoples' physical and mental integrity, life, safety, and protection against discrimination on grounds such as race, gender, sexual orientation, national origins, color, age, ethnicity, religion, and disability; and individual rights such as privacy and rights based on protected characteristics.

Conscientious objector   An individual who has claimed the right to refuse to perform military service on the grounds of freedom of thought, conscience, or religion. In the United States, conscientious objectors are assigned an alternative civilian service as a substitute for conscription (i.e., military service), or are assigned to non-combatant, non-armed roles in the military (e.g., as medics).

Constitution's Original Sin   Refers to the institution of slavery being justified and included within and protected by the Constitution of the United States.

Criminal syndicalism   A doctrine of criminal acts for political, industrial, and social change. Such acts include advocating crimes of sabotage, violence, and other unlawful methods of terrorism. Criminal syndicalism laws were enacted to oppose economic radicalism by criminal or violent means.

De facto   A Latin phrase meaning "by action."

Defendant   A party against whom a lawsuit has been filed in a civil court of law, or who has been accused of or charged with a crime or criminal offense.

Defund the police   The phrase commonly used by the social movement to reform systemic racism in police departments that advocates moving some funding of police department budgets and diverting those funds to other social institutions, such as social welfare department, mental health professionals, and similar organizations to better confront social problems. It would be used, for example, to defuse domestic violence confrontations by deescalating such events rather than having police deal with them as law enforcement situations.

De jure   A Latin phrase meaning something being done "by law."

Dicta   Legal terminology (plural for dictum); a statement of opinion considered to be authoritative, although not binding, given the recognized authoritativeness of the person who pronounced it.

Discrimination   Applied prejudice; negative social attitudes translated into actions whereby public policy enforces the subordination of minorities' rights.

Disenfranchise   To deprive someone of the right to vote or to deprive someone of the rights and privileges of a free inhabitant of a locality, state, or country.

Doctrine of incorporation   The legal theory allowing the Supreme Court to apply the Bill of Rights to the states under the Fourteenth Amendment's due process clause.

Double jeopardy   The prosecution of a person twice for the same offense.

Due process of law   The constitutional limitation on government behavior to deal with an individual according to prescribed rules and procedures. Based on British common law, it prohibits government from depriving an individual of "life, liberty, or property," as protected by the Fifth Amendment to the Constitution with respect to the national government, and by the Fourteenth Amendment against such violations by the states.

Equal protection of the law   The constitutionally guaranteed right that all persons be treated the same before the law.

Ethnocentrism   The evaluation of other cultures according to preconceptions that are based in the standards and customs of one's own culture; the belief in the inherent superiority of one's own ethnic group. It often promotes xenophobia and has been the usually unspoken assumptions justifying racial and ethnic discrimination in law.

Exculpatory material   Evidence favorable to the defendant in a criminal trial which exonerates or tends to exonerate the defendant of guilt. It is the opposite of inculpatory evidence, which tends to present guilt.

Executive orders   Actions issued by a president, assigned numbers, and published in the federal register, that are akin to laws passed by Congress and that direct members of the executive branch to follow a new policy or directive.

Exempt   An individual, class, or category of individuals to whom a certain provision of the law does not apply.

Federal abstention doctrine Any of several doctrines that a court of law in the United States may (and in some cases, must) apply to refuse to hear a case if doing so would potentially intrude upon the powers of another court.

Fourteenth Amendment The post–Civil War amendment, ratified in 1868, that declared that all persons "born or naturalized in the United States" are citizens. It overturned the 1857 decision in *Dred Scott v. Sandford*, which had declared that Blacks were not and could not be citizens. In subsequent decisions, the Supreme Court gradually most of the first ten amendments to the states via the Fourteenth Amendment.

Genderism The social and cultural belief in there being only two genders—male and female—and that all aspects of one's gender are inherently linked to the sex assigned at birth by the biology of the individual.

Human right A right that is believed to belong justifiably to every person; for example, the right to equality and freedom from discrimination; to life, liberty and personal security; to freedom from torture and degrading treatment; to marriage and family; to the right to your own things; to freedom of thought and freedom of expression; to public assembly; the right to democracy, social security, and workers' rights. Collectively, they are expressed in the United Nations' Universal Declaration of Human Rights.

Identity politics A tendency for people of a particular religion, race, sexual orientation, or social background to form exclusive political alliances on that basis, moving away from traditional, broad-based party politics. It uses such shared identity for political empowerment to mobilize a constituency to seek recognition of their identity as a political goal and as a strategy to achieve their political goal.

Inalienable rights Rights that are not transferable or capable of being taken away or nullified by government.

Injunctive relief   A writ or court order stopping an agency or governmental official from taking an action that petitioners argue before a court would be harmful.

Jim Crow   The former practice of segregating black people in the United States.

Judicial review   A power, exercised by U.S. courts, to examine legislation and to strike down those laws that judges believe violate the U.S. Constitution.

Jurisprudence   Taking legal action in courts of law or the system of applying judicial judgments (e.g., reviews).

Jus sali   Citizenship based on place of birth.

Jus sanguinis   Citizenship based on blood or parentage.

Landmark decision   A Supreme Court decision that sets a precedent, distinguishes tests or other guidelines that determine subsequent court cases on a legal matter.

Litigation   The process of taking legal action.

Magna Carta   An act signed in 1215; it is the first written document presented to King John of England (1166–1216) that Parliament forced the king to sign, limiting the monarch's powers. It was the basis of English citizens' rights, for example, the right to assemble to protest a grievance against the government.

Naturalization   The legal act of making an individual a citizen who is not born a citizen.

Nolle prosegui **with leave**   An unusual legal procedure whereby a North Carolina prosecutor was able to neither dismiss nor reinstate a case, but to leave a case open, potentially indefinitely, and to reinstate the case without further permission by a judge. It was ruled an unconstitutional procedure on the basis of the Sixth Amendment's requirement of a speedy trial.

Per curiam   A legal term for an action taken by a higher court reviewing the decision of a lower court in which the decision is rendered by the court (or at least a majority of the court and often by a unanimous court), acting collectively rather than being authored and signed by an individual jurist.

Plaintiff A person who brings a legal action (e.g., files a suit) against another person or entity, such as in a civil lawsuit or criminal proceeding.

Pogroms Violent outbreaks of anti-Semitism that occurred in Eastern Europe and involved looting, pillaging, rioting, murders, and, in some cases, even the total destruction of Jewish ghettos.

Prejudice A mindset whereby the individual or group accepts as valid the negative social definition that the majority society forms in reference to some minority group and is predisposed to apply those negative social definitions to all individuals who are seen as belonging to that group simply on a given basis—that is, on race, color, creed, ethnicity, religion, age, gender, or sexual orientation.

Pretextual An adjective meaning constituting a pretext; dubious or spurious denoting or relating to a minor offense that enables authorities to detain a suspect for investigation of other matters.

Prima facie A legal term meaning "based on first impression"; accepted as correct until proved otherwise.

Privileges and immunities The clause in the Fourteenth Amendment on aspects of citizenship designed to protect citizens from government, but there is widespread disagreement on their actual scope and the relationship to the privileges and immunities conferred by state citizenship.

Progressive Era The period of widespread social activism and political reform across the United States that spanned from the 1890s to the 1920s.

Racial profiling A pattern of behavior of police officers based on racial appearance.

Racism The discriminatory treatment of people who belong to a different race from one's own, and justifying the sometimes violent behavior towards them.

Reconstruction era   The period in U.S. history lasting from 1863 to 1877 that had a profound impact on American civil rights.

Remand   An action taken by a higher court reviewing the decision of a lower court by which a case is sent back to the lower court for new action following the dicta or guidance of the higher court as to some point of law, often involving a constitutional question or issue involving a constitutional challenge based on one of the amendments to the U.S. Constitution.

Regime politics   The determination of a substantive basis of emergent party conflict; defending certain regime principles that view the common good manifested in particular ruling beliefs, habits, and institutions broadly associated with a segment of society.

Rights   Legitimate claims that an individual can make against government, the most extensive of which apply to citizens. Rights are thought to be correlative with duties. A citizen who has the right to seek governmental protection thus also has the obligation to serve in the military when needed.

Stakeholder   A person or organization with an interest or concern in something, especially a business; or one who is involved or is affected by a policy or course of action. Stakeholders are often parties to civil rights and civil liberty challenges to administrative rules, executive actions, laws, or policies of government.

Stare decisis   A Latin phrase meaning "let the decision stand"; it is a doctrine or policy of following the rules or principles of determining points in litigation according to precedent.

Statutory interpretation   The right, especially of U.S. courts, to interpret the law.

Suffrage   The right to vote in political elections.

Tort   A wrongful act or an infringement of a right (other than under contract) leading to civil liability.

Venire   A writ issued by a judge (also venire facias) to a sheriff directing the summons of prospective jurors; the entire panel of prospective jurors from which a jury is selected. When a defense wants a jury brought in from another area, it is called a change of venire.

Writ   A form of legal command in the name of a court or other legal authority to act or to abstain from acting in some way, for example, an injunction or a writ of certiorari.

Writ of certiorari   A legal order by a higher court to review a case. Certiorari is Latin meaning "to be more fully informed." A writ of certiorari orders a lower court to deliver its record in a case so that the higher court may review it.

Writ of habeas corpus   A court order requiring jailers (e.g., a prison warden) or an agency to explain to a judge why they are holding a prisoner in custody; to deliver the imprisoned person to the court issuing the order. It literally means "to produce a body."

Xenophobia   The excessive fear of the foreign or foreigners.

Yeshiva   A Jewish religious school.

Zero tolerance policy   The Trump administration's policy to have the Department of Homeland Security enforce illegal immigration measures dealing with expedited removal and related issues of illegal immigration that justified the separation of children from their parents, including babies who were being breastfed, or other family members in detention and awaiting expulsion for unauthorized immigration.

About the Author

Michael C. LeMay, PhD, is professor emeritus from California State University–San Bernardino, where he served as director of the National Security Studies Program, an interdisciplinary master's degree program, and as chair of the Department of Political Science and assistant dean for student affairs for the College of Social and Behavioral Sciences. He has frequently written and presented papers at professional conferences on the topic of immigration. He has also written numerous journal articles, book chapters, published essays, and book reviews. He is published in the *International Migration Review, In Defense of the Alien, Journal of American Ethnic History, Southeastern Political Science Review, Teaching Political Science,* and the *National Civic Review.* He is the author of thirty academic books, nineteen of which are academic volumes dealing with immigration history and policy. His prior books on the subject are *Party and Nation: Immigration and Regime Politics in American History* (2020); *The Immigration and Nationality Act of 1965: A Reference Guide* (2020); *Immigration Reform: A Reference Handbook* (2019); *Homeland Security* (2018), *Religious Freedom in America* (2018), *U.S. Immigration Policy, Ethnicity, and Religion in American History* (2018), *Illegal Immigration: A Reference Handbook,* 2nd ed. (2015), *Doctors at the Borders: Immigration and the Rise of Public Health* (2015); series editor and contributing author of the three-volume series *Transforming America: Perspectives on U.S. Immigration* (2013), *Illegal Immigration: A Reference Handbook* (2007), *Guarding the Gates: Immigration and National Security* (2006), *U.S. Immigration and Naturalization*

Laws and Issues: A Documentary History (ed. with Elliott Barkan, 1999), *Anatomy of a Public Policy: The Reform of Contemporary American Immigration Law* (1994), *The Gatekeepers: Comparative Immigration Policy* (1989), *From Open Door to Dutch Door: An Analysis of U.S. Immigration Policy Since 1820* (1987), and *The Struggle for Influence* (1985). Professor LeMay has written two textbooks that have considerable material related to these topics: *Public Administration: Clashing Values in the Administration of Public Policy*, 2nd ed. (2006), and *The Perennial Struggle*, 3rd ed. (2009). He frequently lectures on topics related to immigration history and policy. He loves to travel and has lectured around the world and has visited more than 150 cities in fifty-one countries. His previously authored books in the ABC-CLIO Contemporary World Issues series are *U.S. Immigration* (2004); *Illegal Immigration*, 1st ed. (2007), 2nd ed. (2015); *Global Pandemic Threats* (2016); *The American Political Party System* (2017); *Religious Freedom in America* (2018); *Homeland Security* (2018); *The American Congress* (with Sara Hagedorn, 2019); and *Immigration Reform: A Reference Handbook* (2019). His most recent books dealing with immigration are: *The Immigration and Nationality Act of 1965: A Reference Guide* (2020) and *Party and Nation* (with Scot Zentner, 2020).